Northamptonshire
Within Living Memory

WITHIN LIVING MEMORY SERIES

Other Counties in this series include:

Bedfordshire	Somerset
Hertfordshire	Staffordshire
Shropshire	Surrey

Northamptonshire Within Living Memory

Compiled by the Northamptonshire
Federation of Women's Institutes from notes
sent by Institutes in the County

Published jointly by
Countryside Books, Newbury
and the NFWI, Northampton.

First Published 1992
© Northamptonshire Federation of Women's Institutes 1992

COUNTRYSIDE BOOKS
3, Catherine Road,
Newbury, Berkshire

ISBN 1 85306 202 2

Cover Design by Mon Mohan
Produced through MRM Associates Ltd, Reading
Phototypeset by
The Midlands Book Typesetting Company, Loughborough
Printed in England by J.W. Arrowsmith Ltd, Bristol

Contents

Foreword

Over the past 30 years developments in Northamptonshire have brought changes that would have seemed inconceivable in the period covered by this book.

The coming of the M1 Motorway and high-speed train links have put a once rural county very firmly into the range of London commuters. The development of Northampton itself has enclosed villages into suburbs and many villages are populated not by country folk, but by people born and brought up in towns.

This is one reason why this book is such a valuable addition to the social history of our county, giving us a record of what life was like when Northamptonshire was truly rural. Many recollections come from people who have lived their whole lives in one area or even one village and for whom the changes have been immense. From the coming of electricity and piped water to the closure of schools, village shops and even churches.

There have been changes in agriculture with the arrival of mechanised farm machinery, in industry with the decline of the shoe trade and the rise and fall of the steel industry. There have been improvements as well in the provision of health and welfare, education and working conditions to correct the balance, but, the spirit of Northamptonshire remains in its small village communities and open countryside. Despite the industrial changes Northamptonshire still produces some of our finest shoes and retains its rural appeal to the many thousands of people who make their home here.

Sue Bird
Co-ordinator

Acknowledgements

Northamptonshire Federation of Women's Institutes would like to thank all W.I. members who supplied material for this project through their local Institutes.

Unfortunately we were not able to include extracts from every submission; to do so would have meant some duplication of content, and of course we had to take into account the total amount of space available in the book.

But all the contributions, without exception, were of value: deciding the shape and content of the book. We are grateful for them all.

I would also like to thank Doreen Chown and Helen Wooler for their patient transcription of the handwriting to typescript, and Sue Suttle and Pip Challenger for their help with the delightful sketches which introduce each section of the book.

Sue Bird
Co-ordinator

TOWN & COUNTRY LIFE

NORTHAMPTONSHIRE'S TOWNS AND VILLAGES

⌐⊃

Riding the trams in Northampton before the First World War, an afternoon's shopping in Kettering in the 1930s, the village of Deanshanger when old ladies still made and sold pillow lace for sixpence a yard from their cottages, the canal people at Stoke Bruerne – these are just some of the memories of towns and villages before increasing traffic, new building and modern amenities changed the face of Northamptonshire for ever.

MEMORIES OF NORTHAMPTON 1910–1940

'When I was five in 1913 I frequently visited Northampton where my grandparents lived. It cost one penny to ride on the tram from Abington Park to the town centre in Mercers Row where the trams were turned round. The trams from all parts of the town converged here, and I was fascinated to watch the driver or conductor change the trolley pole round for the return journey. The trams in the early days had open tops, but later changed to covered ones. The seats had movable backs which the passengers could move to enable them to look the way they wished. The tram started off with a great clanging, it could hardly be called a hooter but was a great noise which effectively cleared all pedestrians and traffic.

In The Drapery were the best shops. Adnitts was one owned by a local family – ladies' outfitters, but no "ready mades". There were rolls and rolls of materials and shelves full of ribbons and haberdashery. Right at the far end of the shop were the hats. At that time my hats were of straw and were decorated with cornflowers, poppies or daisies. As one entered the door a shop walker was there to usher you to your counter and help you to a chair. They were high chairs so that customers had a good view of the counter. The money went into a wooden ball which went on rails to the cash desk. A farthing might be all that had to come back and sometimes this was replaced by a packet of pins. The assistants all wore black dresses and many of them lived under a strict regime over the shop.

There were other outfitters shops in The Drapery. Brices was not quite so select as Adnitt's but good, and Shepherd and Manning was another local family business. They held a good range, and specialized in hats. There was also McCullough's which was always the venue for my mother when she wanted warm underwear, which included woollen combinations. My own underwear and outer wear she made herself – broderie anglaise knickers and petticoats and an under petticoat which had a flannel bodice and crocheted woollen bottom, usually pink, in shell stitch. My best dresses were always of velvet and I wore long button boots made of shiny glacé kid.

Also in the Drapery was a penny bazaar (anything for a penny!). This had a fairly narrow entrance and penetrated a long way back. There was a display the whole length of the premises, which was above waist level and not easy for a small child to see, but there were always some small toys or trinkets to please a small child. There was another penny bazaar in Gold Street. I think this was one of Marks and Spencer's first shops.

I spent the years from aged five to 14 at Long Buckby where my father's work took him. He had work at Frederick Cooke Ltd, who made what were supposed to be some of the world's best boots and shoes. They made riding boots for Royalty. The factory was in a one storied building, modern for those days, and if there were any messages for my father, I could walk straight in and find him. There were other shoe factories too, where very high quality hand sewn shoes were made. One of the factories is still there, and would, I should think, be of heritage status. Some of the work went out to men who worked at home in the "back shop" and we were always able to go in to watch them work, stitching the shoes together. As far as I remember they had a thread in each hand which they pushed into holes already made, thus changing hands. The needle was a bristle. Finishers were men who put a wonderful polish on the soles and heels. This was quite hard work; it was not just one application but several.'

'I was born in 1922. My home at St James, Northampton was on the edge of river meadows, now dominated by "Wogan's Lighthouse" and industrial estates. Our playgrounds were these meadows, where in due season we hunted for lady-smocks and "molly blobs" – marsh marigolds. In high summer they were golden with buttercups, not much use for grazing as they were always liable to flash flooding. The Nene was then choked with bullrushes. Water lilies floated tantalisingly close to the banks alive with dragonflies, water rats and the odd kingfisher. In the winter following heavy rain then frost, sheets of ice brought literally hundreds to slide and skate in safety, the water being only inches deep.

Our winter games were hopscotch, marked out in chalk on the pavement, marbles, whip and top, and skipping, which we did in

11

the middle of the road. Motors were a rarity in the side streets, we could easily move for the milkman's float or the coalman's cart.

If you were real "Chapel" you went to the "Tin School", built at the end of the 19th century, when nonconformists didn't want their children corrupted with Church school dogma. This school existed until the early 1930s, and the Corporation bus depot stands on the site. I remember the day when we moved to the brand new Spencer school at Dallington, carrying all our own exercise books. After about two years the education authorities then decided to send some "Jimmy's End" children to Spring Lane school in the Boroughs area of the town. This was viewed with horror by our parents, and we were given a separate cloakroom from the other kids, in the hope we didn't catch their nits. We had to walk through narrow slum streets, past open door tenements, I recollect the smell today, one rich with the indescribable odour of poverty.

During this time the shoe trade was in severe depression, most men working two weeks on and one week off work. I was lucky being an only child, with a father who neither drank or smoked. Many of my friends came from large families where hand-downs and bread and dripping were the norm. My mother was adept with her "Singer" and made all her own and my clothes. Most families had someone who could mend all the shoes.

I used to walk across the fields to St James Mill for eggs once a week for one shilling worth; in the spring when hens were laying well I had 20 for this amount. The bucket would then be filled with islinglass obtained from the chemist and eggs were put down for cooking use to help out in the winter. I also used to visit the butcher for a roasting joint, the price about two shillings. These were my Saturday chores for which I was given one penny. This was carefully spent, a favourite was a bag of sherbet and a "Hard" stick (licqorice) which would last all day. Another was a gob-stopper, which turned your tongue lurid colours. Chocolate went too quickly, but a visit to the railway station meant you sometimes were lucky to receive a penny bar from Fry's machine.

There was a cacophony of sound when shoe factory sirens went off at 7.30 am and again at mid-day for the dinner break. There were no canteens, men almost tumbled out of doors at a run in order to get home, eat a meal and be back again in the hour. Some had cycles which could be left propped up against the wall with no fear of thieves, but no other transport was laid on. Every man also had his Thermos flask of tea which he could drink as he worked, no food was allowed. Being from a "Chapel" family this filled my life. School twice on Sundays and later evening service too. Dondridge was quite a big chapel and operettas were produced every year by the Sunday school choir to which I belonged. Many evenings taken up rehearsing for this. Anthems were practised for anniversary services in the summer, when we marched around the streets behind the Boy's Brigade Band. A new straw hat would be the hope of every girl for this event, or at least a new ribbon trimming. On Tea Party day we were taken by special train to Brampton, Pitsford or Piddington where a field was hired and we had sports, then sat in circles for tea, bread and butter and "tea party" – plain madeira slab cake. As time went on the "Stop me and Buy One" man's tricycle often came along too, and did a roaring trade with penny snofrutes. In the winter another favourite was the Band of Hope where we sang temperance hymns with gusto; afterwards there was a magic lantern show for which we paid a halfpenny.

About this time, too, I remember seeing the Jarrow marchers, and I was not allowed to wear my "Sunday Best" that day, on reflection as a mark of support I suppose.'

'How the streets of old Northampton have changed since the advent of the car! Now they are dull grey linear car parks, but before the war they were full of life and colour.

Each weekday morning after husbands had cycled off to work and children had been despatched to school, the housewives were out, sweeping the path, scrubbing the steps, polishing doorknobs and knockers, blackleading bootscrapers and exchanging the latest gossip. In the meantime the milkman would appear with his pony and trap, the shining copper measures on hooks along the side and the milk in churns.

Next came the baker with his horse and cart and the delicious aroma of newly baked bread, unwrapped and unsliced, of course. How we loved cottage loaves with all that extra crust to sink our teeth into! Another popular person was the LMS railway delivery man who was often seen making his stately way along the street perched on the dray behind his huge much-loved shire horse. There was a rush to be first with a shovel after he had passed by and delivered the goods! A great contrast was the Walls ice-cream man on his tricycle bearing the legend "Stop Me and Buy One". The sound of his bell would bring children flocking if they were fortunate enough to have a penny for a Snofrute.

The postman made three or four deliveries daily, and the police-man plodded his beat morning and evening. Delivery boys pedalled furiously along on their heavy bicycles bringing groceries, meat and vegetables ordered earlier in the day. Another regular visitor was the lamplighter who came every evening with his long pole to turn on the gaslamps. The lamp-posts were very useful for the boys who tied ropes to the arms at the top and swung round at dizzying speeds.

The "ash box men" (these were pre-dustbin days) came twice a week with their odiferous open cart, and the coalman, the rag-and-bone man, the knife-grinder and the chair-mender were occasional callers, as were pedlars, tinkers and gypsies, and once, causing great excitement, an organ-grinder with his monkey.

On Sundays the street was quiet. No workers were to be seen and no children played. A solemn Sabbath calm prevailed. In the morning residents clad in their best made their way to church or chapel – there was a sharp division in those days – sometimes encountering a housewife from a poorer home carefully making her way to the neighbourhood baker with the precious Sunday joint to be roasted ready for her husband's return from the nearest public house. The day was sometimes enlivened by the Salvation Army conducting a service in the middle of the road.

Out of school hours the streets, which were then safe playgrounds, were filled with children's activities. Hopscotches were carefully marked out in chalk, circular ones on the road, rectangular ones on the pavement. Tipcat, a game known to have been played in medieval times, and ball games such as sixes and cannon were played all the year round. Sides in competitive games were always called English and French, a reminder of national enmities dating back to the Napoleonic wars and earlier. Springtime would bring out hoops, whips and tops and skipping-ropes; and a quiet game of jacks, sometimes called five-stones and dating back to the Romans, was ideal for a hot summer day. Another relic of Roman times was the shrill cry of "Cavey" giving warning of the approach of a rival gang, from the Latin "cave" meaning "beware".

Saturday mornings were special. The weekly pocket money, usually a penny, had been collected, and it was time for a visit to the corner shop. What to buy? It required careful consideration. In the window were trays of Bluebird toffee and banana split, glass jars of dolly mixtures, jelly babies, peardrops, aniseed balls, liquorice whorls, and most splendid of all – gobstoppers. So the children made their choice, watched while the sweets were weighed and transferred to a paper poke, handed over the precious penny, and made off with the week's treat.

Then there were the special occasions which brought extra interest to the street. Guy Fawkes and Christmas carolling have not changed much, but Good Friday had its own little ritual. Early in the morning we would listen for the boy bringing round hot-cross buns in a cloth-covered tray on his head, ringing a bell and crying his wares, and we really did have a baker's dozen – 13 buns for a shilling.

14

'Late in 1940, I came to live in Northampton. We lived in Newland. It was an interesting street with a mixture of houses, shops and other businesses. At the southern end of the street was the Market Square, with the fountain, where, on Sunday evenings in summer, there was usually a political speaker or two. Also, there was the Peacock Hotel with its beautiful wrought iron balcony which was another place for speakers. On winter evenings, you could buy hot baked potatoes from a barrow. In those days, the market was held on Wednesdays and Saturdays and the stalls were cleared away at six o'clock when the market closed, so the Square was often used for big parades and other events. The Salvation Army held an open-air service there every Sunday.

To the north of Newland was the church of the Holy Sepulchre. It had a thriving Sunday school and youth organisations. At Christmas, there would be a pantomime and, on the Thursday after Easter Sunday, there was the Easter Sale, with a good entertainment put on by everyone connected with the church – Girl Guides, Boy Scouts and church workers of all ages took part. I used to walk through the churchyard every day on the way to school and in spring there were hundreds of crocuses in bloom – a lovely sight.

The Emporium Arcade, with its many shops and workshops, had three entrances on the west side of Newland. On the east side was Princess Street, with the Baptist church and the Masonic hall, and Lady's Lane with all sorts of shops, houses and factories. Several residential streets led off Lady's Lane and most of the people worked in the nearby shoe factories of Lotus and Randall's. In those days, you could always smell the leather in Northampton; there were so many shoe factories, tanning companies and leather merchants and the people who worked in the shoe trade followed their parents and grandparents into it.

Within a hundred yards of our house, everything we could possibly need, from a loaf of bread to a piano, could be purchased. In Newland itself there was a wonderful old-fashioned hardware shop which sold gas mantles, pot menders and spare parts for oil lamps; then there was the lino shop; the draper's; a sweetshop and tobacconist; a newsagent's where you could get ten aniseed balls for a penny; a fish and chip shop; a barber's; a cycle shop; a taxi company; a café; a tailor; an antiques dealer; a cabinet maker; a watchmaker; an off licence where people took jugs and bottles to be filled from barrels of beer in the cellar; a printer's; a furniture shop; a commercial hotel; three public houses – The Hare and Hounds, The Central Tavern and the Fireman's Arms; the 20th century Working Men's Club; the Temperance Hall Cinema; a supplier to the shoe trade; a leather merchant; a shoe factory; a dentist; and the Borough

15

Coroner, Mr A. J. "Pat" Darnell, who was a familiar figure about the town in his top hat and frock coat. At the bottom of the street, near the Market Square, you could see the *Chronicle and Echo* being printed and sent out. As a child, it was quite thrilling to hear the roar as the presses rolled.

HARLESTONE UP TO THE 1930s

'As a child at Harlestone I spent a lot of my time talking to quite old men on our farm and workers on the Spencer estate. Hence I learned of village life and happenings in former times and many anecdotes which, I was assured, were quite true!

All transport was by horse; roads were just tracks with no curbs or footpaths. The stone which was used to repair the roads was dropped in large heaps by the roadside, broken up by ex-convicts and rolled in by the cart and waggon wheels.

The village had a brass band which, I understood, mainly played on the Fox and Hounds lawn. The champion ploughman, a Mr Golby, lived in Lower Harlestone, as did the champion hedgecutter, a Mr Irons. There were two Co-op shops owned by Harlestone and Industrial Society and also a Co-operative farm and dairy. The Spencers in those days were very prominent Liberals and gave great support to the village business activities.

A Mr Spring who ran the laundry in Upper Harlestone built himself a sizable greenhouse and grew quite a large crop of tomatoes. Very soon he had a ready sale for them with great satisfaction to him and his customers. In the village, a gentleman who was not a particular friend to Mr Spring and who was also a District Counsellor, wasted no time in informing the Rating Office. A member of the Rating Committee came to see Mr Spring, who was very annoyed and most offensive, and when asked if he grew tomatoes to sell he replied: "What do you think I grow the . . . for, to throw at people!" – He was duly rated!

One person before the First World War successfully made counterfeit half-crowns!

One summer's evening a farmer was driving home in his horse and trap and saw three or four of his men sitting on the side of the road. He stopped to speak to them and was told it was the birthday of one of them. He replied that if they could take their wheelbarrow into Mannings Brewery in Northampton, a distance of four miles, and fetch a four and a half gallon barrel of beer and be back to Harlestone in two hours, he would pay for it. One agreed to try and was back within the allotted time – and the farmer did pay for it as promised. Quite a feat considering the state of the roads at that time. They set up the barrel on the old preaching cross and drank it before going to bed.

One has to realise that life in Harlestone in the early 1920s meant being without electricity, gas or any other present day amenity. There was no piped hot water, no bathroom or interior toilets, no refrigerators or freezers, etc. Cooking was done by solid fuel or paraffin. Lighting was by candle or paraffin and the general policy of the village centred round the Duchess and the Parson. The Duchess of Grafton lived in the big white Harlestone House overlooking the lake and the Reverend Pattinson at the adjacent rectory.

Building bricks, tiles and pipes, etc were produced in Spencer's brickyard and piped water was pumped to most of the houses in the village by either petrol engine or windmill – the water works being another department of the Estate. The village had its own sewage bed at Lower Harlestone, which was quite efficient and overseen by William Craddock at the mill. The mill itself was quite busy, grinding grain mainly for animal feed. The Malting Yard opposite the Fox and Hounds housed a mineral water factory, known in those days as "Spruce" – the proprietor always being known as "Sprucey". The Malting has long since ceased making spruce. A local man, Mr Albert Shaw took it over and started a coal business there, which soon proved to be a success, supplying the surrounding villages.

The carrier – Mr Fred Dunkley, visited Northampton twice a week taking parcels, packages and passengers to and from on Wednesdays and Saturdays, always picking up sheep and cattle skins from Mr Dickins' butchery on Wednesday mornings – I might add, it was a covered van with a special tailboard to carry the skins outside to avoid poisoning the occupants! The journey would take at least half an hour. He always put up at the Cross Keys public house in Sheep Street. The only other means of travelling to Northampton, apart from walking or carrier's cart, was by rail from Church Brampton, station, which was, of course a mile to walk either way. The station was added after the railway was built for the benefit of members of the County Golf Course at Brampton.

AN AFTERNOON IN KETTERING 1930

'On a grey and misty November Saturday afternoon in the 1930s with my legs encased in brown leather leggings fastened with long rows of boot buttons down each side, I set off with my mother to shop in Kettering. After (to me, aged about seven) a long walk, we reached the crossroads in the middle of the town, where a large policeman, with arms outstretched, was directing the few cars, errand-boys on bicycles loaded with basketsful of parcels, and horses and carts.

Into Woodcock's Department Store which was on the corner of Montague Street and Newland Street, where ribbons, gloves and socks were bought and the assistant put the money and bill into a brass cylinder which was attached to a wire overhead pulley. It went rattling away to a cashier on some remote upper floor; eventually it came slowly back and change (in farthings!) and the receipt were politely handed over.

Across the road to Hooton's Penny Bazaar – lit by gas-light and smelling musty – where I bought two tiny china dolls, jointed and with long hair for a penny. Along to Cobley's the grocers; full of spicy, mouth-watering food smells, and I was perched on a high stool by the shiny wooden counter, regaled with little pieces of Cheddar and Leicester cut from enormous rounds of red and yellow cheeses with a wire, whilst dried fruits and rice, scooped from large sacks were weighed. They were poured into dark blue paper folded by the nimble practised fingers of the grocer into bags, himself enveloped in a long and spotless white apron. High up on the shelves were big canisters of tea with labels like "Assam", "Darjeeling", "China" stencilled across in ornate gold lettering; and great slabs of yellow butter stood on a marble slab, to be cut into pounds and patted into shape with two wooden "bats" and the top imprinted with some "dairy" symbol.

Along the High Street and to the market; crowds of people laden with bags and baskets, noise, bustle and flickering lights. The raucous yells of the North-country "Lino Man" with the rolls of linoleum propped against the wall of the rectory/parish hall, great lengths of gaudy patterned floor-coverings flung across the cobbles for display by the red-faced and perspiring seller, and room-sized lengths, eagerly bought by customers, for 19 shillings and elevenpence. The "Pot-Man" who, to a child's eyes, was something of a conjuror, to the delight of a vast crowd of spectators tossed up plates, cups and saucers and ended up with all balanced along his arms, making a great business of being about to drop the lot, which, to my disappointment, he never did. Here again shoppers walked away with a complete tea-service all wrapped in newspaper, for less than £1.

The many greengrocery stalls (manned by local market-gardeners) were redolent with the smells of oranges, tangerines, well-polished apples, over-ripe bunches of bananas and the tangy "winter" scent of celery, still coated in lumps of brown earth and crisp and white in the growing dusk of late afternoon. Small, thin and grubby little boys scrambled about under these stalls for "tacked" oranges and broken

18

wooden boxes discarded by the stall-holders which these urchins trundled home for fire-wood.

A flower-stall at the front of the market, where great buckets of shaggy chrysanthemums in all the browns, yellows and golds of late autumn together with evergreen pots of ferns and more exotic blooms for the affluent, attracted many. A sharp contrast being made by a butchery stall, with a blue-striped apronned and cold, red handed vendor, where great sides of dark red, yellow-fatted beef hung together with long festoons of fat pink sausages interspersed with long red polony and shiny black puddings.

A look at stalls selling many coloured woollens made in the factories of Leicester. Three yards of lovely bright red velvet at one shilling and elevenpence three farthings for a party dress for me.

And finally, across Sheep Street, to a bow-windowed chemist's shop, quiet, ordered and peaceful after the clamour and colour of the market, where we were met by the mingled scents of lavender, violet and rose soaps and toiletries and the more astringent smells of medicaments of various kinds. People were being served with bottles, pill-boxes and such, all neatly packaged into little white paper parcels held together with a dab of red wax.

One last stop at the newsagent's on the corner for Arthur Mee's *Children's Newspaper*, *The Rainbow* comic and a penny bar of Cadbury's chocolate, then homewards, with the cries of a newspaper seller on the street corner with the "last edition" of the *Evening Telegraph* and copies of the local sports paper "The Pink 'Un", the tall grey spire of the parish church looking down over the lights, colours and milling townspeople in the Market Place as it had done for centuries.

Home, with laden shopping baskets, high tea, a roaring log fire and "In Town Tonight", with its well-known signature tune "Knightsbridge" on the wireless at 7 pm.'

DEANSHANGER UP TO THE 1930s

'Deanshanger was a pretty village with small cottages, many thatched, several of which were little sweet shops. One lady made and sold black pudding and others made bobbins and pillow lace for about sixpence a yard. There was no electricity, only candles or oil lamps. Sanitation was an outside loo with buckets often at the bottom of the garden. These were emptied once a week in what was aptly called "The Lavender Cart".

In the mid 1930s council houses were built and people from the cottages rehoused but one family, not being used to bathrooms, kept coal in theirs.

Before the motor car arrived, village streets were safe for children to play their games of hopscotch, or tops and whips. This is Little London, Deanshanger before the First World War.

Every day a number of women pushing trucks, prams etc would walk to Whittlebury Woods about three miles away collecting wood for their fires, while others would go around the fields filling their baskets with blackberries, mushrooms and sloes, selling them to the blackberry man who came round each week with his horse and cart. He even bought rabbit skins for sixpence each.

There were not many cars in the late 1920s and early 1930s so it was safe for children to play with hoops, whips and tops, hopscotch, ball games etc. I just remember Queen Mary and King George V coming to Stowe. Farmers took villagers in their horse-drawn carts and waggons to see them. At last along came the Royal carriage and there was Queen Mary sitting bolt upright in all her finery.

We had our village characters, Bill Bambrook for one, often seen with his little cart and sweep's brushes off to sweep a chimney, and there was the drunk trying to rake the moon out of the brook-thus the village got its nickname, "Moonshine".

Then there was Yorky (Bill Williamson). He came to the district in 1948 and lived in a tent in Silver Spinney on the Deanshanger-Wicken road, later moving to a hovel on the Buckingham road near Thornton. He did a good trade with his portable grinding machine attached to his bicycle. Yorky was well liked and locals would visit him to hear his many stories. A friend of Yorky's came round each

20

year selling shopping bags. Alas, Yorky died and his friend never came this way again.

Deanshanger was prone to flooding. On one occasion, Duck End, as it was called, was cut off and farmers rescued children from school and people from Patricks Lane in farm carts and tractors. Carpets from the houses were dried on the boilers at the nearby oxide works.

Sunday School treats were held either at Passenham rectory or Dove House Farm. Festivals were well attended. Christmas would see the children doing their Nativities. The school carol service was held in church. On Christmas night the Methodist chapel would push their organ on a trailer round the village singing carols. All doors would be opened to listen. The churches were decorated beautifully for all festivals and they also had a very good choir. Ash Wednesday and Ascension Day the children marched up from school and then they got a half-day holiday.

Humphrey's of Old Stratford ran a bus service in the early 1920s, and the remains of the old wharf and warehouse were taken over by E. Hayes, boatbuilder of Stony Stratford. The entrance to this large basin was crossed by a large swing bridge; quite a number of these bridges were along the canal.'

GRETTON 1930–1960

'Gretton has always been a self-contained closely-knit community. Life was not easy during the 1930s. Wages were low. Work was found in the nearby ironstone pits, on the farms or the railway lines. Young lads badgered the farmers for odd jobs, gladly helping to make the hay, gathering the harvest or tending cows by the roadside. Employment for women could be found at the small clothing factory; girls vied with one another for baby-minding or shopping errands.

In spring-time, a walk to the woods to gather primroses and bluebells was a pleasure. In summer, thoughts turned towards the river, children paddled in the shallows, swimmers enjoyed the deeper water.

Throughout the autumn, as the days shortened, children played in the streets with hoops, skipping ropes and marbles and games of hopscotch and hide-and-seek, or maybe attaching a button on a string to tap on windows, were the games they enjoyed.

On cold winter days, the family gathered round the table for their evening meal, maybe stew with plenty of potatoes, or hot dripping toast, perhaps bread and jam, comfortable and warmed by the glow from the grate.

As time went by, the nearby steelworks expanded and work and wages increased. Although most needs could be supplied by the village shops, a weekend trip to the nearest town was a treat. Families boarded the mid-day train, returning in the evening loaded with goods.

The postman trundled down to the station at 7 am with his wheelbarrow, picked up the mail and trudged up Stoney Lane to the post office. This he did three times a day. The post office was kept by an elderly brother and sister in their front room.

Some of the happiest times for children were the annual events like the May Day festival. A procession of children carrying May garlands followed the May Queen on her horse-drawn throne, parents gathered to watch the maypole dancing and the celebrations ended with a feast of sandwiches and buns.

On Easter Monday, family outings and visits from friends gave a general holiday feeling.

During the summer, Sunday school treats were enjoyed. Sometimes races and games, followed by a tea, was the order of the day or the children rode in wagons as the horses plodded steadily through the fields to a picnic at Kirby Hall.

The first weekend in August was the traditional Village Feast. Great preparations were made as this was the time of family reunions and visits of friends, the highlight being the return of the fair. For a whole week, children and adults enjoyed the fun.

As Christmas drew near, pigs were slaughtered and thoughts of succulent joints and other good things filled the mind. One of the pre-Christmas events was the Fur & Feather Whist Drive, which was a tense evening for nervous players.

Apart from these highlights, there were other activities. Football and cricket clubs, the whist league, band practice, the Pig Club (to which members paid a small sum to insure against loss), dances, socials, whist drives and parties took place in the old school.'

TOWCESTER AS IT WAS

'When thinking about Towcester as it was, everyone remembers the cinema. It was built at the start of the war in 1939 by the Hesketh family for the present Lord Hesketh's grandmother, who had her own box. I remember the plush carpets and the manager, who wore a dinner jacket. When the cinema closed it was used for bingo and wrestling before it was pulled down in 1983.

The Town Hall on the Market Square was used for dances until 1973 when the SNDC took over from the Towcester, Northampton and Brackley RDC. The betting shop was the grocer's, H.T. Newman and when you entered the shop over the worn step using the latch door, you were met by a warm smell of bacon, cheese and coffee, the latter standing in large tins waiting to be weighed out. A large safe stood in the office. Barclays Bank was Jeyes the chemist, with large coloured bottles on display and pills and potions prepared "out the back". Mr Edwards owned the bicycle shop, with its lovely shiny new bicycles and, later, television sets.

Fareys on the corner of Park Street sold wools from the first room, the second being a veritable grotto of toys. The Indian restaurant was Page's, the baker, cake decorator and cafe. One day Wee Willie Harris came into the cafe with pink hair. Mrs Page looked at him and said, "Do you know what a sight you look!" "Yes, Missis," he replied, "but it brings in the money."

Robersons owned the hardware shop with lots of wares hanging outside and nails sold by weight. Causebrook's the men's outfitters were opposite and were a perfect example of trust and service. Ties, caps and shirts were all neatly laid out in trays. You could take anything home to try on and if it did not fit, take it back – none of this "If it's not on the shelf we haven't got it". Mr Tuckey had a cycle repair shop on the Northampton Road and all the youngsters left their bikes behind his shop. We all stood in awe of him but I really do not know why.

The snow in 1947 brought skating on Bairstow Lake and stranded lorry drivers had to sleep in the Town Hall, where Mr Page and other locals took them meals. Towcester was often flooded at both ends, near the cinema and the police station.

The rugby clubhouse was in the old fire station in the brewery yard, where Malt House Court now stands. Guides and the youth club were held on the top floor of the old workhouse, which was the old council depot and is now Gilbert Scott Court. The primary school is now the library and all the children walked to the workhouse for school dinners. Meals were also prepared here for other village schools.

The green called Sawpitts outside the primary school had railings all round but these were taken down during the war as part of the war effort. Dancing round the maypole was held here. Towcester grammar school pool was at the bottom of the school playing field, surrounded by corrugated iron sheets, and only the pupils could swim there. They had a holiday rota and the key had to be collected from the headmaster. St George's Day, 23rd April, was celebrated with the raising of the flag in the playground, and Founders Day for William Sponne meant a long crocodile of children going to the parish church, where Canon Curtis gave his address with such grand gestures that when he said "Here lies William Sponne", we all hoped that one day he would surely move.

Buses ran daily between Towcester and Northampton but only twice weekly to the villages, so getting home to the farm after school meant a two mile walk with very few cars passing by. If someone did stop to give you a lift it was someone you knew and no cause for alarm.

In the autumn we walked the hedgerows collecting rosehips for twopence a pound; these were collected from the schools. Mrs Minnie Robinson sat in the doorway of her house in Queens Road all dressed in black, making lace, and Mr Law made shoes in his house opposite the police station. His shoes were all hand-made, including the trainers worn by Roger Bannister when he broke the four minute mile.

A Horticultural Show was held on the old August Bank Holiday, with side shows, stalls, a flower show and a fancy dress competition. Towcester races were very popular. People arrived by train and walked to the racecourse. This brought business to the town and Prince Monalulu was a regular celebrity.

I lived on a farm outside Towcester and many prisoners of war stayed on after the war ended in 1945 and worked on the farm, helping to grow potatoes, sugar beet and kale for the cattle. The Greens Norton youth hostel was used as a POW camp. The prisoners built the roads to the new council houses in Sycamore Road.

Every Saturday morning my father got ready for market. He wore brown breeches, highly polished brown boots and brown leather leggings which I remember lacing up for him with the silver hook that hung on the mantelpiece. In the summer when I was nine or ten he was busy haymaking and I caught the local bus into Northampton with a large basket of eggs. I went to the bank with his cheques and collected cash; exchanged the eggs for haddock at the fish man's; bought fruit from the market, then caught the bus home. Walt Lawrence, the owner of the bus, never went home without all those he brought into town.'

YELVERTOFT IN THE 1960s

'In 1965 we were part of a second wave of incomers to Yelvertoft, buying a newly built bungalow on an old lane which was bordered by fields, two farm houses and a cottage. At the far end, the road petered out and a tree-lined footpath led down to the brook, bridged by two planks. Generations of small children spent hours damming its slow flow or hunted for minnow and stickleback in the shallow, watercressed reaches. Donkeys were kept in the neighbouring field where they rested between engagements as "racers".

When my sons were small we used to walk down past the farm

land at a spot to the end of the lane where the land sloped down and became a water meadow as it met the brook. This provided another interesting area to spend time in because of the numbers of wild flowers growing in the high grasses. We used to try to find Yelvertoft castle in the mounds and bumps which were all that remained of a very early manor. Nothing of this is left to take future generations of children to enjoy; the mounds have been levelled and the land raised so that it no longer floods, the host of meadow flowers is no more.

Here and there around the village were farmhouses. Most of these have been pulled down or sold as residences; only one or two now house farmers. My feeling in 1965 was that the old heartbeat of the village was measuring the seasons of the farming year and that visible activities in the village reflected this – cows going home to be milked; sheep being herded for shearing or beef cattle for market.

At this time the households of the village were well served by a series of travelling shops. The Co-op van, a baker's and grocer's van, called twice a week, but the van of all vans belonged to Mr Swinfen. It was small, sturdily built and dark green in colour. Mr Swinfen would stop, get out and raise louvred sides to reveal a fine display of goods, just like a market stall. Although hardware and heating or cooking fuels were mainstays, knitting wools and tins of peaches sat on the shelves beside kettles, pans and cleaning materials. There were and are two milk rounds. The village based one was owned by a dairy farmer and although the round still exists, the cows are no more. Whilst we continue to boast of a post office and general stores we have lost our butcher's shop along with its home-made sausages and freshly boiled ham.

When we arrived I regularly used the bus to get into Rugby and it would also have been possible to catch the train. Yelvertoft station stood close to the Sir Edward Lutyens cottages at the edge of Stanford, so it served both communities as "Stanford and Yelvertoft" on the Rugby-Leicester line. It was axed by Beeching and the house and waiting room are now a small country club. Within living memory milk churns were taken from the village to supply Rugby. Goods, fuel and people made their way to the village, their journeys from the station often taking longer than the train ride itself!'

ON THE CANAL

'Watching the crowds of people that visit Stoke Bruerne in the summer months, it would be easy to think that before the days of trippers this must have been a very sleepy village. Without doubt, one can walk from one end of the village to the other on certain winter days and see not a living soul. The arrival of the Grand

Union Canal has been well documented but the last 50 years have brought changes of possibly more importance to the lives of ordinary people.

However, our earliest memories are to do with the canal. One member recalls the barge women in their black bonnets and skirts, with lock key hanging at the waist. All the barges then were horse-drawn and a tug was needed to pull the boats through the Blisworth tunnel. The horses were led over the boat road and met up at the far end. Bill Bustin and his father operated the tug until they were superseded by self-powered boats, when he turned to chimney sweeping. A large man in a trilby hat, rumour has it his trousers were made from army-surplus blankets.'

'From a very early age, every Sunday summer evening in the 1930s my parents and myself walked to the canal at Blisworth Arm to watch the barges and butties tie up for the night. In those days the barges were horse-drawn. The horses wore straw hats to ward off the flies and both horses and barges displayed gleaming brasses cleaned so much that they shone white. The barges and butties also displayed their array of hand-painted ware and decor.

The horses were stabled for the night in the stable between the cottage and the Navigation Inn at Blisworth Arm. My father was one of eight children born in that cottage and shared a bedroom with his brothers above the stable, so Sunday night meant very little sleep as the horses would kick and snort most of the night. Sunday evenings it was quite a meeting place for Blisworth and Milton Malsor folk.'

'The Grand Union Canal ran through Yardley Gobion and narrow-boats brought coal, which was loaded onto carts and delivered to the villagers.'

'The Grand Union Canal is about three miles from Long Buckby and we often walked there for family outings. Our fathers fished in it. The "barge children" had to attend school for certain periods of the year and had to live with retired grandparents on the "cut" whilst their parents continued carting coal or other things along the canal. They walked to school in all weathers and I think were the only scholars who brought their lunch. The girls (I do not remember seeing any boys) wore long, full print skirts and heavy lace up boots. Their hair was plaited and pinned around the head.'

THE SQUIRE
AND THE POACHER

When it was customary to curtsey or doff your hat to the local gentry, the Big House was a major influence on local life, often to the good. It wasn't only the gentry, either, who expected acknowledgement from their social inferiors – it could just as easily be the rector's wife or the Sunday school teacher. At the other end of the social scale, the poacher was a popular figure, particularly when times were hard and a fresh rabbit or two meant a good meal on the table, and every town and village had its characters or eccentrics, accepted as part of life.

THE BIG HOUSE

'At the beginning of the century, and before, the Rev Henry Crawley was rector of Stowe. He was a benevolent old gentleman, of moderate build, clean shaven and who always wore a stock. He had three or four horses and rode, but did not hunt. Women in the village used to curtsey to him, some of them 40 yards before they reached him and he would often produce packets of tea from his pockets. He always carried a tin of Balsamic lozenges which he would hand round.

Ella Burton remembered the Crawford-Woods coming to the Grange in the 1890s, and holding a birthday party for their eldest son on 5th November 1895. "It still remains to me the grandest firework display I can remember. The eldest son was born on 5th November, at a guess five years before. The party had been for children, but all the village was asked to the fireworks and refreshments were handed round to all and sundry. Though we had many lovely parties at the rectory, there was something different about this one. While the family remained at Stowe we had a party every 5th November, but that first one was the best."

'Although not an estate village, Clipston had its gentry and I heard tell how all the females of the working class were expected to drop a curtsey, even in the muddy road, when one of their "betters" passed by.'

'Welton Place played an important part in village life. It was occupied by the Garrard family. Two of the daughters ran the Guides and the

Brownies; they had a hut built in the grounds for the meetings. There were five daughters in the family in all and when each was married a red carpet was laid from the front door of the house, through the garden, over the village street up to the church door. A village cricket team was formed and played on land belonging to Welton Place. The team was disbanded in the 1960s when the property was sold and the house demolished.

Some villagers tell of a Russian prince who lived at Welton Manor in the care of Admiral Nicholson. He was about eight years old and was not allowed out – but on Saturdays and Sundays a few children were invited in to play with him. It was said that the boy had seen his parents killed at the time of the Russian Revolution.'

'At Easton on the Hill there was quite a distinction between the upper and lower classes. The clergymen, farmers, schoolmaster and business folk were all looked up to and held a place in village life apart from the workers on farms etc.'

'When Gayton boys met any of the ladies of the village, ie the Sunday school teacher, the postmistress or the rector's wife, they had to doff their cap – failure to do so could result in that particular lady reprimanding their mothers. These ladies did help to run the village and kept a certain amount of order and respect.'

'Mrs Gina Watts Russell remembers the village turning out to welcome her when she arrived at Biggin Hall at the end of the Second World War. She and her husband, David, heir to the estate, met when they were serving in Cairo. This welcome continued a tradition. In the case of her parents-in-law, villagers and tenants pulled the carriage from the Hall to Benefield church when they returned from the London wedding and their honeymoon in 1913.'

'Mr Wroughton, of The Lodge, was Master of the Pytchley Hounds in the 1920s and on one occasion, when hounds met on Creaton Green, a young couple, staying nearby, came with their baby daughter, sitting up in her pram like a little queen. Now the ladies of Creaton all loved a baby and this one was no exception; but her mother wasn't so happy at the crowd and shooed them away! But then this was a very special baby, because she grew up to be a Queen – Elizabeth II and her parents were the then Duke and Duchess of York.'

VILLAGE CHARITIES

'Before the advent of pension schemes, the poor and elderly of Brigstock village were helped by the generosity of local benefactors. The village fellmonger would donate one cwt of coal to each "poor" person, and a soup kitchen was run at Fermyn Woods Hall for the widows and the poor. The widows were also invited there for a Christmas "treat" as were the village schoolchildren, and, in the 19th century, the owners of the Hall had bequeathed money to build a row of six cottages for widows. Several similar rows were built at different times, but now only one remains standing. In the centre of the village stood another group of cottages, known as "Union Row" or "Workhouse Hill", presumably also for the poor, but these were demolished following a fire in the 1950s and now form part of a garden.

Nearby is the largest of the allotment areas in the village, the rent from which goes to a village charity. At one time, two other fields were also used as allotments, but have now been built on. At the corner of the allotments stands an acacia tree, one of several trees around the village commemorating royal events, the most notable being the oak planted for the coronation of George V in 1911.

THE POACHER

'In the early 1920s my father Lewis Ayres and George Turnham were charged with poaching rabbits on the Helmdon to Syresham road. When charged, my father said they were only looking for a dinner. They were each fined £2, which was a large sum of money in those days. My father told me that times were very hard and they had to catch rabbits to eat and also to sell to make a bit of extra money. He had a duck, which he used to put in a drain under the road. The duck quacked and frightened the rabbits out of the other end of the drain, where they were trapped.'

'There was no real need for poaching at Stowe, though there was one poacher by the name of Todder Lovell, who came from Bugbrooke. "He went everywhere; his speciality was tracking down hares in the snow."

Most locals had permission to shoot and snare because they worked on the farms. Mr Dickens remembered his father used to shoot on Joe Starmer's land, some 600 acres (now the Old Dairy Farm) and the only payment sought by Mr Starmer was "a couple of rabbits". These might have been shot or ferreted. Ferreting was very common – in one case we were told 30 to 60 rabbits a week "paid the rent".

Stringing rabbits was a method by which they were driven into a long net along the hedge and then their necks were wrung. A windy, drizzly night was best for this. During the 1940s, when other meat was in short supply, rabbits were taken to Ryton on Dunsmore and sold for six shillings each.'

'Most households at Gretton kept a pig and a few fowl, together with an allotment or a garden supplying vegetables and fruit, adding a little luxury to their somewhat sparse diet. Poaching a rabbit for the pot was a risky business. One well-known poacher always took his daughter on his expeditions, she wearing a leather belt under her long black coat, often returning home with half a dozen rabbits hooked onto the belt. She knew no gamekeeper would dare to lift a lady's skirt. The rabbits would easily sell for sixpence or more.'

VILLAGE CHARACTERS

'Paddy Freshwater who lived in a Romany caravan in Holcot Road, Brixworth was a well known charactor at this time. His suits which were hand-made had upon his special instructions 14 pockets. On the occasion of the annual appearance of a fairground during All Saints Feast he very generously invited all the local children to mount the roundabout and when it was full and at full speed Paddy disappeared, an old score apparently settled in a most satisfactory way.
    Tramps (many of them gentlemen in the true sense of the word) would visit the workhouse for a bed, carry out their manual payment and continue on their way. The workhouse children, always well scrubbed and obedient, lived a life of strict discipline and hard work and were made aware of the their lowly position on life's social ladder. One imagines these children now to be among those of the highest regard, clean, honest and hardworking.'

'The tramps used to pass through Duddington. Whenever I heard one approaching my mother would give me a penny to run over to our stone wall with and place it in his cap. I can't remember my mother ever turning away a tramp from our door without at least a slice of bread covered with dripping or cheese. The tramps used to carry a very dubious coloured billy can which was topped up with steaming tea.'

'Great Houghton boasted a taxi service. This was run by Archie and his large square car. I don't remember hearing Archie actually talking or having a conversation with anyone, and I am not sure how he managed to make a living as his services were not all that frequently called upon. The most noise he made was to emit loud belches in between gulps of ale while sitting in the corner of a room in the White Hart, which provoked a chorus of "Steady Archie" from his fellow villagers, who would probably be playing cribbage, dominoes or skittles.

The village had many other characters. There were the three brothers Gilpin – eccentric gentlemen all – who turned the land around their tall, old house into a sort of market garden. The middle brother (nicknamed Konk because of his large, honey nose), took a horse and cart laden with vegetables around parts of Northampton. He had a wonderful time as he would receive a cup of tea here, a dinner there, and had all the public houses on his route. His lovely old grey mare, Dolly, would wait patiently at every stop and it would be mostly dark by the time he meandered his way back so it was fortunate that Dolly knew exactly the way to go home without too much guidance.'

AROUND THE VILLAGE

You might have stopped to rest a while on the village green, or gazed into the village brook, chatted with the roadman or the postman, or watched the cattle being herded along to market. Then, if you were a man, perhaps an hour or two in the reading room catching up with the newspaper.

THE VILLAGE GREEN

'In the 1930s the village green at Evenley had a road crossing it from the Red Lion to the opposite corner. The road was eventually grassed over but traces of it can still be seen during very dry weather. There were several very large elm trees on the green, but sadly they were lost later of Dutch elm disease. Cricket was played on the green by the young men of the village, a tradition that still goes on. There was a road around the green and the cottages faced onto the green on three sides.'

'At Nether Heyford the Parish Council held a candle auction for the use of the green for grazing catle and even geese. A pin was stuck in the lighted candle to time the auction.'

THE VILLAGE HALL AND THE READING ROOM

'Miss Elsey, the river bailiff at Fotheringhay, would go to the river every Sunday from June to March, the coarse fishing season, and, with the farmer's permission, collect a "bob a rod" from the fishermen. In this way she collected between £200 and £300 a session for the building and equipping of the village hall.'

'Helmdon doesn't possess a village hall, only a reading room. This was given to the village by the Fairbrothers in 1887. It was for the men to use and this rule has never officially been altered. The better-off people donated newspapers and weeklies and it was open every day of the year, except for Christmas Day, Good Friday and, unofficially, the Thursday of Banbury Fair. At first, the "gentry" used to sit at one end and the working men at the other. This room was left under the jurisdiction of the rector and churchwardens and was not endowed. Monday evening is still the Working Men's Club night, when they hold their billiards matches.'

'The reading room at Ashley, sometimes called "The Club", was a very popular meeting place for the young men of the village. There were billiards, card games and a library. Women were admitted only when whist drives were held.'

'A reading room was provided for the men of Grafton Underwood. They could go there and read or play dominoes, billiards, darts, skittles and cards. No ladies were allowed inside. In 1940 when the Army was in the village, it was used by them as an office and later on as a home for evacuees. After the war the reading room was discontinued.'

'Land in Stoke Bruerne was owned by the Grafton estate. The great house at Stoke Park, along with its beautiful pavilions, was built in Palladian style for Sir Francis Crane in the 1600s. Sadly the original house burned down in 1886. Stoke Park passed into the hands of the Vernon family. Wentworth Vernon built the reading room for the men of the village as a place where they could go to read their newspapers. In 1957, after the Park estate was broken up, the late Mr Christopher Taylor realised the meeting room could be lost forever, so he bought it. A parish meeting was called to arrange a management committee and 20 people were appointed. They all put money in to pay the costs of having the reading room transferred to the village hall. Since then a great deal of work has been done to improve the facilities and it is well used.'

'The Duston Women's Institute was formed in 1924 and developed into a popular organisation which met in the village hall. The hall began to be a focus for village social life and opened up an exciting new life for the women. They were able to learn new skills from one another and, as their houses were also beginning to be improved and easier to run with many new amenities, they found they had more time for leisure and tennis clubs, garden parties, croquet parties, and the cinema and shows in Northampton. These same women also developed a social conscience and an awareness of how they could help others to live improved lives – a Child Welfare Association was opened in 1933 under the direction of the local Medical Officer of Health and the Health Visitor, and a voluntary working group organised the running of baby clinics where the babies were not only weighed but lectures were given to help mothers learn how to feed, clothe and care for their babies.

A keep fit group was formed and, after they had made themselves suitable costumes of the same colour and design, they would put on displays under the direction of a member of the League of Health and Beauty. Of course, radio had arrived in 1926 and gradually everyone seemed to have either a crystal set and headphones or an early radio with a loudspeaker like a trumpet – they became a feature of everyday life and made people more aware of national and international events. Many women still had long hair and would plait it into buns over the ears like the radio earphones. In fact, they became more fashion conscious now and their clothes became more colourful – the days of the black skirt and white blouse or the even earlier beaded jacket, were lost in the past. Stockings changed from black woollen or pure silk to light coloured artificial silk or acetate, and short hair became fashionable with the "bob", the "bingle" and the "shingle". Life became much more enjoyable for village women in the run up to the Second World War. No wonder they loved the village hall, which had given them a place to get together and then from which to branch out and learn to do other things.'

THE VILLAGE LAUNDRY

'There was a high class hand laundry at Nassington, first started in a barn above 35 Church Street, secondly in buildings at the rear, and finally below the village green. The only machinery was a washer which held about eight full sized sheets, but everything white or boilable was done in an enormous copper, heated by coal. The seven

33

and five pound irons were heated on a large coke stove which held about 50 irons.'

TELLING THE TIME AND THE NEWS

'My parents looked after the church at Middleton Cheney for many years. Dad was a warden and also rang the bells for 50 years in all. He would ring the dinner bell in the middle of the day in the early years of the century. He used to be working in the fields at the farm but he would take a watch and at five to twelve he'd ride his bike back to the church so that the men working in the fields would hear the chimes and then they'd know it was lunchtime. They didn't have watches, you see.'

'When I was a child at Denford in the 1910s, we didn't have watches and would know what time to come home from play by the trains passing through. There was one railway line one side of the river across the meadows (the Great Western) and the Midland line ran the other side of the village. There was a clock on the church, of course, but the only other way of knowing the time was hearing the buzzers from the Islip Furnace or the foundry (Smith & Grace) for the workers there.'

'The Town Crier at Irthlingborough was Dick Cuthbert who lived in School Lane and would ring his bell and call "This is to give notice", and then go on to tell the town of special events such as a sale of work at church or chapel, possibly of a dance or party or even of lost and found items.

Another way to advise of news was the school bell, which rang when a death occurred, followed by the number of peals to denote the age of the deceased and, invariably, the townsfolk would know who it was.'

THE VILLAGE BROOK

'Harpers Brook played an important part in Brigstock village life earlier in the century. Water from the brook was used to turn the mill wheel which in turn drove machines which ground the corn etc and turned the saw mill.

The working horses and cattle drank from the brook and the timber merchants' horses had their hooves washed there.

In winter the brook always froze and both children and adults skated on long lengths of the water. In summer many children learned to swim in the brook's clear water.

One lady remembered an eel trap from which her mother collected the eels, took them to the wooden draining board in her kitchen where they were skinned and subsequently eaten by the family.'

THE POSTMAN

'In the 1920s the postman cycled up to Stowe from Weedon. He used to place bets – I remember my mother investing sixpence each way on Tipperary Tim in the Grand National and it won at 100–1!'

'I remember the postman walking across the fields from Glapthorn to Benefield to deliver letters, stopping for a coffee before walking back. In the autumn he would pick mushrooms for us.'

ON THE ROAD

'In the autumn at Easton on the Hill a large pile of flintstones would be spread on the road for the horses and carts to flatten during the winter, and so make the roads good for another year. This was very dusty in the summer and hard on the feet! Later on came the hot tar machine and gravel to spread on top of it. It was wonderful when the roads were macadamed and the open gutters along the street covered.'

'At one time at Stanion we had a roadman by the name of Mr Betts and he looked after the village, keeping it clean and the paths weed-free. He walked around with his wheelbarrow and shovel and there was no rubbish or dirt anywhere.'

'My great-uncle, Richard Hines Wood or "Timber", was the roadman at Harpole, from the last bungalow at Southview right along the bottom of the hill not far from Heyford. He used to keep all the grass verges cut. He was well known by all the cyclists going to and from work in Northampton and was quite a character. He used to sit on his upturned barrow to eat his lunch.'

'The roadman at Ashley kept the footpaths and gutters clean and saw that the drains ran freely, also the gullies from the roads to the ditches. He covered the whole parish in this way.'

'Tuesday was busy in Denford as cattle, sheep and pigs from Ringstead, Raunds and Stanwick were driven through the High Street on their way to and from the market at Thrapston. Kitty remembers that everyone made sure their gates were shut on that day! There were three drovers with the cattle, one went down School

Lane and then ran along Church Lane and came up Church Walk to head off any stray cattle. Kitty's family would be outside their house to stop any going down Front Street, another man would guard the end of Church Lane, and the other one, Meadow Lane. The first one would run past the animals and be ready to keep them from going up Child's Street and so on until they were safely through the village.'

'The A509 through Bozeat village was so quiet that twice a day cows from the Church Farm cowsheds were herded along the road to the fields opposite. Four times a day (men went home to a mid-day dinner in those days) the village roads were full of workers from the three shoe factories either cycling or walking to and from home. There were no school dinners so children were also about at dinner-time. The few men who took a packed lunch to work could always be seen outside the factories playing football to while away the time till the factory work started again for the afternoon. There were no post vans delivering mail to the outlying village farms, this was delivered by the village post lady who cycled round. Warners Garage ran a fleet of lorries to pick up churns of milk from the farms in and around the village. The lorry drivers also had to lift and load two and a quarter cwt sacks of wheat for transport to Whitworth's Mill. Travelling fairs were to be seen on the road through the village. Each August one stopped here in time for Bozeat Feast, a celebration of the anniversary of the dedication of St Mary's church.'

GASLIGHT

'At the bottom of Smiths Hill, Irthlingborough, to the left, was the Gas House and the cottage of Mr Stokes, who worked the Gas Works, adjoined.

The gas was obtained by burning the coke until it was very hot and then they "drew it off". When this procedure was taking place, it lit up the town of Irthlingborough. The fumes were so strong that when children had chest problems. Dr Robb would have the kiddies sent to the Gas House to clear their chests. Apparently it worked.

Before gas was installed in buildings, houses and factories were lit by paraffin lamps and also candles. Factory workers would take their own candles to work. When gas was installed into houses, they only had one lamp in the downstairs living room with one jet. The meter was in the kitchen which took a penny at a time. The local community soon ran short of pennies and neighbours would be back and forth, borrowing pennies or exchanging threepences or sixpences. Considering that a shoe worker's top wage was £2 a week, this was quite expensive.'

'Long Buckby was served by gas and we had street lamps which a lamplighter came along to light. When there was a moon the lamplighter had time off. The moon was called the parish lamp.'

THE LOCAL BOBBY

The local constable was part of the village scene, on his bicycle or on foot as he went about his regular patrols. The children were in awe of him, as justice was meted out for any infringement of the law, knowing that more often than not they would be in just as much trouble at home if word got back to their parents!

'The Easton policeman lived in the village. He watched the children and any misdemeanour was noted in his black book and that was all the warning they needed for most of the time. Offences such as jumping over paddock walls or throwing pebbles on a zinc roof were all taken very seriously.'

'The village policeman came regularly to Stowe, by bicycle from Weedon. He would meet the Sergeant outside Cavalier Cottage at Upper Stowe. They sometimes went in for a cup of tea.'

'I was born in the early 1920s when my father was the rural Police Constable at Moulton. We lived in a row of cottages in West Street and in those days the policeman and his family were very much part of the community. A constable's brief in those days was first the prevention and then the detection of crime and to deal with and keep down complaints both major and minor in his area of beat. Moulton was and still is a large village but the area in those days encompassed Moulton Park (a sub-parish) and stretched almost as far as the Red House on the main Kettering Road. Latterly he moved to Boughton, a smaller neighbouring village, but then there was the addition of the villages of Pitsford and Brixworth which it was his responsibility to police.
    The police house was manned for 24 hours of the day, by mother who took messages in my father's absence on patrol. In the days after the First World War the night beat was patrolled on foot (per eight hour shift visiting designated points) and by bicycle on the day-time shift. He had to deal with any matters requiring attention during patrol and then with any callers at the house afterwards – almost a 24 hour on call service. As can be imagined the policeman's wife and family were not always popular with neighbours especially if some misdemeandour had been committed.
    Again in the early 1920s, rural policemen were permitted to have

their own dog section. The animal was the property of the policeman and he was allowed to take the dog on patrol only during the night beat on foot. We had a pedigree Airedale, named Spider, who was expertly trained by my father and obeyed him absolutely. As we lived in a row of cottages with open backs and gardens, a particular neighbour took exception to the dog straying on to his area when it was a puppy and he very often chased the dog away. As the dog grew older she could not bear the man and one night my father took the dog on patrol as usual and called back at the house for some reason in the middle of the night. He told Spider to go into her kennel and she obeyed. Later on the neighbour had to visit the outside lavatory during the night and Spider took her revenge by sitting outside the door, thus keeping him there until my father returned at 6 am and called her away. One can imagine that although my father apologised for this we were definitely not popular with those neighbours as a result.

Another story to illustrate the call-in aspect of the job. One Sunday lunch time an elderly, very fat man came puffing up to the house with tears in his eyes saying "Come quick, come quick, she's after me with the horsewhip". It was well known that the man, the local carrier, was also a heavy drinker, who from time to time beat his small long suffering wife when he was in his cups. My father's remark was "Good for her, she ought to have done this years ago. You can take care of yourself surely."

Again another part of the rural policeman's job was to know everybody on his beat and of course he was his own crime prevention man and accident and motor patrol officer. There was not a great deal of motor traffic in the 1920s but it was increasing in the 1930s and there were traffic accidents with injuries which had to be dealt with. Also, of course, there was no central CID and crime and sudden death etc had to be dealt with on the spot by the local man in the first instance.

Stories abound about local characters long since dead and I recount just one from the Moulton days. The local builder had the job of fitting a window in an old stone barn which was used by the local doctor as a coach house and stable. It still stands and was originally a meeting place for some nonconformist sect in the middle of the 19th century. The good doctor was inspecting the work when the time came for payment and he commented to the builder – "Sure, Mr B. this is not square" (because the old stone work was very irregular it was very difficult to achieve a neat and standard opening). The builder, a gruff sort of individual, said "Look, when I make a mistake it is there for every damned fool to comment on, when you make a mistake they are put under and no more is said about it."

Stories are rife about Boughton Green, the site of an ancient horse fair which lies between Moulton and Boughton. There is a ruined church in the dip on the Moulton side of the green and many trees which make it quite an eerie place at night. In the days I speak about there were three white gates at the three corners of the green – one on the Kingthorpe side, one on the Boughton side and one by the ruined church on the Moulton side. These gates were mostly closed and the story goes that some fellows had been drinking at the Five Bells at Kingthorpe and were walking home to Moulton. When they got to the Moulton gate it mysteriously opened for them and they were quite sure that this opening of the gate was performed by a spirit or ghost. They made the best speed they could back to Moulton and recounted their adventure later in the village pub. In fact the gate was opened by the "man in blue" who happened to be there on night patrol and who performed the act silently and without comment.'

DOWN AT THE LOCAL

'The Hare and Hounds at Great Addington had stables where ponies and traps were kept earlier this century. Mr D. Payne was the landlord and carrier. On the occasion of the Archdeacon's visit, Mr Payne was taking the Archdeacon to Cranford station when, on turning out of the pub yard, the wheel fell off the trap! Boys used to sit outside the pub and direct the traffic at the junction and drink the old men's beer.'

'There were still two pubs in Denford Ash in the early 1950s, but it was probably in the next few years that the Rose and Crown became a rather nice general store. I remember the Cock Inn used to have a skittles table. The "cheeses" were made of wood, as were the pins, of course. This table still has an airing annually at the church fete. I believe this type of skittles is only common in this part of the country.'

'There were two public houses in Braybrooke. The Swan Inn in the 1950s was kept by Graham Moffat, the "Fat Boy" of Will Hay fame. The village fruit and vegetable show originated in the Club Room. This was popular for many years, later moving to the village hall. The Sun Inn by the church, closed in 1967, was known for its beer and skittles and was frequented by the locals. It had many characters and was the home of the skiffle band, with washboard, tea chest mandolin and various other home-made instruments. On Boxing Day the band accompanied by hobby horses galloped to the mock meet of the Hunt at the end of what is now Newton Way.'

OUTDOOR BEER HOUSES

'There used to be five pubs in Everdon – only the Plough is left now but there was also the Plume of Feathers, the Red Lion, the Crown and Anchor and the Barley Mow. There were also outdoor beer houses where you could get a drink. One was at Glebe House and the other at Home Farm, Little Everdon. Here. men could stop and get a drink as they walked to work in Weedon.'

'Off licences, or outdoor beer houses as they were called, were only licensed to sell beer. Opening hours were as follows:- Weekdays 10 am to 2 pm and 6 pm to 10 pm. Sundays 12 noon to 2 pm and 7 pm to 10 pm. There were six altogether, at Irchester, two of which were in private houses, the latter selling the beer at the front door – a hinged wooden flap served as counter and when not in use it hung against the wall. All the beer was sold from the barrel, customers bringing their own jugs. Price was three pence to fourpence ha'penny per pint.'

'No 1 High Street, Gayton was a licensed "Jug and Bottle" premises where you could buy intoxicating liquor which was poured into your own jug or bottle for you to take home to drink. They also sold other items such as tobacco and cigarettes. Until the 1960s the Queen Victoria had a shop in the southside front room which sold everything.'

CLUBS AND CHARACTERS

'Creaton used to have two pubs. The Horseshoe Inn was so called because there was once a landlord who was a blacksmith. This inn was burned down, having just been rethatched in early 1962. The other pub, The Bricklayers Arms on the main road, has its own claim to fame. In 1902 John Blunt became its landlord and he remained there until 1962 when he died at the age of 93. He was the oldest landlord in England – Blunt by name and blunt by nature! The Bricklayers was the venue of three special club dinners each year. The Ex-Servicemen's Club, the Pig Club and the Sick Club. Having fed and "oiled" the inner man, entertainment was next – "home-made and completely predictable"! Always the same people and always the same song! Other characters who frequented the pub were "Clocky", who mended watches, and Rags, who played the concertina and sang "When you have money, life is all honey, gaily your friends all knock at the door, when you've no money, isn't life funny – nobody knows you when you are poor!"'

THIS GATE HANGS WELL

'I came to Cotterstock in 1947 and remember the Gate Inn with the river Nene, a lock, a mill and the mill race nearby. The inn is now a private house but then it had sawdust on the floor and a sign outside which read:

> This Gate hangs well and hinders none.
> Refresh and pay and travel on,
> But if perchance a storm appears
> Furl up your sail and anchor here.'

THE BUTCHER AND THE BAKER

Recalling the village scene of the past, the shops and services that existed to serve their immediate community spring at once to mind. Here you would probably find a butcher, a baker, a general store, a blacksmith, a wheelwright, a post office and so on. The bakehouse in particular holds many happy memories of past Sundays, for in the days before every housewife had her own reliable oven, it would be the baker who would undertake the roasting of the joint and the Yorkshire pudding, as well as baking cakes and pastries.

IN THE VILLAGES

'Barby had its own shop, post office, baker and butcher. Before the days of refrigeration, the butcher, at the end of the day, had to remove his stock from the shop and take it to his own home where he had a large cellar. When the baker was in the village, local people would take their Yorkshire puddings, meat and cakes to cook in the hot oven. The wheelwright, undertaker, roadsweeper and smithy were all resident in the village. The blacksmith was also sexton of the church. Every day, he climbed the church tower to wind the clock up. He also lit the boiler in church on Sundays. The bier was pushed by him at funerals.

Water was obtained from three pumps in the village, one pump having better drinking water than the others. Milk was supplied by one of the local farmers, who delivered to the door with quarter pint, half pint and one pint measures poured into householders' jugs.'

'I remember when Denford had several shops – a butcher's, which had home-made lard and dripping which was lovely, a post office which sold cheese, bacon and so on, and another shop in the High Street, Webb's, which sold all sorts of things from dolls and beads, which I remember were in a glass case, to biscuits and sweets. Oil for lamps was available at this shop, too. You could get milk and home-made butter in the village from the Talbot's farm. I remember taking a can and going at the right time and standing on the step at Talbot House until it was our turn.

The ovens at the bakehouse were busy on Sunday mornings, not full of bread but with the villagers' Sunday dinners. With most families being large, the Sunday roast would not fit in the small ovens in the cottages and for a few pence the baker, Alec Manning, was pleased to offer the use of his bread ovens. He used to deliver his bread to surrounding villages by a wickerwork handcart and in the summertime he had to cool the wheels down by throwing buckets of water over them to make the iron bands around the wooden wheels contract again to fit.'

'Seventy odd years ago Creaton was still a fairly self-sufficient small village. There was a shop-cum-post office on the main road (A50). Two butchers could be found, one of whom only opened for business

Milk came to your door direct from the farm in the days before pasteurisation – and the milkman's cart with its large metal churns looked very different from those we see now.

42

on Wednesdays and Saturdays. The other, Turlands, was housed in a small rectangular building just below the church. Inside, on the right of the counter was a hollowed-out "apse" in the thick walls. On enquiry, I was told a crippled relative used to do the books, and in order not to take up unnecessary space the "apse" had been made – rather a chilly seat!

At the bottom of High Street was the bakehouse, where bread, cakes of all descriptions etc were baked and sold, and on Sundays the good people of Creaton would take along the Sunday joint to be cooked in the oven, while the families were at church. Further up the High Street, Mercy Cattle sold sweets, vinegar and paraffin in her front room. On the green there was a cobbler, and later on Mrs Webb, a Londoner who married into a Creaton family, having been trained in dressmaking and tailoring, was a boon to many a person, not only in Creaton.'

'Two shops are recalled at Great Addington. One in All Saints Cottage by the church was owned by "Old Sarah" who was dotty and used to wander up and down the street muttering prayers. This was a general store and usually in a muddle. Mrs Wilson sold sweets and tobacco, another eccentric, her shop was next to the bakehouse where Ginger Wilson could cook your Sunday dinner for twopence.'

'There was a blacksmith at Welton, Mr Harrison, whose forge was under the horse chestnut tree next to the dairy. I can remember the smell of the hot metal now and the sound of the hammer, mixed up with the sweet milky smell of the cows' breath as they were driven up the street twice a day to be milked, and my mother's grumbling at the cow pats they dropped. There were two pubs, a post office, a general store, where the golden syrup was kept in a barrel with a tap – and one day some child turned it on! There was a dressmaker, a cobbler, a carpenter (who was also the undertaker), a midwife and a bakery and the policeman came round on a bicycle.'

THE BUTCHER

'In the early 1930s at Yardley Hastings, on Monday mornings, older boys and some of the girls would gather outside the butcher's slaughter-house, near the school, waiting for the "Bullock Cart" to appear. Drawn by a horse, this would come from one of the local farms bringing a beast for slaughter.

The animal would be unloaded into its special pen inside the building and a noose slipped over its head. The other end of the rope was then threaded through a ring, specially secured in the centre of the floor, and then out through a hole in the wall, ready for "the big pull". At a word from the butcher, the farmer, the children and anyone passing at the time would space themselves out along the rope and pull and pull until the beast's head was down on the floor near the ring. Then the butcher would pole-axe him. None gave it a second thought at the time. It always happened nearly every Monday morning. Sheep and pigs on Tuesdays!'

THE POULTRYMAN

'Mary Turnham's grandfather had the first commercial van in Helmdon from Henry Oliver's, Mercers Row, Northampton. He used this van for his egg, butter and poultry business. Norman Osborne, who worked at Oliver's, stayed at Helmdon to teach Hedley Owen to drive the van.

She remembers Christmases between 1920 and 1939. This was a busy time for her grandparents, Arthur and Edith Humphrey. Poultry was bought from surrounding farms and kept in barns. Her grandfather also bought prize-winning birds from the local shows. During the Christmas period of about three weeks, they employed many local people to help with plucking and drawing the birds and Will Duncombe did the killing. The feathers were put in sacks to be sent to Wisbech on the train. Mary and her grandfather were usually weighing and labelling the birds before taking them down into the cool cellar or the front room which was cold. Many of the birds went to the shoe factories and clubs in Northampton as well as to shops and hotels. Mary usually delivered local birds on her bicycle. When the work was finished, they all had port and mince pies in the kitchen and the hand bell ringers would come and play.'

SUNDAY DINNER AT THE BAKEHOUSE

'In the present age of such convenient cookers, it is hard to imagine the method by which many villagers enjoyed their Sunday dinner – NOT called lunch (that was at eleven o'clock!) – dinner, that special meal of the week when all members of the family sat down together and during which problems were ironed out; important plans made; new clothes requested and highlights of the past week remembered. Sad that the pace of the present day does not present such leisurely times together.

It was usually the man of the house who made the journey to the bakehouse, carefully carrying a large baking tin (often approximately 18" × 12") containing a good depth of batter with a joint perched rather precariously on a stand above. One after another they walked along the street, sometimes hurrying and, therefore, splashing batter everywhere because, help! – ten minutes to eleven was the time for the tins to go into the oven, all at the same moment. The men, of course, stayed in the bakehouse to discuss issues of the day and the previous football matches etc. Having made sure all was well, one by one they would drift off to the local for opening time at twelve. So the return journey of the "Bake-pudding and meat" had to be undertaken by Mrs or one of the older children.

From the age of nine, it became my task, well over 50 years ago and what a responsibility, too! What a gorgeous smell of baking met you at the door and what an array of puds were out on the well-scrubbed tables awaiting collection *before* 12.45 pm. All this for a penny – until one Sunday, young as I was, I sensed all was not well with the baker. Was he upset? Was he ill? Was he angry? There was a "fishy" smell, too – funny, somehow. All was soon revealed when the owner of a pudding arrived and, lo and behold, on his tin was a herring – much dried up. In no uncertain terms, that person was told not to come until meat could be obtained as all the meals had absorbed the vapours from the fish and, to say the least, were not very palatable. Never mind, though, that week everyone had their penny back.

So the hot pudding and meat were cut up then and eaten hot; during Sunday evening, cold pud and slices from the joint; warmed up on Monday with bubble and squeak and any left went into cottage pie on Tuesday – all from the Sunday dinner.'

'My grandfather was the village blacksmith at Roade, and so was my father until he ran away to join the army during the First World War. One of my earliest memories was during the early 1920s, of my grandmother in her long black skirt and white apron, running down the street on a Sunday morning with the roast beef and Yorkshire pudding, all steaming hot and cooked to a turn, from the village bakehouse, where the local baker cooked Sunday lunch for dozens of families, for a few pence. My father used to tell me how he and his brother climbed in the pantry window on a Sunday afternoon and pinched lumps of Yorkshire pudding, and Grandma used to say "Funny! I thought I had more pudding than that."'

'There were four bakers at Irchester including the local Co-op, and in 1946 the price of white bread was small fourpence ha'penny and large sevenpence.

Parts of the village were without gas until after the Second World War so two of the bakers fired their ovens on Sunday mornings at ten o'clock ready to receive Sunday dinners to be cooked – the price

The village bakehouse at Cold Ashby, where Sunday Lunches could be taken to be cooked.

of this was twopence per dinner. The meat was brought in the tin ready to be cooked, surrounded by batter for the Yorkshire pudding. Anyone living on the outskirts of the village brought the batter in a jug. One of these bakers, retired now of course, says he knew everybody's dinner! Not so the other baker (Co-op), because one mother of a rather large family, arriving a little later than usual, found to her dismay someone else had taken her large tin and she was left with a small one.'

'Many Bigstock villagers remember taking their Sunday lunch to be cooked in the bakehouse ovens on the corner of Bridge Street and High Street. At twelve o'clock a steady stream of women and children would carry their joints of meat surrounded by Yorkshire pudding to the bakehouse where, for a few pence, their dinners would be cooked and an hour later both meat and pudding would miraculously be done to perfection and even more surprising, each meal would be passed to its rightful owner. But I have heard one story of a small girl walking a quarter of a mile with the family Sunday lunch only to be told by her mother she had collected the wrong tin!

During the week cakes and pastry could also be taken to the bakehouse. One lady remembers being admonished by her mother when there were very few cherries left in her cherry cake when cut at tea time – small daughter had fished them out of the mix when carrying it to the bakehouse!'

THE BAKER AND TEA DRINKING

'Twice a year at Easton on the Hill there was an event known as Tea Drinking for the school children. The bakehouse catered for these events. One of them was the annual school treat, the other was May Day. In the latter case, the children paraded the village with a garland, singing songs about the merry month of May. Needless to say, it was usually a cold day so most children were wrapped up warm in scarves and top coats. On these two Tea Drinkings, the baker made very large long loaves for ease in cutting up the mammoth number of slices of bread and jam – also huge fruit, seed and Madeira cakes were made. These, with gallons of tea were soon disposed of with much relish. At Harvest Festival the bakery put a display of sacks of flour and large "quartern" loaves in the church.

During the war years, it was compulsory to add potato meal to the flour mixture. This produced a very dark loaf which we ate with thanksgiving. Despite its appearance, it was still sustaining and wholesome.'

THE GENERAL STORE

The little shops that sold everything were the backbone of rural life before the car made the town shops accessible and the supermarket came to stay. Some of these shops were ahead of their time in the services they provided, while others were as idiosyncratic as their owners.

THE SHOP NEAR THE STOCKS

'The first shopkeeper anyone can remember at Little Houghton was Little Miss Smith who lived there with her uncle who was a carpenter.

At Christmas, Little Miss Smith would put toys and sweets in her window and stand a bench outside so that the children could stand on it to look into the window.

One day Henry Shrewsbury got up to look in and put his head right through the glass of the window. His father, Bumper Shrewsbury came upon the group of children including his son and, not knowing it had been his son who was responsible for the damage, told the children that if they could not behave themselves better they should get out of the village!

The next person to keep the shop was Miss Nellie Luck, daughter of the blacksmith (Auntie Nellie to me, she being my grandmother's cousin). In those early days of this century it was more than a grocery shop, she also kept haberdashery, wool and some ornaments and glass. In hot weather she kept her butter on a ledge down the well to keep it cool.

All her stock was brought to her and on Wednesday afternoons she closed the shop and went to town to pay her wholesalers, see what was available, do her banking and shopping. On these trips she would often bring back articles of underclothing for people who could not get into town.

There was no bell on her shop door, but a piece of iron sticking up above the door which, as the door opened and closed, scraped over another piece of metal fitted like a spring above the door. This scraping made a peculiar loud creaking note which warned her of a customer's arrival.

Her name – E.E. Luck, – was, by her brother Alf (also a blacksmith), set in split pebbles into the concrete step outside the shop door (this has now been covered up by the new steps).

Inside the shop were lots of big bottles of sweets, bulk containers, big tins of biscuits etc from which she would weigh up the customers' requirements. There were wooden drawers, deep ones with brass handles, and, of course, the old fashioned scales with weights.

All supplies such as tea, sugar, butter, cheese and lard came in bulk and were weighed and wrapped or bagged by Miss Luck whilst you waited. A chair was provided to the left of the door.

My mother told me that in her father's day men bought tobacco by the penny weight-the penny one side of the scales and the tobacco to that weight purchased, and the men would look amongst their money and make sure they saved the heaviest pennies! I cannot imagine that the weight differential was so great but certainly some of the old pennies did look larger than others.

In wartime, when you entered the door you found yourself behind a long heavy, brown, coarse hairy curtain which, at night time (she kept open until 9pm on Saturdays) you could not open until the door had been shut. The door and windows both had shutters which she took out each night and put on the outside of the windows.

These acted as a blackout, but were also the sign that the shop was closed.

Miss Luck kept the shop from before the First World War until the 1950's. At first she did not live at the shop but at the blacksmith's house with her mother, and her brother Alf lived at the shop with his wife and young family. She never married, but she had a sweetheart who was an Australian. He went back to Australia and she stayed here.

Miss Luck was followed in the shop by Johnny Bowles, who lived there with his mother, the Churchills, the Stantons and now Del and Margaret Scott.'

AHEAD OF ITS TIME

'Half a century ago in Syresham we probably had a store which in effect was well before its time. Its trademark was "Kings for Everything" and it could and did supply everything. It had its own brewery, brewing beer and lemonade, and these bottles are now very collectable items, especially as they had marble stoppers. The brewery was a local landmark and during the Second World War was used by the local Home Guard as a look-out post. The beer was delivered in their own lorries and they also ran mobile shops, travelling round many local villages. People will remember their distinctive red vans with "Kings for Everything" painted on the side. The top of these mobile vans had racks to hold the beer and lemonade. The shop was very large and sold not only provisions and groceries, but much more besides. Many people remember all the huge tins of loose biscuits and choosing your own varieties to be weighed up. The bacon and cheese was also cut up on the premises whilst sugar, dried fruit etc was bagged up on the premises. What wonderful smells can still be conjured up from this store.

In addition the shop sold all types of furniture, carpets and every conceivable household item. Clothes, shoes etc could all be purchased there and many other haberdashery items. Everything could be got under one roof in the village shop. Sadly the shop is no more, the building has been converted into houses and flats and a store place. The brewery was demolished some years ago and houses stand on the site.'

SHOPKEEPING IN THE 1950s

'In 1949 we left Kettering for Geddington, where we bought a shop and cottage, next to the church. Part of the building was 12th/13th century, the original forge and bakehouse (we believe) serving the castle. It was thatched and had a "crutch" roof. It also had a well in the cellar with a constant supply of pure cold water; this spring also served the village at the well under the Cross. The property was built on a hill, so there were plenty of steps. The walls were over three feet thick. The kitchen fireplace, where huge logs had been burned years ago, was large enough to hold a Bendix washing machine, a cooking stove, a hot water boiler (for the central heating), and a coke bunker (holding one and a half cwt of coke). Above was an oak beam, over two feet square, from which we removed over 200 hand-made nails.

I had never done shop-work before and I was very nervous at first, especially as many things were still on ration – sweets, cigarettes, soap, cheese, etc. I was warned that Woodbines were for regular customers only; the first morning I opened, on the doorstep were two ladies demanding Woodbines. This was a problem as I didn't know who were regulars! I almost lost my voice that first day, but after that I began to enjoy it.

Fred helped, doing the accounts, filling in the endless forms, and not least counting the coupons. There was no cash and carry; travellers called and they really wanted your custom. Goods were delivered with the account, which you paid at the end of the month. Anything special, medicines, cakes, films or goods in very short supply, Fred collected from Kettering.

I started getting little gifts for the children, who came in with sixpence or a shilling wanting a present for Mum. I also sold fireworks, which I didn't care for. Many children, the boys in particular, brought in their pocket money, tuppence usually, to enter in a book for collection on 5th November.

We had many a smile, and frustrations too. Customers would call when the shop was closed (often in the middle of a meal), "Please can Mum have a dummy, a babies bottle, or a teat". One lady regularly came for her cheese ration when we were closed and she only lived a few doors away; she was not very popular. Once she brought half a dozen sweets back and asked me to change them as her son (30 years of age) did not like the green ones. A child came in one day for half a pound of human paste – she meant almond paste, it was just before Christmas.

Soon after we settled into the shop we realised the thatched roof needed repair; we decided to have it rethatched. Easier said than done. We scoured the whole district for a thatcher. The Bythorn thatcher had retired and he said "Try Olney". We went to Olney, no one knew of a thatcher. Then near the market place we saw a policeman. He didn't know off hand but then he had an inspiration – the publican opposite had had a house thatched a year ago, so over the road we go as the church clock was striking six. There was the publican opening the door. We followed him in, the policeman leading into the bar and the moment the publican saw the policeman he greeted him, reached for a tankard and started to pull a pint. "No," said the policeman, "not yet, this gentleman is looking for a thatcher." We got the address but no luck, he had a contract to thatch 20 pubs for the brewers. One amusing thing happened though, during our early conversation with the policeman. We suggested we called at the police station to ask there. "No point," said the policeman, "half the force are on holiday, and you are talking to the other half." In the end we found that the "Dukes" thatcher was free-lance, he kindly came and did the job. About this time the whole village was "put on the sewer", and town water fed to the whole village. Goodbye night-cart, goodbye our own water supply from our own well.

A ten year old boy, who lived near, had a habit of coming into the shop just on closing time, leaning on the counter, gazing into space, and asking for "Quarter pound of sugar and two pounds of tea". One day when my husband was serving he asked for two shillings and eightpence worth of aniseed balls (they were then, I believe, 16 a penny). We had a dear old vicar who came in every week for half a pound of extra strong mints; he suffered dreadfully with indigestion, his housekeeper was a shocking cook.

We sold Lyon's ice-cream, enjoyed in the summer by the ladies at the local factory; two girls would come with a large basket for 20 or 30 sixpenny ones. After ten years I had trouble with my legs (too much standing), so on doctor's advice we sold up and returned to Kettering.'

THE POST OFFICE 1930–1960

'I first came to Moulton in 1928 as assistant to Mr Martin who ran the post office and a general store in West Street, close by the village school. About a year later the business changed hands and the new owner, Mr William Tite, was pleased when I agreed to stay on and help him in his new life as he had previously been a valet and knew little about shopkeeping.

I remember those early days selling penny and halfpenny-worths of sweets to the children and groceries to their mums, stamps and postal orders from the PO counter and manning the telephone exchange all at the same time. It really was a two person job, but it was just not possible for us both to be in the shop all of the time- there were jobs to be done elsewhere as well.

The telephone exchange, I must explain, was a manual one. By the time that the automatic exchange was built, a year or so before the war, the number of subscribers had risen to about a hundred. I remember some of the early numbers: Mr Hooley was No 1, Lucas the builders No 2, the doctor No 3, the vicar No 4. Mrs Manfield at Moulton Grange was No 9.

Whatever we were doing – usually halfway through serving a customer – if the bell rang, Mr Tite or I had to drop everything and answer it, ask for the number required and plug it in. This led to delays in serving if I was alone in the shop. As it was a 24 hour service we had an arrangement to deal with night time calls. Generally Mr Tite went to answer them but if the bell rang more than once in a night and he was sleeping I would get up to it. The night bell was just outside the bedroom door and whoever heard and answered it would tuck a hanky under the clapper so that the other would know that the call was being attended to and could return to sleep. This worked very well and saved the postmaster from hurrying down if I was already doing the work. One night, however, I forgot to remove the hanky and another caller tried to get through without success. We had an official enquiry about that lapse!

Then there were the postmen. The main usually arrived before 6am and the postmen were always there waiting to sort it. They were an assorted bunch, four of them. One, John Robinson, finished by about 10am and took a break for breakfast. He then came on again and cycled to Boughton and Pitsford and on to Chapel Brampton to empty all the post boxes then seal the bag and on to Brampton station where he padlocked it in the guard's van of the train (after taking out any letters for Moulton which he delivered on the way back). Back in Moulton he then had to meet the bus at Eynon's corner and collect the mail, unlocking it on the bus platform. Finally the second post had to be delivered around West Street.

The afternoon delivery was from about 3pm so he certainly had a very long day. No vans in those days, just a bicycle. I don't think he ever forgot his keys. If he had done so there would have been no delivery and the mail would have had a nice bus ride to Kettering and back. All this was for a wage of little more than £2 per week.

Another postman was Ted Whitney who took the post of the Grove, the farm lodges, Holcot, Hannington and all the lodges down the Kettering Road in the morning, again in the afternoon, emptying the boxes on the way, including trips to Overstone Sywell and Mears Ashby. He was a friendly, helpful chap always whistling on his rounds. 'There'll always be an England' was the favourite tune. He was sometimes careless about closing garden gates. One he left open repeatedly and one day the owner stood waiting: 'Postman, what do you think I got that gate for?' Then said Ted, scratching his head, 'Oh! I should think for about 30 bob.' Ted was also the village lamplighter for a long time.

Oh yes – the telegrams. When one arrived it had to be delivered by hand, which meant that Mr Tite used his bike. If anyone was passing by whom he knew to be reliable he would ask them to do the delivery for him. Payment was sixpence for up to a mile, over that a shilling, more if it was right over to Walgrave. We always covered Boughton and Holcot and did Walgrave on their halfdays. The village lads after school and on Saturdays would hang about the shop door hoping for the chance to earn a copper or two by these deliveries. They were on to a good thing – but we knew who we could trust.

I am a Baptist and went to the chapel along West Street and made many friends there, but Mr Tite and his family went to the parish church where he was in the choir and when his daughters were old enough they sang too and became Sunday school teachers.

I stayed with the Tites until 1960 although Mr Tite gave up the post office due to ill health. He died in 1959 and I stayed on to help Mrs Tite to clear up the business and move to another house.

Thirty three years of my life . . . and I enjoyed every minute of it'.

'As an adventurous five year old in 1927, being looked after by my grandmother, I tried using our telephone, thus causing chaos at the telephone exchange (Mr Drage, Roade). Our phone numbers were 1Y1 Roade and 1Y2 Roade, the only numbers I knew. Mr Drage had to contact my parents who were working on the buses and were at the Northampton terminus.'

FIRE AND FLOOD

Horse-drawn engines, hand pumps and bucket chains were still the line of defence against fire within living memory, and putting out a fire was often very much a community effort. Against floods, of course, there was no defence and the rivers that provided so much fun for skating in the winter were a threat to life and property when the thaw came or heavy rains fell.

FIRE IN WEST STREET

'One Sunday morning in Moulton in 1938 as the congregation sat listening quietly to the sermon, a message was brought into church and handed up to the vicar in the pulpit. He read it, pronounced a hurried blessing and told us that a serious fire was raging at the doctor's house in West Street and help was urgently needed. How right he was – and the whole village turned out to do the best we could to help. Doctor's house, a lovely stone and thatch building, was doomed but the surrounding cottages were also in danger. Bucket gangs were formed to raise water from a well and pass along to men up on the roofs to dowse the thatch and beat out sparks to prevent the fire from spreading. Other gangs (we girls among them) ran to and fro across the street taking household goods and furniture from the cottages to the safety of the Farm Institute or the Principal's house which were just opposite the fire. The village engine – a hand pump – broke down and lost a wheel on the way through the village, so was not a lot of use. The town engine, when it finally arrived, concentrated on the main fire but neglected to tackle one which was beginning in the next house, also a fine stone building. This one could have been saved if it had received attention in time, but at least the cottage homes of many villagers were saved by our efforts.

A new house was built for Dr Smart on the same site but luck was really against him. A few years later bombs were dropped on that part of Moulton, probably jettisoned by a German bomber looking for Coventry, and a huge crater was left in the garden right next to the new house causing considerable damage to the property.'

THE CAT THAT MEWED

'Sometime in the 1930s in Greens Norton there was a fire in the High Street. There was a row of three cottages which burned down. I was wakened up to see the fire. Apparently, the alarm was raised by a cat mewing. All the human occupants escaped, including an invalid lady, but the cat perished. Everyone was very upset about that.'

THE BAKEHOUSE FIRE

'Where the Pavilion Chinese Restaurant stands today in Irthlingborough, 90 years ago it was Tom Parker's public house. Directly opposite this was John Parson's bakehouse. Mr Parsons was a very good baker and, mid-morning on Sundays, the husbands would take the baking pans with the meat and the batter mix to be cooked in the large ovens. Often, the housewives would pop an onion in one corner and possibly a shaved apple in another. Lunchtime would arrive, to see the same husbands with a towel collecting the baking pans all wrapped up.

Mr and Mrs Parsons lived with their children, and also the lad who helped in the bakehouse, in the cottage adjoining, with their sleeping quarters running over the bakehouse.

One Christmas, however, the bakehouse was very busy cooking cakes and poultry for the people of Irthlingborough. No one knew exactly how it started but opinion was that the oven, which was cooking through the night, was overfull and that fat probably splashed onto the gas jet and caught light. However, the building was soon blazing, with the family trapped upstairs. The parents escaped with the children, leaving the youngest, a baby, in the same room at the back of the house with the lad who worked in the bakehouse. The lad then seized the baby, wrapped it in blankets and lowered it down over the kitchen roof to safety. He then jumped down himself, wearing only a nightshirt.

When a fire occurred in Irthlingborough, the 'Church School' bell was rung to alert the town. The children rushed from all over to assist, with the fire engine being filled by means of a hand pump from the pond on Back Way, which was situated at the back of the Church School and College Street/Victoria Road. The fire station (described as 'no bigger than a cupboard') was conveniently placed next to the pond, but the plodding carthorse which was to pull the engine was unfortunately tethered in Marsh Lane and had to be fetched. As the horse only moved at his own speed, by the time it had travelled Station Road, The Cross and College Street, the fire had often burned out by the time the cavalry had arrived.'

'THE FACTORY'S ON FIRE!'

'When I was about ten years old at Roade in the 1930s, I was wakened one morning at five o'clock by hearing my mother shouting to my father 'Tom, Tom, get up quickly the factory's on fire.' The factory was at the end of our road, making it into a cul-de-sac, and we lived four houses away from it. I looked at the wall of my bedroom and saw this livid red glare, and heard roaring and crackling. Dad jumped out of bed, threw on some clothes, and with a couple of neighbours tried to move a lorry that was parked between two of the buildings, but the heat was so fierce, and there was no key to move it, and although they tried to push it to safety, it wouldn't budge. In the end it caught fire and so did the other building. When the fire brigade arrived they could find no water for about half an hour, so that by the time the fire was brought under control, most of the factory was gutted. My mother spent a busy morning making gallons of tea for the firemen. My one abiding memory of the fire, and it is as clear as the day it happened, is going to the back door of our house to get a back-view of everything going on, and coming face to face with a poor old frightened donkey. It was in the vicarage paddock and the noise and uproar had frightened it into our garden.'

FLOODS AT DENFORD

'There was skating on the frozen floods across the meadows most winters. I can remember strapping skates on over my shoes. Mr Percy Weekley, who was an expert skater, used to tow everyone behind him. I recall one occasion when my sister went through the ice and came home rather wet! I remember, too, going on the frozen river. The road at the ford was often flooded after the winter snows or heavy rainfall.

Over the years there have been several people drowned around here. One day a friend and I saw a body in the river but someone going in to Thrapston to work said they would report it, which they did. Being young at that time, we didn't realise that a person reporting something like that got two shillings and sixpence for the information!

There were flash summer floods in June or July in the late 1950s, when there was a tremendous amount of rain all at once and the church tower was struck by lightning. Hay bales and loose hay were floating down the river and got caught up in the barbed wire, and people were canoeing right across the meadows. These flash floods disappeared the same day.'

FERRIED BY CANOE

'Grendon is divided by a stream, a tributary of the river Nene, and until the 1980s there was frequent flooding at the lower end of the village called Blackmile Lane. At times the canoes from the Hall were used to ferry people and supplies to the houses in the lane. Flood signs and warning lamps were kept at the Hall to be put out when the road flooded. Several houses at the lower end were frequently flooded, but after a great deal of lengthy discussion with Anglian Water they agreed to widen and realign the brook to make a better flow and this also necessitated a new bridge being built.'

THE WINTER OF 1947

The long and harsh winter of 1947 still evokes memories of villages cut off in huge snow drifts and the struggle by a war-weary and rationed community to continue the daily routine through several months of Arctic weather.

WOULD IT EVER STOP?

'I have vivid memories of the winter of 1947 as, at the time, I lived in Kettering and worked in Rushden. Every morning, I left home at 7.20 am., and cycled into town where I left my bicycle at a friend's house and then caught a bus at 7.40 am. This bus went all the way to Rushden but, unfortunately, everyone had to get off in Irthlingborough and wait for 20 minutes or more before they could get on again. This was rather soul-destroying so several of us used to walk into Higham Ferrers, by which time the bus would have caught us up. The fare for a weekly ticket was seven shillings and six pence for six days, so, every sixth week, the unused part of the tickets could be traded in for a free one.

At the end of January, the snow came and it looked as if it would never stop. I remember walking through snow up to the top of my legs and the buses did not run for two weeks. In those days, it was possible to go to Rushden by train from Kettering, changing at Wellingborough. On one memorable day, the train took two and a half hours to reach Wellingborough because all the points were frozen. On arrival at Wellingborough, we were told that there were no trains to Rushden as the snow was too deep, so we set out and walked! I arrived at the school where I taught at 12.20 pm, having left home at 7.20 am as usual, though not using a bicycle. When I arrived, the headmaster looked at me and said 'Do your registers and then go home.' I set off to walk back to Wellingborough and a kind motorist gave me a lift. The train took 20 minutes to reach Kettering.

The snow lay in the streets for six weeks and even the busiest main streets were covered with packed snow until the middle of March.

We made the most of the conditions and had some happy times tobogganing on the snow-covered hills and lanes, but we were very thankful when the thaw finally came and life returned to normal.'

WALKING WAS BAD

'The winter of 1947 – I was only 15 at the time and sent home early from work. It was snowing heavily and I was told the buses were going to stop running. My parents weren't so fortunate, along with a lot of others. My mother, I remember, called in to the grocers, James Bros, on the Market Square for some provisions in case we were unable to get out. She then walked home six miles to Denton. Walking was bad because the snow was getting deeper. My father who came even later also had to walk home. By that time, no one could see exactly where the road was and they were walking into deep drifts, a terrible journey home, arriving very late in the evening, wet through (I believe this was a Monday). The next day we discovered we were snowed in, Denton being in a dip. There were drifts ten feet high on the Northampton road. Everyone was out digging. The baker being at Yardley Hastings, we had no bread. The men started digging towards Yardley and Northampton but we were snowed in for three days. Everything was on ration and some people had nothing at all. There was no coal. If you were unlucky enough to have been expecting a delivery that week, everyone would rally round and help out, as everyone knew everyone else.

We youngsters of course loved all this. If you did possess wellingtons, that was great, you could tread in all the new snow. My brother and the rest who went to school in the town were also

Towns and villages all over the county were cut off for several weeks in huge snow drifts in 1947. Though food and fuel were a worry, tobogganing was a popular sport during this enforced leisure time.

58

having marvellous times. We all sledged all day down the village green from the top near the village pump to the horse trough, and across the road, the village green being a very steep one.'

THE COALMAN CALLED THE DAY BEFORE

'Cold Ashby was snowed in for four days. Luckily the coalman had been the day before so on-one was cold, and with two bakers in the village no-one would starve. Men were shovelling snow all day to try and make a passage through the village. Snow was up to some of the bedroom windows of the cottages.'

AFTER THE THAW – AND ANOTHER DISASTER

'In 1947, after the snow came terrible floods in Woodford and Hinton. Pool Street in Hinton was like a river.

In 1967 a great whirlwind hit the village, doing much damage. A pram with a baby in it was blown up into the air but miraculously the baby escaped unhurt. Workers demolishing the station buildings had a lucky escape. They decided to leave work early as the boy responsible for providing lunch had forgotten it – 20 minutes after they left, the building where they would have been eating collapsed.'

CHURCH AND CHAPEL

Sunday was a special day, whether you attended church or chapel, with the chance to forget about the work which filled the rest of the week. Many people attended church two, or even three times during the day and the rector was the most influential person in the village, next to the squire. Children, of course, attended Sunday school, and looked forward eagerly to the annual outing or treat.

SUNDAYS

'Sundays were very active. Worship was expected and singing was enjoyable. At Hargrave there was the Church of England and the Wesleyan chapel (now demolished) which each had two services and Sunday schools for the children. It was possible to fit in both denominations by going to church in the morning and chapel in the afternoon then making a choice for the evening. Church bell-ringing was a regular half-hour call to prayer and a popular activity for the ringers. Roast beef and Yorkshire pudding (made with a penn'orth of skimmed milk) was cooked at the bakery on Sundays until 1924 – twopence per tin and the smell was tantalising as they were collected and carried away at speed. Sunday was a time for family walks in "Sunday Best". For youngsters and young adults it was a time for grouping and pairing to share secrets and discover themselves. A regular stroll was to the three Shires (Northamptonshire, Bedfordshire and Huntingdonshire) meeting point where there was a concrete trough to which was attributed a little bit of magic. Step in, turn three times and wish.'

'The very large vicarage at Evenley was some distance down the road to Brackley. Sundays in the past can be remembered as a time when The Book was placed on the table in the cottages.'

'Our Sundays were spent at Sunday school and at church. We always had special clothes which we called "Sunday best". We hardly ever wore them except on a special occasion. If we went to visit my grandmother on a Sunday we were never allowed to knit or sew and the only book that we were allowed to read was the Bible.'

'More people used to go to the chapel in Denford than church at one time. We had a Sunday school and there used to be several classes. We went at ten o'clock and again at two o'clock. I remember that the children had cards and we were given a red star if we were there on time and a black one was put on if we were late. If you got 104 stars, you got first prize, which was a book. There was Prize Day, when there was a special service when mothers and fathers could come. Sometimes we had a Sunday school Treat and went up into the fields and had games and a tea. I remember we used to scramble in the grass for sweets although I'm afraid I didn't find many.

Sometimes, after chapel, some cousins of my mother used to come back to our house and we'd have a sing-song. I had a little organ, which my mother bought from Mrs Robinson at the shop when I was about nine, which had no stops but had to be pedalled, and I had music lessons from a lady in the village. I used to take threepence and a candle and have half an hour's lesson. I remember I went to someone in Thrapston for some lessons later on. I also had some lessons from Mrs Spendlove in the village, who played the church organ.

I can remember after chapel on a Sunday evening, Mum and Dad would sometimes take us children for a walk, sometimes up Brickhill Lane, sometimes up Out Mere way, we'd go right round the Green lane, go one way and back another. We used to go up Brown's Lane, across the field to the left and over the football field, through the "Belt" (a long, narrow field) through the Cattle Arch, up the next field and down Brickhill Lane. Or another favourite walk was up Rose Hill, over the railway and into Brickhill Lane. We used to enjoy those walks.

I used to like to go round the Westfields – that was up Ringstead Hill, across the fields to Ringstead and back by the river. Sometimes we would go down Meadow Lane, over the first bridge (the second bridge was where we used to paddle) and then to the high bridge over the big meadow to Woodford, over the church field, and over the railway line to Islip.

I do remember how dusty the roads were in the summer and a man coming round with a water cart to lay the dust. In the winter when we had floods, the big meadow was very good for skating. The road at the ford used to be flooded sometimes.'

'The church of St Denys at Cold Ashby, built in stone in the early English style, with four bells, one of which bears the date 1317 making it the oldest in the county, played a big part in the life of the village. Services were taken by the vicar, who came from Thornby. There was Sunday school at 10.30am, a service at 11.00am then home for dinner, most likely cooked at one of the bakers. Back for Sunday school at 3.00pm with a service in the evening at 6.00pm on alternate Sundays. The choir would sing at both services and be paid a penny for their efforts. When someone died there were several women who "laid out" the deceased, the carpenter would build a coffin and a plank was laid in the roadway to rest the coffin on if the journey from their home to the church was a long one. The lychgate, built in 1883 and inscribed "Death is the beginning of Life", was opened for the coffin to be taken into the church; this gate is still only used for funerals to this day. The Sunday school trips were something the children looked forward to with delight. Some were simple picnics held at Honey Hill just outside the village and in later years there were visits to Wicksteed Park on a bus.

The chapel was formally consecrated as a Congregational church in 1943 but the cause had flourished in the village for 100 years or so before that. The chapel had previously been a wool barn, but no longer used as such was given to the village to be used as a place of worship in 1860 by a local farmer.

At one time the Church Army had a caravan in the gardens of the vicarage. The people of the village fed the army and they were allowed to sleep in the school room. After school the children of the village would go along to the caravan and sing with them; "What a friend we have in Jesus" was a popular hymn.'

THE PARISH CHURCH

'Mrs Holloway's grandfather, who died in 1930 aged 83, said that when he was a boy the church at Helmdon had a gallery. Before the organ was installed a minstrel played the bass viol to accompany the hymns. In later years, the present organ was pumped by Mr Sheppard, who was blind. He used to walk across the field footpath from the chapel to the church. Mrs Gascoigne, the blacksmith's wife, played the organ.'

'The church at Whilton was lit by oil lamps which had to be kept in trim. A coal stove was lit to provide heating by flues under the floor. The choir consisted of one man and several boys; there were no girls. When a death occurred in the village the death bell was rung as soon as possible afterwards. This meant tolling the bell once for each year of the deceased's life. The sexton was then responsible for digging the grave.'

'The children at Woodford were encouraged to be thoughtful and helpful, and on Easter Sunday the children from both the church and the chapel Sunday schools would take baskets of fresh eggs, which were later taken to Northampton General Hospital and distributed.'

'St Andrew's church at Arthingworth dates back to the 12th century. Money from one five acre field in the vilage was used for the upkeep of the church bells and the money from that field still goes to the church.'

'Our family had close connections with the church at East Farndon and my grandfather was the sexton for over 40 years and my grandmother cleaned the church. It was heated by two coke stoves, one at the end near the belfry door and another halfway down the back aisle. Grandmother once had her hair and eyebrows singed by the heat when she opened the top to tip the coke in.'

'Even a small village like Yardley Gobion had its divisions. People who attended church would not go into the chapel. Everyone in church had their own pews and provided their own kneelers. One penny was put into the church collection.'

'In the early years of the 20th century a blacksmith, John Harris, who had a smithy next door to Ivy Cottage, was also sexton and churchwarden of Great Addington church. He kept the musical instruments used in the church under his bed.'

'My mother played the organ in church at Denford for more than 20 years, both before and after she was married. I remember pumping the organ occasionally before electricity came to the village, and having to keep going lest the music "die" on the congregation. The Methodist chapel, now empty afer being used as a factory for many years, had more worshippers than the church at one time.'

'The church at Gayton was well attended in the past, but attendance seemed to lapse during the Second World War years and never picked up again. There were full choirs at both morning and evening services. The church bells were rung every Sunday morning and evening and at Christmas the handbells were rung at different houses. In 1931 the bell were rehung and on one of the bells the name of a churchwarden, Mr J. Major-Lucas, was engraved. He, together with Mr W.A. Ratledge, another churchwarden, are buried side by side in the churchyard.'

'Stanion church had two coke stoves, one just outside the belfry and the other down the first aisle. My mother looked after the lighting of the stoves and started about six o'clock on Sunday morning to get the heat into the church. Mother also did a lot of church cleaning and even got down on her hands and knees to scrub the stone slabs.

We had four bells in the church and Mr Lewis Gray rang three of them (one in each hand and the other by his foot), leaving the other bell for anyone in the choir to ring. The church clock was wound up every night by Mr Gray and often I went up with him to help with the winding. We had to climb the steps to the belfry and they went round and round in the pitch black until you reached it. The remains of the clock now stand in the church, including the big handle which wound the clock up.'

'At the turn of the century, Barby church was very much the centre of the community, with all children attending Sunday school regularly. The children, on meeting the rector, would have to curtsey to him. Should children fidget with their bonnet straps during the service, the rector would send them home until they were able to sit still. At Christmas time, the rector was very generous with prizes for the children who had attended regularly and kept their books clean throughout the year.

The church had a large band of bellringers who rang for services, weddings and ringing in the New Year. The choir was especially busy over Christmas with services and carol singing around the village. School children attended church on Ash Wednesday, followed by the rest of the day off from school. At Easter, the rector gave all the children Easter eggs. Harvest Festival was a big event with villagers wheeling barrowloads of fruit, flowers and vegetables to adorn the church. The produce was sold by auction the following day or sent to a home owned by the rector.

A major event connected with the church was the village wake held in August, "Barby Wake – Dark at Eight", which celebrated the patronal festival of the Blessed Virgin Mary. The festivities took the form of a flower show, dance, whist drive and a fair installed on the green with roundabouts and swingboats.'

'At Creaton old Charlie Brown and his sons were all very keen campanologists and they knew all the bell towers in the country more or less! Christmas and New Year were always welcomed with gladsome peals, as was any occasion such as a Coronation. And, of course, no wedding was complete without a peal of bells. Any death in the village would find Charlie, or one of his sons, tolling a passing bell – thrice times three for a man, twice times three for a woman. Once the sex of the deceased had been "told", then came the sonorous tolling of the age.'

'At Nether Heyford a lychgate stands guard over the village churchyard. This lychgate was built in 1885 and still contains the four-wheeled bier made by a villager and used to transport the coffin either by pony or bearer from as far away as Upper Heyford. The coffins, too, were made by a local undertaker. The church bell has not been tolled since before the Second World War but when in use the tolling rhythm was three by three for a man and three by two for a woman, followed by the slow passing bell.'

THE CHAPEL

'The Baptist chapel at Braybrooke has remained much as it was throughout the early years of the century. The services used to be taken by lay preachers but in 1965 our own pastor took over. In the old days the Sunday school anniversary was quite an occasion, when the children sat on a platform in front of the pulpit and sang special songs, followed by a tea. The Harvest Festival also attracted large congregations. An attractive display of fruit, flowers and vegetables, not forgetting the lump of coal and glass of water, was arranged at

64

the front on trestle tables. On the Monday evening friends from our daughter chapel at Desborough came in a special bus and returned home laden with goods from the auction. Once a year the Rothwell Mission Band came; they played hymns outside the Swan Inn and then marched to the chapel to take part in the service. Outside the chapel is the river Jordan, where history says people were once baptised. Some years ago the stream was diverted, improvements made and in 1986 a dam was built to the west of the village in the castle grounds. Prior to this, in times of storm and melting snow the water frequently overflowed the banks and the chapel and low-lying houses flooded.'

'I remember particularly the Easter Monday teas at the chapel. People came from all around and there were probably over a hundred there. The ladies from Denford chapel prepared the tea and there was a chapel service before and another in the evening after the tea. A group of men called The Crusaders came from Raunds to sing.'

'The Baptist chapel at Gretton held their Anniversary celebrations for a whole weekend. All the girls wore pretty new frocks which mother had planned for months ahead. The festival ended on Monday with the band leading a grand parade of children carrying a banner, with members of the chapel bringing up the rear.'

'Many children at Welton went to church in the morning, chapel in the evening and Sunday school in the afternoon. The singing always seemed better in the chapel.'

'During the sumer months at Irchester, parades, or tea drinkings as they were called, were arranged by the Methodist chapel for the children. Each child brought a tea cup and saucer tied up in a large handkerchief. They would carry flowers and walk around the village singing, ending with tea in the chapel Sunday school room. Another outing, also arranged by the Methodists, was for all the senior citizens of the village. This started with tea in the school room, then everyone piled into a line of buses waiting to take them for a ride around the countryside. Everyone looked forward to it.'

SUNDAY SCHOOL

'The Sunday school Treat was held each year in the rectory grounds at Everdon. We had a tea and then ran races for little prizes. Afterwards we all had a present – a small book or something like that. There was also the Choir Supper. The choir stalls were all full, the boys in front and the men behind; it was a pleasure to go to church for the singing. The Choir Supper was held when Rev Frank Churchill had killed his pig – there was plenty to eat then.'

'Sunday school Treats are well remembered occasions. In Nether Heyford the Baptist children had the edge on us all in the summer. After their tea they were privileged to enjoy a ride in the big waggons owned by Farmer Siddons – drawn by the patient cart horses which had already done a long day's work in the fields. The church children trooped down to the Manor Farm behind the church, where Farmer Busby lent his field and shed for a picnic tea. He gave us rides on the back of his hunter, fixed up a rope swing from the lower branches of a tree and turned a blind eye when the boys had a forbidden paddle in the brook. There were singing games and races and scrambling for sweets (misery for a quiet only child not used to a lot of rough and tumble) and a lovely happy evening when the mothers joined us as they finished their working day.

Later on Wickstead Park became the favourite venue for the treat and coaches full of mothers and children rumbled up to Kettering to enjoy the playground, paddle boats, miniature train and the gardens.

The treats were so popular that a few children would manage to get into more than one Sunday school for a few weeks, going mornings to church, afternoons to chapel, perhaps to a service as well in order to make the minimum number of attendances needed for an invitation to the treat. During the depression years when Dad was maybe out of work and agriculture was in the doldrums this could well have been the only holiday a child might get.'

'Sunday school was held at Race school at 9.30 am., followed by a church service at 11 am. At 2 pm Sunday school started again to teach the Commandments and the Collects. At 6.30 pm it was back to church with parents.

Every autumn, prizes of prayer books or bibles or religious books were presented to the scholars.

Summer Sunday school tea took place on the rectory lawn. Each child took a plate and a mug. They were given a jam sandwich, a piece of lemon and seed cakes tied up in a cloth (like a man's hankie) and tea to drink. Home-made games – such as Aunt Sally – were played. At hometime, unwrapped sweets were thrown down and all the children scrambled for them.'

'The Sunday school Treat at Long Buckby meant being transported (or walking) to a field where games were played and tea provided.

Occasionally, we received the hospitatlity of a neighbouring chapel. The tea usually consisted of bread and butter followed by slab cake or sometimes seed cake. For any Christmas party, jelly and custard were usually added.'

'Whitsun was the time of year when the Sunday school at Lois Weedon held its Anniversary. All the girls would have a new voile dress, with a sash, and a hat for the occasion. This would then be our new summer outfit. The chapel Sunday school always seemed more lively than the church one – once we went on an outing by coach to Edgehill, and another time we ventured as far afield as Stratford on Avon, where we went on the river and had tea provided by a chapel in Stratford.'

'Chapel picnics at Brigstock were held in the fields behind the village, followed by games and races. Church Sunday school was always held in the school itself and not in the church. At some point in the 1910–1920 period, the church Sunday school folded and the mothers all put their heads together and said "Our children are going to know Sunday from weekday" and so we all had to go to the Chapel Sunday school.'

CHAPEL GREEN

'Motor-racing enthusiasts all over the world will be familiar with Chapel Curve which is part of the Silverstone motor racing circuit. Few of them know that there was a Methodist chapel and a group of cottages huddled together beside a copse in a tiny settlement called Chapel Green. A double-fronted house, Maggotts Moor Lodge, used as a gamekeeper's cottage, stood a little way off at the entrance to a riding into the Whittlebury Forest. Legend has it that a chapel dedicated to St Thomas a Becket, no longer visible, was built in earlier times, hence the name Chapel Copse. The Methodist chapel and the cottages on the green were all demolished in 1939, somewhat urgently, to make way for the building of a war-time airfield. After the war the Royal Automobile Club acquired the land with its runways to found the now famous Silverstone motor racing circuit, home of the British Grand Prix.

Lily remembers, on summer Sunday evenings she and her school friends, in those far off unsophisticated days of the 1920s, used to walk more than a mile by field and footpath to attend service in the tiny chapel. They were Florrie, May, Ellen, Violet and sometimes Dora if she managed to get ready in time. As far as Lily remembers there were no boys in the party. I imagined high jinks on the way home but apparently not. The little twelve year old girls were quite content to be on their own.

The chapel was a very small room in part of a cottage occupied by Mr Jim Philips. There were proper pews, a reading desk and a small harmonium. Services had to be held in daylight as there was no lighting.

Mr and Mrs George Payne lived next door to the chapel. George's brother Harry had one of the cottages at nearby Luffield Abbey Farm, with his wife, Liz, and three sons Frank, Arthur and Lewis. Harry played the harmonium and led the singing. He was very strict with the children and woe betide anyone who behaved irreverently. Sometimes Mrs Payne deputised for her husband by playing with one finger. The Payne boys grew up in the tradition of going to chapel and they all had good voices, especially Arthur who was greatly in demand for village concerts. Their father offered to teach them to play music but Lewis regretted that none of them took up the challenge.

The chapel was part of the Towcester Methodist Circuit and was a favourite place for preachers to go on a Sunday, especially as Mrs George Payne put on such a splendid tea in her cottage next to the chapel.

The highlight of the tea was Albert Markham's doughcake from the village bakery in Silverstone. Markham's delivered to the outlying farms and cottages three times a week by horse and cart. John and Linda clearly remember driving the horse and cart through rough farm roads with many gates to open. They sat on a high seat above the carefully protected bread which was tidily stacked in the well of the vehicle, and carried to the houses in market baskets. After Luffield Abbey Farm and its cottages the next stop would be Chapel Green, then through other farms to Lillingstone Dayrell.

Emily Hinton remembers her father taking her to chapel when she was a little girl. She enjoyed the walk across the fields and will always remember seeing the preacher arriving on horseback.

So now when you listen to Murray Walker commentating on the progress of Nigel Mansell or Ayrton Senna negotiating Copse Corner, Maggotts Drive, Becketts Corner and Chapel Curve, spare a thought for the people who lost their homes and their little chapel to make way for the war effort and afterwards the Silverstone motor racing circuit.'

HOUSE & HOME

THE WAY WE LIVED THEN

When we remember the good old days it is as well to also remember the hard work that went with them. The kitchen range was warm and welcoming, but it required regular blackleading and cleaning and oven temperatures were something of a lottery on a windy day. Often newly built council houses were looked on as the last word in modernity in their village, but even they had shared pumps and outside loos. Electricity, running water, mains sewerage – all were blessings warmly welcomed only a generation ago.

FARMHOUSE LIFE IN THE 1920s

'I was born in the mid 1920s in a large Victorian farmhouse (where I still live) situated midway between two villages and not far from Kettering. I have seen almost unbelievable changes in the home, on the farm and in the countryside during my life here.

Electricity was brought to the village in the late 1920s, but it was not until the spring of 1951 that it was brought to us. Until then, life was very difficult to say the least and the work often hard and dirty.

For cooking we had a large black range, nicknamed the Black Dragon. Every week all the flues had to be raked and brushed out and the steel rubbed with emery cloth until it shone like silver. The rest was blackleaded and when dry was buffed with a soft brush.

When the oven was going to be used, the smoke hood had to be closed down as also the flue box, and then came the tricky bit of how to stoke the fire to get the right oven temperature; also, this depended on the direction of the wind as to whether there was a down draught to upset things.

We did not heat our irons on the range as we found that the handles got too hot and set the iron holders alight, so these were heated on a paraffin primus stove instead. To test for temperature a drop of water was put on them to see how quickly it sizzled off.

My father always wore *stiff* white collars and fronts, and they were the giddy limit to get up. We usually left them until we'd got about half a dozen. After washing they were starched with Robin cold starch and rolled tightly in a clean cloth and left for a little while, and then the fun began. The starch would "toast" on your iron and you would have to scrape it off with a knife, and then you were lucky if you didn't get a smut on the cloth from your iron holder.

Washday was a mammoth task. First of all the 45 gallon copper in the back kitchen had to be filled with soft water from a huge cistern under the kitchen floor; there was an extension pipe from the pump against the sink. The copper was heated mostly by wood which had been sawn in convenient lengths to fit the furnace.

After the clothes had been washed and boiled they were rinsed and the whites "blued" – the blue was tied in a little flannel bag and swished in the water. If you put too much in, instead of whitening the whites, you "ditched" them. After rinsing, they were folded and put through a mangle (that had heavy wooden rollers) taking care to avoid putting pearl buttons through otherwise you had a session of replacing them as they would be smashed.

Thank goodness, blanket washing didn't have to be done every week. It was all systems go on a warm windy day. The water was heated in the copper and then carried in buckets to a galvanised dolly tub placed over a drain in the yard. Soap powder was added and then the blankets were "possed" with a posser, then rinsed, roughly folded and carried in bath tubs to the mangle, which was in the dairy, and afterwards carried to the line.

This copper was also once used for brewing beer; after the beer had been made it was poured down a pipe situated in the kitchen, along and down to the cellar to fill the barrels.

For lighting we had oil lamps and candles. It was quite a ritual in the morning to fill them, turn the wicks and to see that the glass chimneys were clean and not smoked. Not only were the house lamps to be done, but also the farm hurricane lanterns. Later we had Aladdin lamps with mantles (these gave a white light) and last of all we had a Tilley pump-up lamp.

Going to bed with a candle was quite an experience. If you went upstairs too quickly or opened a door sharply and there was a sudden draught, the wretched thing blew out and then you had to fumble about for the matches. The candle also had to be carried level to avoid spilling the tallow.

We had coco matting on the quarry tiles in our "top" kitchen which was too heavy to carry out for beating every week, so after rolling back, damp sawdust was sprinkled on the tiles to keep the dust down. Most of the carpets had to be done with a brush and dustpan or a Ewbank sweeper.

We did have a bathroom, with a bath and toilet only (no hand basin) but all the water had to be pumped up to a huge tank in the roof from either the hard water pump or the soft water pump; it was hardly ever the latter as this was kept for washing etc. When one wanted a bath, the hot water had to be carried up in buckets from the back kitchen. We managed like this until the mains water was brought to us in 1962 and then we had a new bathroom and the back kitchen modernised and central heating installed.

Before 1949 when the village was put on the mains water supply, the whole village had to rely on pumps for their drinking water. Some were more fortunate than others by having a pump to a row of houses, while others had to fetch it in buckets from pumps in the street. The village baker was one of the unlucky ones, who had to fetch water for bread making in a galvanised open tub on iron wheels. Water butts were used for collecting rain water off barns and outbuildings. One particular row of houses had a windpump that pumped water from the brook – this was not very hygenic as cattle used to stand in it during the hot weather.

One little luxury we did have was warm beds in the winter, thanks to Mother and the warming pan. Red hot embers were taken from the fire and put in the pan (avoiding any that were smoky as these made the sheets smell). Then, while we were undressing, Mother would be pushing the pan up and down the bed. If she left it too long in one place the sheets got scorched.

Clothes – oh dear! I can remember both my brother and I having to wear combinations ("combies" for short) and me liberty bodices, but I did flatly refuse to wear them when I started secondary school, alhough some of the other girls did. My father and grandfather wore flannel top shirts and undershirts, the latter being hand made in Welshpool flannel. I was introduced to herringbone stitching at a very early age, likewise knitting on four needles, because my father always wore breeches and leather leggings, so these needed long hand-knitted stockings made in rib to cling better.

When I was a child we kept quite a few cows for calf rearing and the milk that was surplus was "set" in large shallow pans in the dairy. After twelve to 24 hours the cream was skimmed off with a skimmer (a fairly large metal saucer with perforations in it).

After several days, when enough cream had been collected, it was put into a large barrel-type churn (that had been scalded with boiling water), the lid clamped on, and you were ready to begin. A man always did the churning as it was much too heavy for a woman. Sometimes it came quickly and sometimes a drop of boiling water had to be added to "liven it up".

When it did come, the butter was taken out and put into a large bowl and kneaded to get all the surplus buttermilk out, then rinsed with cold water, kneaded again and then salted to taste. The butter was then weighed up in half pounds and made into pats with two patters known as "hands". These were placed on squares of greaseproof paper to set and then packed for sale.

Sometimes there was some of the first milk after a cow had calved and this was known as "beastings". A delicious junket-like pudding was made with this by adding a little sugar and sultanas and baking in the oven. The skimmed milk was mixed with barley meal for the pigs.

Talking of barley meal, my father ground all the wheat or barley needed for cattle feeding with a grinding mill which had two huge circular stones with little grooves and knotches in them; this was driven by a traction engine. When the grooves and knotches got worn and wanted recutting it was done with a hammer and chisel and was called "stitching" (my grandfather was a miller as well as a farmer).

Among the country delicacies the older people enjoyed were rook pies, after the shooting of the young rooks in May, pigeon pies and lambs' tails puddings. I shall always remember our shepherd collecting the fattest lambs' tails after a tail cutting session and they looked revolting, even after being scalded and skinned and cooked well – they must have been rather gristly!

Even during the war a lot of the houses in the village weren't on the sewer, and had to be content with the bucket system. These were emptied during one night each week. Sometimes at lodges or farm cottages the toilet or privy was an earth one up the garden.

My grandparents' outside toilet was in a shrubbery with some high trees in which guinea fowl roosted. These were kept as intruder alarms and the blood curdling row they kicked up was unbelievable if they heard the slightest sound.'

COTTAGE LIFE IN THE 1940s

'As a new bride, I came to live in Walgrave 50 years ago. It was war-time and housing was difficult so we started married life in two rooms in my mother-in-law's home. I found village life much different from Northampton, where I was born and bred, but after I was "accepted" I found the villagers friendly and helpful.

There was no piped water at that time, and drinking water had to be pumped up and was kept in a covered enamel pail, water for general purposes was kept in a zinc bucket and my mother-in-law taught me how to throw a small roped bucket into the soft water well and draw it up full. It certainly made one realise how much water we used for flushing the cisternless loo, which was outside, and for washing clothes and bathing, etc. The only washing machine we had then was a dolly tub and pegs, something that I never quite got the hang of but, looking back, perhaps I wasn't allowed to for, much to my annoyance, my washing was often fetched before I was awake, as washdays could commence as early as 5 am. Bath night was on Friday; the built-in copper had to be filled and a fire lit underneath and, because the copper didn't hold all that much, we had to 'manage' by topping the bath water up with a drop more hot for each one and there were four of us. I was privileged for some reason and allowed in first. The same copper had to be lit for boiling the clothes on washday, always Monday, and irons were heated, mainly by fire, on Tuesday afternoons.

We did have a small gas cooker, but frying was not allowed on that. We used an oil stove, situated in what used to be a "shoe maker's shop" attached to the house. It was eventually converted into a bathroom, complete with a flush toilet. I had been married twelve years by this time and we thought it to be the height of luxury.

We were fortunate as electricity was brought into the village around the time that I was married for, until then, there was only gas lighting in one room downstairs and also in the two main bedrooms. Owing to the cost and the war-time blackout, oil lamps or candles were the main source of lighting. It was off to bed, carrying a candlestick complete with matches to be handy in case of need. There were no electric blankets then, but a brick, having been kept in the side oven of the open fire all day, would be wrapped in a piece of blanket cloth and put in the bed to heat it. There was no heating in the bedrooms, and it was a long cold trek to the outside loo, so chamber-pots were fashionable and useful, and often froze in winter-time!

We did have constant hot water in the winter as a kettle was always kept on the hob at the side of the open fire, and a trivet would be there too, on which to place saucepans containing vegetables, stew, or a filling suet pudding. Vegetables were grown on the front garden where we now have a lawn, and the milkman trundled his churn along and transferred the milk, still warm from the cow, by measure into your jug.

Floors were covered by lino in the bedrooms and coco-matting downstairs. This was lifted weekly to sweep up the dirt that had literally gone through where the pegged rugs didn't lay. These rugs, laid down at every conceivable place, were made from pieces cut from old clothing and pegged onto hessian, or washed sugar sacks, and were taken up each day and shaken outside. No electric cleaners existed in our house, only a brush and dust pan, the use of which often gave rise to a severe attack of sneezing.

For entertainment, we had the radio, or board games. Women's Institute or a devotional meeting were highlights and these still continue; but we could go to town on the bus for a mere ten pence return and, if we didn't think to lock the door, it didn't matter, for honesty was then a keyword.

I still live in the same house now (with all its improvements) as I did then, and the younger generation never tire of listening to "life as it was" and I often wonder what they will remember of their lives and living in the present time.'

LIFE IN THE COUNCIL HOUSES

'I lived in one of a row of council houses along the Leys in Roade in the 1920s. In those days the road was just a stony, muddy country road, and there were only a few houses and bungalows, besides the ten council houses. The latter were thought very up to date, despite the fact that there were no taps and we had to get our water from a pump situated halfway along the row. The toilets, of course, were outside and it was jolly cold out there sometimes in the winter with, if you were lucky, a candle, sometimes with just the light of the moon. The rent for the houses was about two shillings and sixpence a week. This went up a few pence when they put in water and later electricity. Until then we had an oil lamp, and a candle to go to bed. There's something about the light from an oil lamp – soft, warm and gentle, different from the glare of electricity.'

'My parents lived in a council house in Kettering in 1923 when I was born, but within a few years they were proudly buying a double fronted house at a "good address". Mother told us that a government subsidy of £100 was available then, which was almost a quarter of the purchase price.'

'In Arthingworth in 1953, eight council houses were built. The rent for one of these in 1957 was £2 19s 6d per week.'

'Nearly 40 years ago we moved from Sussex to a new council house in Bozeat. After about a week, we were visited by a journalist from the *Wellingborough Evening Telegraph*. She surprised us by asking if we had dared to step outside the house. She then told us that, unknown to us, there had been angry protests about strangers being given a council house. Apparently the villagers were not pleased and in those days strangers stuck out like sore thumbs among the village folk.'

WELLS AND WATER

Being able to turn on a tap in your own home and see clean drinking water or hot water gushing out was a dream unobtainable for most people only a few decades ago. For most, essential water had to be physically pumped up or drawn up from the well, which might be at some considerable distance from home. Others took their bucket to the local spring. Mains sewerage, too, has for most people ended the walk to the privy at the bottom of the garden and the visit of the nightsoil man – though perhaps the vegetables on the allotments have suffered in the process!

PUMPS AND WELLS

'Until mains water was brought to Shutlanger the village was supplied by three pumps and one well. The well was of the familiar type found in fairy tales, with a handle to turn and a bucket on the end of a chain. There was also a running brook for drinking water. In 1952 electricity was brought to the village. Up till then cooking was done by coal and paraffin. Mains drainage did not make an appearance until 1964.'

'Mains water did not reach Wootton until 1946 and there was no gas, sewerage, or electricity systems. Every drop of water had to be pumped up by hand. Some houses had their own wells and one or two even had a pump in the kitchen but the majority had to trudge to the public wells at the corner of Quinton Road, the bottom of Church Hill or halfway up Water Lane. Many of the houses were in a poor state of repair and a number had been divided up with several families living in one house. Families welcomed the milk delivery by Louise Frost, but everyone tried to stay indoors when the nightsoil cart did its rounds to empty the garden privies.'

'In the few years from 1949 to the mid 1950s tremendous changes occurred in Stoke Bruerne. First, in 1949, came electricity, followed by mains sewerage and tap water, then television. "We really thought we were on the map then," as a friend puts it. It is hard to judge which of these "services" made the most impact, but the availability of water must have been a wonderful boon. Previously the village was served by standpipes, taps set at certain access points. When these dried up, which seems to have been a regular occurrence, journeys had to be made to the well near the entrance to the Blisworth tunnel. One lady remembers her grandfather putting a wooden yoke across his shoulders to enable him to carry two pails of water. Another recalls that from her parents' cottage she had to cross a stile to reach the well, and no matter how high she lifted the bucket it always hit the top of the stile, resulting in the loss of precious water.'

'I had, from a very early age, spent holidays with my aunt and uncle at Great Houghton. Life in this village was so very different from my home environment in the outskirts of industrial Birmingham. The village has now grown with the building of modern houses but in those days it was a fairly small community and with so many families being related it really was like one big family. During my holidays I would probably put on a few pounds and go home with quite a golden tan. However, there were things about staying with my aunt and uncle that I did not like at all! Drinking water had to be brought into the cottage by bucket from a water pump and in the back yard stood two huge barrels which collected rain water as it drained from the roof, and this was used for washing purposes. I hated this because of all the little insects swimming around in it and probably often went a little unclean in between baths in front of the kitchen fire. And not having any electricity or sewer laid on was just about the end from my way of thinking! The smells come back to me – the nicer one being from the pretty oil lamps.'

'Water at Gayton came from wells and springs, and there were standpipes at various points in the village and lovely water it was too! Later when some wells in the fields at Goggs Farm were connected by pipe to the village, a few houses had taps over their sinks – what luxury.'

'At Little Addington there were five pumps; one provided the water for the cattle trough and the rest were for the village folk to collect their water. One pump was inside a cottage, one in a garden which has only recently been demolished. They're now a collector's item.'

'Electricity came to Easton on the Hill in 1934 and piped water in 1954; sanitation quite a few years later. Water was drawn from wells or pumps situated in various properties on each side of the village street. The main village pump was in what is now the car park of The Cavalier (Slaters Arms). It was lovely clear drinking water, sparkling and delicious. The wells never ran dry, even during the hottest, dryest seasons.'

'The farmland around Nether Heyford was well supplied by springs and it is said that even in times of exceptional drought, Heyford never ran dry. The water was considered by some to have medicinal properties and some old folk attribute their longevity to Heyford water. One "ancient" reckons that mixed 50/50 with Scotch it was the best medicine obtainable. However, the coming of piped water and sewerage systems in 1952 brought benefit to all who depended on pumps from springs and wells for their water as well as the weekly emptying of their outside privies. There was still a water ram operating from a spring in the hills.'

'Before 1956 the residents of Whilton obtained their water from wells or pumps. In many cases a group of families would share one pump or well. Before retiring for the night, the kettle would be filled and a bucket of water brought into the house. Sticks for kindling would be put in the oven by the fire so that they would be dry by morning. Whoever came downstairs first would prepare the fire with paper and sticks and then light them. This would provide the heat for boiling the kettle which hung on a hook over the fire. The tea could then be made. (If anyone was given a very hot cup of tea, the customary saying was, "This was made from water boiled on sticks".)

The earth lavatories in the garden were often near the pig sty, which gave a certain amount of warmth.'

WATER FROM THE SPRING

'In my aunt's house at East Farndon all the water for bathing and washing had to be heated. Drinking water was fetched from the spring opposite the house. This was easy for us, not so fortunate for people who lived further up or down the village. The drinking water was kept in two large pails in the big stone-floored larder.'

'I was also brought up in East Farndon, in a cottage with no running water and oil lamps or candles for lighting. The cottage was painted cream outside with black beams in the walls, and had a thatched roof covered with corrugated iron sheeting. Tubs for soft water stood in the garden to catch the rainwater, mainly for washing, in an old copper in the kitchen corner, which had to be lit with a fire underneath. It was also used for bathing in a large tin bath, which was kept hanging on a hook at the back of the house.

During periods of drought, my elder brother and I had to fetch small baths full of water, from the village spring, to fill our tubs up. Our drinking water also came from the same spring, fetched in pails. We fetched pails of water for older people and we were given a penny for each pail between us.'

THE NIGHTSOIL MAN

'Main sewers were constructed in 1957 at Grendon and until the houses were connected or your property had a septic tank, the nightsoil man came round twice a week, usually during the morning when he used to meet the milkman delivering the milk at the same time!'

'Water distribution at Great Addington was by wells and pumps situated at strategic points throughout the village. Constant maintenance of the pumps was required to keep "rats and other things out". Squire Lane, who lived in the manor house, installed the first water pipe fed by local springs. Mains water finally arrived in 1938. Sewage disposal was by tipping your bucket out on your allotment! By 1930 nightsoil removal was in operation – and complaints were made that collecting it at eight o'clock, breakfast time, was objectionable.'

'Piped water came to Braybrooke in 1952. This was followed in 1955 by the mains sewer. Previously it was the cesspits or the nightsoil man coming round in the middle of the night.'

'Evenley Estate was sold in July 1938 after the death of Major Allen, whose family had owned the estate since the turn of the century. It was during Major Allen's time that electricity was laid to the cottages and there was an Evenley village water supply. This came from a well in the field off the Brackley Road near the allotments. Above the well was a wind pump. The village wells were also still in use. Sanitation appears in the sale catalogue as "pail closets". The contents were buried on the allotments, which may account for the very good vegetables the men were able to produce.'

'Denford was amply supplied with wells, but it was hard work pumping the water. After the mains water was connected, many wells were filled in. Outside toilets were commonplace, and the nightsoil man came about once a week to do what was necessary. One lady remembers the first time she visited her future parents-in-law's home, after a hockey match. She went upstairs to change out of her shorts and, to find hot water in the taps and a toilet upstairs, she thought was absolutely marvellous. She remembers a small bedroom at her own home being converted to contain their first flush toilet and going upstairs and pulling the chain in sheer delight at this modern convenience!'

'I was surprised in 1929 to find that Greens Norton had running water and sewerage, though many of the cottages in the courts shared a standpipe and only the houses lining the streets had access to the sewer. Apparently this work took place during the First World War. The men digging the trenches for the sewer pipes went on strike for more pay. They were granted an extra halfpenny, making the rate a princely fourpence ha'penny an hour.'

LOSING THE COBBLES

'In the late 1920s a proper sewerage system was provided in Welford. Mains water and electricity came in the mid 1930s. The installation of these services resulted in the cobbles that formed both the backyards and the pavements of many of the houses in the village being removed – much to the relief of many of the younger members of the community; being set to weed the cobbles was a regular punishment used by harrassed mothers!'

BLAME THE AMERICANS!

'Mains water was installed at Denford Ash in 1950 but the supply was erratic – the excuses given to us included that the American troops at Chelveston were using water for showers, and we, being the highest point around, did not get priority for cooling the milk and watering the cattle.'

THE HOUSEHOLD ROUTINE

⟨⇔⟩

Washing, ironing, cleaning – the daily routine repeated itself week after week in the home, and hard work it was. Without modern amenities, washday really was a whole day devoted to washing, starching, blueing, mangling and drying, with ironing by flatirons

heated on the kitchen range to follow. And for the men, a day's work was often followed by an evening on the allotment, growing the vegetables that were essential for the family budget.

WASHDAY

'Washdays in the 1930s–1940s was a major event. Most households had a copper of some sort, gas or, in older houses, a bricked-in solid fuel one. Mother also had a vacuum clothes washer; a copper funnel-shaped gadget on the end of a wooden pole, this came with its own galvanised barrel with fluted sides. Can you imagine the steamy kitchen because the gas boiler was heating the whites and then this early version of a washing machine which was operated by energetic plunging up and down in the water of the washer. To add to the heat the oven would be on to cook jacket potatoes, which was always Monday's meal, with cold joint and left over Yorkshire pudding. The wet clothes were then mangled half dry ready to hang on the line.'

'Water butts caught the rainwater from the roofs at Grendon, soft water being much better for washing. Most houses had an outside washhouse with built in copper, otherwise coppers were built into sculleries. These were used for boiling clothes – almost everything was cotton then. There was a mangle with its huge wooden rollers for wringing out before hanging the washing in the garden. Irons were heated in front of the range fire.'

'The first job was to fill the copper and baths or tubs with soft water. Several butts were set outside the house to catch rainwater. The fire which usually drew well would be lit and kept burning with rubbish, even old pieces of leather were sometimes burned. If the wind was in a certain direction the fire would go out and it would be some time before it would burn. White articles were boiled, rinsed in cold water then put into water to which a "blue bag" had been added. Before hanging out the washing would be put through a mangle with two huge wooden rollers which were turned by a handle. A sturdy wooden copper stick was used to lift the washing from one container to another. Some housewives had a ridged zinc rubbing board and a tub and "dolly stool". The latter was a small wooden three-legged stool on a long handle with projecting arms. The clothes in the tub were churned around by twisting the dolly. These were two methods of dealing with the soiled washing. Ironing was carried out using flat irons which were heated on an iron grill which hung in front of the fire. There were different sizes and shapes of iron for cuffs, gathers etc.'

'Monday at 7 am the fire under the copper was lit. The copper was filled the night before with soft water, rainwater from the iron pump in the washhouse. Sheets were boiled in the copper. Most cottages and all farmhouses had a washhouse, some a separate little building. The washhouse contained a copper, stone sink are some a pump. The rainwater was collected off the roof and stored in a large bricklined square well under the kitchen. In the very dry summer of 1921 the well was dry and it was scrubbed clean. There was a tap with cold water (not mains as today) from an artesian well.

My mother and her helper, using a galvanised bowl with a wooden handle ladled the boiling water into a bucket and then into a large wooden trough-like tub. Whites were washed first, ending with socks and coloured clothes. From the wash tub for rinsing into a round tub on four legs with a rubber mangle; this tub had hot water from the copper and cold tap water with a blue bag swished around in the water making the water blue. This did not make the sheets etc blue, but it was said to enhance the whiteness.

The clothes were dried on a washing line in the garden, or in bad weather on a rack in the washhouse or kitchen. The rack was on a pulley; usually pulled up to the ceiling.

Sheets and pillowcases went through a mangle which had two heavy wooden rollers and was turned by an iron wheel. Ironing was done with a flat iron heated on the kitchen range. Clothes etc were aired on a wooden clothes horse placed round a fire or kitchen range.'

DRY CLEANING

'Dry cleaning? Not to worry. At Creaton Mrs Trussell in a small cottage in the Jetty, cheerfully took it in, doing it in front of the open fire – with petrol, her husband sitting by contentedly smoking his pipe!'

THE DAILY ROUTINE

'The cottage at Benefield where I and my older sister, Annie, were brought up was just one front room downstairs with a long passage to the pantry. Upstairs there were two rooms. So much happened in that one room, cooking, washing and bathing. A pot on the fire provided hot water and, for Monday wash-day, there was a washboard, dolly-tub and mangle. The washing was dried on two lines in the little front garden and, at the end of the back garden, which was reached by coming out of the front door and round the side of the cottage, was the earth closet, emptied at night. Also in the back garden we kept a pig, hens, rabbits and guinea pigs.

Heating was from the one fire in the range, lighting from one oil lamp and candles which were carried around in jamjars. In the same front room we hung the bacon and hams after the pig was killed and cured.

We had our special jobs, blackleading the range, cleaning the knives and "wooding" – parts of the local wood were allocated to families where they could cut their faggots. When a doctor was needed a message had to be taken to Oundle five miles away, then the doctor would cycle out. Club cards were taken to school with contributions. Clothing, coal and the doctor were paid for in this way.'

ROUND THE FIRE

'One of my most vivid childhood memories is of the family sitting around the fireside on a winter's evening, listening to the older members relating tales of the past. The blazing fire, the kettle singing on the hob and the oil-lamp (the wick of which I had watched my mother trim so carefully) casting shadows into the recesses of the room, all combined to make a perfect setting for story-telling.

Here I heard of my Granny's life; she who was born in the Hungry Forties and who knew what it was to be hungry and cold and ill-clad and who had worked hard all her life and had never been to school. Her youngest son, born in 1886, was my father and, as he puffed away at his pipe of Digger Mixture, he would spin many a yarn. In the mid 1920s, he decided we would have a crystal set to enable us to listen to the wireless. I remember sitting spellbound, wearing ear-phones, to hear "Daventry Calling" or "London 2LO".'

ON THE ALLOTMENT

'There were a large number of allotments at Irchester, or garden fields as they were called. Most workers grew their own vegetables and flowers too, as there was hot competition at the annual horticultural show held at the Working Men's Club. Mr Dunmore, a local butcher, councillor and football manager presented the cups.

Digging for these allotments always started on Good Friday (weather permitting) as, being Easter, it meant four full days holiday which also meant digging could be completed.'

'Most of the men at Grafton Underwood had allotments and there was great competition to see who had the first new potatoes and peas, usually around the time of Grafton Feast, the middle of July. At harvest festival time the church would be full of vegetables and these would be sold off the following evening in the school with even greater competition – whose vegetables would make the most for the church and the hospital?'

'Everyone at Everdon had an allotment – you never needed to buy vegetables. People would ask "Are you all right for so and so?" and then you would find some left on your doorstep. I had to go and help Father on his allotment. There wasn't a lot of time left for "tomfoolery".'

BATHNIGHT AND BEDTIME

Bathnight, often Saturday night so that everyone was nice and clean for Sunday, meant a tin tub in front of the fire, laboriously filled with hot water and later emptied out in the garden. Then a candle to bed, the flickering light all that was available to banish the shadows. The light from an oil lamp or candle was soft and flattering, but if you were trying to work by it, particularly on something as delicate as lace, a little ingenuity was called for. How happily we clicked on our first electric light.

READY FOR SUNDAY

'Things were improving in the 1930s in Gretton. Electricity was brought to the village, and a row of Council houses were built on the Backside. The lucky tenants were the envy of those who thought themselves deprived and overlooked. Maybe the houses were spacious and up-to-date but, like everyone who was not lucky enough to have their own pump or well, water must be carted from village pumps or wells for all household needs. Saturday was bath night, water was heated in the copper or on the grate in the cottage living room. In some cases, where it was not possible to provide Sunday outfits, clothes were washed at the same time, ironed and pressed, ready for Sunday, when families attended church or chapel and enjoyed a walk in the afternoon, having eaten the Sunday roast which was baked in the bakehouse for a few coppers, and hastily whisked home at mid-day.'

'Bathnight for us in the 1920s at Harrington was Saturday night. The young children usually had theirs in a hip bath placed near the kitchen range, the hot water from a kettle or the copper. There would be clean clothes Sunday morning.

At first we had a saucer of salt in the bathroom with which we could clean our teeth, but then we had Gibbs powdered toothpaste.

A farmhouse I remember had a bathroom with a bath, hand basin and flush lavatory. The bedrooms had a washstand with a china basin and large jug of cold water, a soapdish, a chamber pot on the lower shelf of the washstand and often a china bucket with cane handle and lid.

A rectory and farmhouse I often stayed at had one small bedroom for a bathroom, with a wooden floor and the hip bath in the centre. There were cans of cold water and the hot water had to be carried up from the kitchen.

Each morning the lamps were filled with paraffin oil. The glass chimneys, often with black smoke on them, had to be cleaned. One went upstairs to bed with candles. The candle holders were like a deep saucer with a handle, cleaned by pouring boiling water on the spilt wax, which then melted.'

IN FRONT OF THE FIRE

'I was the daughter of a farmer in the parish of Sywell. Our nearest neighbour was a mile away and living was very primitive as opposed to the present day.

We had no running water, it was supplied by a spring and had to be pumped up by hand, as and when it was needed. Needless to say, the water was wonderfully clear and pure!

We had no electricity or gas either. Cooking was done from a Triplex grate which consisted of two ovens and a hob for cooking pots and kettles etc. It was fired by coal. We used this during the winter months and in the summer we used a Florence oil stove to accomplish the same chores. Lighting was supplied by oil lamps and candles.

Baths were taken once weekly, usually on Friday evenings. A zinc bath was placed in front of the kitchen fire and the water was carried in from a large copper in the diary yard, where it had been heated. After our ablutions it all had to be laboriously emptied, bucket by bucket, and the bath was then wiped clean and hung on the wall outside until needed the following week.'

TO GET A BETTER LIGHT

'Electricity was installed at Barby in 1929. Before that, a lady in the village who did lace work gained a better light by placing a candle behind a bulbous bowl containing water to concentrate the light.'

SHOPPING AND CALLERS

⟨⊙⟩

Far from having to go out for all your shopping, it was quite common for the traders to come to you. You would, of course, visit your village shops if they were near and handy, but otherwise you could always call on the carrier to take an order in for you and have it delivered to your door. There were regular callers and pedlars too, greeted with delight by the children who might be able to earn a few coppers for rags or claim a windmill toy for jamjars.

HOME DELIVERY AND SHOPPING

'About 50 years ago we had a village carrier at Stanion, Mr Jack Smith. He went round the village and Weldon collecting grocery orders for his customers and then went to Kettering in his van and got the orders from Home and Colonial or Liptons. When he delivered them to his customers he charged only a few pence. Later on, he went round Stanion and Weldon with a horse and cart, selling fruit.'

'To get our food supplies, other than dairy produce and eggs, we made weekly trips to Wellingborough, travelling by horse and trap. Whilst Dad was busy at the cattle market, Mother would go the rounds of the grocer, haberdasher, chemist or what have you, then we usually visited my grandmother before returning home to Sywell.'

'Evenley could boast an off licence, post office and shop, which was on the corner of School Lane. Paraffin was on sale there and most goods are reputed to have absorbed the smell and flavour of it. Besides the shops in Brackley, the carrier called once a week for shopping needs. Anything from half a yard of elastic could be ordered and delivered the following week. There was also a muffin man who called at the village.'

PEDLARS AND CALLERS

'Now and again in the 1920s a pedlar lady from Kings Cliffe would walk through the forest and down Wood Lane to Duddington. In her basket she carried wooden wares made by the wood turners in her village. She hawked pegs, egg cups, spoons and bowls from door to door. My mother always bought something from her.'

'In the 1930s a tinker selling pots and pans called around the village at Yarwell. His horse was so thin that its harness would slip about as it did not fit properly.'

'There were several regular visitors to Denford. One was the Windmill Man who would exchange home-made windmills for clean jamjars, which we would go round the village collecting.

Tradesmen's vans calling with the necessities of life were once commonplace, like Mr Thoday and his son, the butchers at Duddington.

Then there was a man with a donkey and a hurdy-gurdy. My brothers used to feel sorry for the donkey, having to pull both the man and the hurdy-gurdy. There was also the Rag Man, who took clean rags, rabbit skins and rats tails for a few pence.'

'Apart from having its own well-established and adequate shops and tradesmen, Clipston was well served with a variety of travelling salesmen. There was the scissor-grinder, who adapted his bicycle to drive a grindstone, the man who sold paraffin, the one selling tapes, cottons, ribbons, darning wools, etc and, best of all, the Trolley Man who came without fail on Saturday afternoons, to the delight of every child with a Saturday penny to spend.'

'Traders who called at Benefield included a butcher, baker, grocer, fishmonger, coalman, knife grinder, a rag and bone husband and wife team, and a man with a barrel organ and a monkey.'

'The rag and bone man came round both in the country and in the town. He had a hand cart, or a better off one might have a horse and cart. He would call out "Rags and bones, rabbit skins." A whole bundle of clothes would produce about threepence and a paper windmill for the children.

The knife grinder pushed his grindstone round on a two-wheeled contraption. He propelled the stone whilst sitting on a fixed seat and pedalling with both feet on alternate pedals. For a few pence he would sharpen scissors, carving knives etc.

In Mercers Row in Northampton the organ grinder would earn a few pennies by turning the handle of his machine whilst his monkey, all dressed up, would caper about to the accompaniment.

Another "push around" was the hot potato or hot chestnut man, who stationed himself on the Market Square in Northampton.'

'A fish man came to Grendon once a week by horse and cart from Earls Barton, and fruit and vegetables came from Bozeat.'

WHAT WE WORE

The clothes we wore are not always remembered with affection. There seemed to be too much of them – though that meant we didn't feel the cold in those days before central heating! Hats were essential wear for men, women and children and no woman would go out of the house unless she had her hat on.

'Before the First World War we always wore thick, black stockings and long-sleeved dresses so our arms were covered to the wrist – no summer dresses like nowadays. We were always bundled up in clothes. We always wore a pinny and if you went to school without your pinny they sent you home again. We used to wear boots, not shoes. The higher your boots came up your leg, the more fashionable you were, but I never got to that degree. Occasionally we went into Banbury to buy a new coat but otherwise Mum made all our clothes, mostly out of cut down dresses. We didn't have new material. My mother never went out unless she was wearing a hat.'

'As a teenager I washed my hair with rainwater and soap, there being no shampoo then. We used to wear black stockings and garters and black shoes. I can remember we were among the first in Denton village to wear light stockings. I also recall three of us girls who all worked at Thrapston having our long hair cut short in the 1920s which caused quite a stir in the village.'

'When we went to church before the war one wore a hat, never trousers, if a woman, and men never wore jeans or the equivalent. No one would dream of going to church in anything but Sunday Best. At Women's Institute meetings, even in the 1950s one wore a hat. Even a trip to Northampton warranted a hat!'

FOOD REMEMBERED

⊸

Fresh doughnuts, hot cross buns, rabbit stew and fresh vegetables from the allotment are all remembered with pleasure. Who needed modern take-aways when you could have fish and chips, hot faggots, saveloys and roasted potatoes?

REMEMBERED TREATS

'Good Friday at Cottesbrook and the boys with their baskets of freshly baked hot cross buns waking us up in the early morning singing their "One a penny, two a penny, hot cross buns".

Friday night, pay night, and fish and chips wrapped in plenty of newspaper and really hot. A piece and a penn'orth for threepence. Supper for six, one shilling and sixpence.

Take your own basin for hot faggots, saveloys, black puddings, roasted potatoes. What lovely smells and no one had heard of take-aways, folk just did it.

With women starting to do jobs outside the home, they took advantage of the baker's oven. Most had facilities for baking customers' tins of meat and potatoes, puddings and cakes, with special joints and Yorkshire pudding on Sundays. Lovely crusty bread smells and the baker himself cooking real doughnuts in a pan of fat, turning them with a long pin – it couldn't have been a hatpin, could it? When ready, poke a knifeful of jam in the side and dunk it quickly in and out of castor sugar – sugar was expensive!'

'At Pitsford, baked pears in syrup from the bakehouse for the fetching for all us children. A loaf of bread and a quarter cheese for every child at school in the hard weather who couldn't get home to dinner, when men had to cut snow walls to the Cross for us to walk through. Soup nice and hot from the rectory Tuesdays and Fridays, free to those who couldn't afford to pay and twopence for five pints for those who could. Tincture of ginger for all old folks to keep them warm in winter. Beer at a penny a quart at the Old Bakehouse, Chapel Yard. Red flannel petticoats for old ladies!'

'At dinner it was the custom to serve a good filling pudding, eg one made of suet, as a first course. The meat course was served next with fresh vegetables from the garden or allotment.'

'A horse-drawn van came round Little Addington and fish and fruit were bought from the van driver. Wild rabbit was often on the menu and like today, honey was a favourite with young and old alike. Marmalade and jam and many varieties of wine were home-made, potato wine being a great favourite.'

'At Yardley Gobion traps were set along the banks of the canal and river, so rabbit stew was a regular meal.'

'Most families kept hens and when the corn was cut and carried we all went gleaning. It was surprising how much we gathered up and it was a great help when everything including animal feed was short. The hens not only provided eggs but when they got past laying they went into the pot, boiled till tender, then browned in the oven.'

'People in Stowe have always grown their own vegetables and certainly up to and during the Second World War and in "shortage" days many kept hens for eggs and also a pig. It seems to have been a healthy diet and probably a fairly substantial one because of the nature of the work in which most men and some women were engaged, that is, manual farm work. When talking of food, older residents brought to mind meat puddings, clangers (a pasty, sweet one end and savoury the other), suet puddings, milk puddings and for a field dinner there might be half a loaf, a hunk of bacon or cheese and cold tea. Sheep's head might also feature on a villager's menu. Home-made butter, cream and at least on one of the farms, home-made pork pies were eaten. Eggs were sometimes preserved by pickling, a method not confined to country areas.

A villager born in 1921 on talking about the family diet when he was a child said: . . . "My father used his gun almost daily, for partridges, rabbits, etc. We had 300 hens, we picked mushrooms, gathered nuts from Everdon Stubbs and blackberries too. We made crab apple jelly . . ."

Nearly everybody to whom we talked mentioned the pigs. These would provide bacon, ham, offal, lard and faggots from a combination of the offal. A Second World War memory was that the pigs were salted for three weeks and then hung from a convenient beam in the kitchen. Mrs Elsie Leeson remembered that her mother had a pig hanging up during wartime (1939/45) when a visiting evacuee wanted to know when they were going to bury it!

Another story concerned Mr Ormond from Wood Farm (now Vineyard Farm) who was taking a pig to market in the back of his car. As he rounded the corner by the old rectory (now Wyndham House) the pig fell out. Mr Ormond proceeded to Northampton market only to discover when he arrived there, that the pig had gone – an episode which he apparently never lived down!

The task of killing the pigs seems to have fallen to various people. At one time, Mr Vic Watson in Upper Stowe had the job, at another someone came up from Flore. At another period, pig-killing was taken in turns, and the meat shared out. In this way, no one family had too much meat at one time.

Milk was supplied by the farms in churns and individual requirements measured out. In the period of the First World War, Mrs Boatwright used to walk from Church Stowe to Upper Stowe to buy skimmed milk at one penny per can for making puddings. She can also remember being given fried bread, jam puff or cake as a reward for running messages across the fields to and from Weedon.'

ICE CREAM AND FISH AND CHIPS

'Twice a day at Roade we used to hear the clip-clop of the milkman's horse as he came round on his milk deliveries, once in the morning before we went to school and once about 4.30 pm after school. If the weather was good we were allowed to get in the cart and help the milkgirl and got great pleasure taking the pints and half-pints to the customers.

The coalman also used to come round once a week with a horse and cart carrying sacks of coal. We see very few, if any of them, these days.

One of my favourite tradesmen was the fish and chip van, where all the kids used to flock with their pennies (old money, of course) for their penn'orth of chips. Sometimes if we were flush, we'd have a piece (fish) and a penn'orth, that would cost threepence. The thing that used to fascinate me, was that in the summer they sold fish and chips one side and ice cream the other, and there was much discussion on the merits of fish and chips, against ice cream. It was a difficult decision, despite the fact that the ice cream tasted a bit fishy. Having said all that, I am now wondering how they kept it cold, since refrigeration was almost unknown then.

If we wanted *real* ice cream there was "Old Walls-y" who came round from time to time pedalling a three-wheel tricycle, in blue and white check, ringing his bell and selling three-cornered fruit ices for a penny and cream ices for twopence. His slogan was "Stop Me and Buy One" and we did!'

A SPECIAL THOUGHT

'Mrs Roberts, a very sick lady and wife of the Squire's gardener, lived in the cottage next to the Royal Oak at Duddington. On arriving home from school, my mother would send me with a titbit for this lady. Perhaps a piece of cake or a bowl of soft fruit topped with cream skimmed from the milk from our dairy. This she did with a special cream skimmer. Mother always churned our butter from this milk, sometimes churning all day and still no butter to show for it at the end.'

KILLING THE PIG

Using everything but the squeak, the pig was the mainstay of the cottager's meat diet until very recently. Most kept a pig or two and got together with neighbours to plan the killing so that, in those days before refrigeration, nothing should go to waste. As one old man said, there was no picture so good on a cottage wall as a side of bacon.

'I have always associated pigs with smell, not however the obvious one, but with the smell of wet overcoats drying before the kitchen fire. These belonged to my father, the village butcher, and to his apprentices. Each Monday during the winter months he would load up his cart with all the necessary equipment needed for pig-killing and together with two large young men would then go to various nearby villages to slaughter the pigs which had been fed to enormous sizes by their owners.

There was much rivalry amongst these cottage pig-keepers and not a little jealously if old "so-and-so's" pig weighed 20 or more score pounds (the weight was always determined in scores – never stones).

These Mondays always seemd to be wet during my childhood and I well remember the anxious look on my mother's face when father finally returned home, tired, wet, hungry and often bad-tempered. The latter chiefly because one of his customers had failed to have the water boiling in the copper when my father arrived, thus wasting

93

his valuable time. There were always several pigs to be killed each Monday – the only day a busy country butcher could spare during the week.

Later, of course, it became illegal to kill pigs except in a licensed slaughterhouse, so I was often an interested spectator at the last squeals of these unfortunate animals. I made a mental note of all this and decided that I would never marry a butcher nor would I keep pigs.

I married a schoolmaster but that did not prevent me from continuing my association with pigs. My husband announcing that he came of good Anglo-Saxon stock (though he was half Welsh), decided that he was unable to exist on the meagre bacon ration allotted to us during the last war, which I believe was about four ounces per week, therefore we must feed a pig. I became resigned to the idea as the end result was certainly a wonderful sight in the shape of hams and flitches of bacon hanging on the kitchen walls. Also we seemed to attract many friends and visitors who were happy to be fed on unlimited quantities of ham and eggs. We also received a visit from the Food Inspector who was rather suspicious of the idea of a schoolmaster feeding his own pig in a rented sty. I was able to assure him that all was in order as he arrived at an opportune moment when I was laboriously cleaning out my clothes boiler after it had been used for cooking pig potatoes. I think he felt quite sorry for me as he departed saying "That's all right, my dear!"

When we came to live in Barton Seagrave the chief attraction of the house in my husband's eyes was the splendid sight of a pig sty in the orchard. We were then able to have two pigs at a time, one of which was sold to the Ministry of Food. It required much careful reckoning to feed this pig to the correct size for the requirements of the Ministry. The British housewife and her family no longer ate fat bacon so the pig must not weigh more than seven score, neither must there be more than an inch of fat on the bacon. These exacting requirements could be estimated by measuring the circumference of the animal, which was an hilarious experience. Some pigs objected strongly to this indignity and refused to remain stationary in order to have the tape measure passed around their middles.

Alas, after discovering that the bacon produced by our friends the Danes was preferred to the home product, our pig farming was abandoned. The sty in the orchard was finally occupied by six light Sussex hens.'

'Buying groceries was very different, especially when you lived in the country. One example is cooking salt – no packets but a large block about a foot square by two foot long. This was bought from the baker for a few pence. On receipt it was cut up into brick sized pieces which were stored in a dry place. When required for use, two of these pieces would be rubbed together to make fine salt which was stored in a jar to be used as required. This was a job for the children and I can still remember the taste of salt one got on one's lips.

When pig killing time came around it was very important to have a good supply of salt. Traditions of pig killing varied from place to place and from household to household. In our case, at Overstone, we usually killed two pigs a year, one in autumn and one in spring, but there must always be an "r" in the month. The butcher would arrive early on a Monday morning. After killing the pig it would be singed, to remove the bristles, over a straw fire. After gutting it would be hung up for two days. The butcher would then come back to cut up the carcase. This was a very busy day for the womenfolk. The fat all had to be made into lard, which was done by mincing it up, an arm-aching job for the children, no electric mincers. It was then put into a large pan to be melted down, and strained into large earthenware pancheons. The best lard to be used for pastry was from the leaf, second renderings were for cooking. The pancheons were stored in the cool dairy for use over the coming months. The crispy bits of skin left, "scratchings", were eaten with bread for elevenses over the following days and very tasty they were too.

Meanwhile, the sides and hams were carried down to the cellar to be cured. We used the dry method, that is dry salt, saltpetre and, on the hams, a little brown sugar rubbed into the meat. This took several weeks until the salt had penetrated right through the meat. The job was done by my father, I think this was partly because it was considered that the meat would go bad if a woman went near it when she had her period.

When the meat was thoroughly cured it was brought up to the kitchen and hung up to dry. When dry it was put into cotton bags to keep it clean and free from flies. Pieces were cut off as required. As I remember, it was very salty tasting and joints were soaked well before boiling. Some of the spring-killed ham was always kept for the following Christmas. As well as the bacon and hams, cheeks and the tongue were lightly salted to make brawn.'

'Many of the cottages at Grafton Underwood had pigsties and the villagers kept pigs that were slaughtered, usually in November, for bacon. This was cured on the premises and then hung on the walls in the cottages. As one old boy said, "The nicest picture on a wall is a flitch of bacon, and an even better one is a ham hanging by the fireplace." Neighbours and friends would be given some of the offal. Faggots were made, the fat rendered down for lard, and even the bladder was dried, blown up by means of a straw and used as a football.'

'George Bradley at Everdon had a pony and trailer and he used to fetch brewers grains from Northampton. Then he sold them round the village for people to feed to their pigs. Nearly everyone kept a pig. The butcher, Percy Balderson, went round killing pigs on Mondays. He was all right in the morning, but often the worse for wear when he got home, as everywhere he went he was given a drink.'

'Most of the village people at Loddington had a sty in the back garden in the 1920s. The pig was fed on household scraps, potatoes and barley – most of the people had two plots of allotments, one to grow cereals and the other for vegetables.

The villagers arranged it amongst themselves when to have these pigs killed, with an interval between each killing. As there were no fridges, they shared out the offal at each killing.

It was a barbaric business considering we could hear the squeals over half a mile away. After the pig had been killed and stuck, it had to be singed and this was done by covering it with straw and setting fire to it. Great care had to be taken at this point not to overdo it and blister it. The pig was then put onto a kind of long, sturdy stool with handles, called a "scratch", and scrubbed with warm water. to get rid of all the charred straw, after which the cutting up began.

Until the war, our pigs were taken in a horse-drawn float to our butcher, who killed it more humanely, scalded it instead of singeing it, and we collected it the next day already cut up. It was then placed in a large, shallow wooden trough called a salting lead. Certain areas of the hams and shoulders had to be pressed very hard to get the blood out, after which a little saltpetre was rubbed well into just these two areas, while the flitches or sides were well salted. It was rubbed and turned daily for some days, before being hung up to dry. The salt was bought in twelve pound slabs from the village baker.

During the war we were allowed to kill a pig, but we had to surrender most of our bacon ration coupons. Our butcher had to come out and kill it for us, and he used a humane killer. Mother being a farmer's daughter, made excellent brawn and pork pies. Home rendered lard was delicious on bread or toast with a smear of Bovril.'

'Money being in short supply, every family had a big, well cultivated garden, which supplied them with all the vegetables they needed throughout the year. They also kept a pig which they killed when it weighed about 300 pounds. They then cured it with salt and saltpetre and that provided them with most of the meat they needed. A pig club was in existence at Harlestone which was virtually a small insurance company. The members paid one shilling per pig at purchase and if, unfortunately, it died they received the purchase price from the club.'

FROM THE CRADLE TO THE GRAVE

⊸⊃

In the days when doctors were only for emergencies and both they and the hospital had to be paid for, self help was often the only course available to people, either tried and trusted home remedies or the confidence of belonging to a local Friendly or Benefit Society which would pay out in times of illness. Birth invariably took place at home, attended by the local nurse or a voluntary 'midwife' and death was signalled to the rest of the community by the doleful tolling of the church bell. Explaining death to a child has, of course, always been difficult, in whatever time you have lived.

WHERE BABIES COME FROM

'We never knew where babies came from in those days, now they know it all when they're so high. My mother was expecting a baby but I didn't know. My Dad came back from Middleton Cheney church, it was a Sunday in 1910 and he rang the bells. "Get your hat and coat." he says to me and my sister. "You're going on a little holiday to Granny Wroxton." (My Mum's mother lived at Wroxton). As it was a Sunday there was no carrier so Dad took his bike and my sister sat on the handlebar. I had to walk (a distance of about six miles). When it was time to come home we came on the carrier's cart. I can't remember if someone met us in Banbury. We travelled from Wroxton on the cart on our own, me and my little sister. I was ten and a half years old. The baby was there when we got home. My mother told me the doctor brought the baby in his black bag. After that I used to watch out for Dr Dwyer and follow him to a house then run home to tell Mum who he had taken a baby to. It was a long time till I found out!

I'll tell you a story now. Mrs Stuchbury used to come in and help deliver the babies, she lived in the village. Well just after I had been born, Lottie Spencer-that-was (Mrs Charlotte Bricknell who ran a pub called the Snob and Ghost near the church) had a baby boy – Cecil. Well, Mrs Stuchbury asked my mother if she could borrow me to show the men in the tap-room, to kid them that Lottie had had twins! Of course I was much bigger than the other baby as I was two weeks older. My Dad was very cross when he got home, he didn't think it was funny that I had gone to the pub!'

'When my sister was born in the 1920s at Kettering, a midwife stayed in the house for a month, doing domestic duties as well as delivering the baby and caring for the mother. Midwives were not compulsorily registered and local ladies were much in demand.'

'When our first daughter was born at Everdon, I had to leave my wife and walk to Badby to fetch the District Nurse. It was 5th May and there was snow on the ground. I had to throw stones up at the bedroom window to wake her, but she soon came on her bike.'

THE CANAL MIDWIFE

'Ann Clarke was the midwife at Nether Heyford – always on call by day or night when she could be roused by a tap on her window with the long pole provided for the purpose. She also served the narrowboat families and her charge was ninepence. You could see her every day at noon with her little white jug fetching her half pint of stout to "keep her going".'

DOCTORS, NURSES AND DENTISTS

'Our doctor in Northampton was driven round in a pony and trap, but by about 1913 he came round in a huge car driven by a chauffeur. He was always halfway up the stairs before my mother could get to the door. He could call out "Where is she, Mother?". He wore a top hat and hung it on the brass knob of the bedstead. One of his favourite pieces of advice was "Give her plenty of bread and lard, Mother!".'

'At about the time of the First World War there was a nurse in Easton but no doctor or dentists in the village (as their services were expensive, these were rarely used anyway). Older people rarely had usable teeth and a bone, honed and polished, was used to core apples etc to aid eating.'

'At first doctors came out from Daventry in a pony and trap. Later they came on bikes or motor bikes. They were willing to come out at any time, night or day, and would perform small operations (tonsillectomy etc) at home on the kitchen table. They would wait for their pay too. People used things like camphorated oil, eucalyptus oil and goose grease for colds etc. Then there were some women who had a good idea of things and they would come and help in cases of sickness. My mother used goose grease which she kept in a basin in a cool place. When one of her children was born, a neighbour came in to help and made her a cake. Afterwards, Mother couldn't find her goose grease. "Oh dear," said the neighbour, "that's what I used to make your cake!"'

'In the 1920s villagers at Brigstock paid a small sum each week into the Nursing Association and were then able to use the services of the village nurse, who nursed the sick in their own homes and was also the maternity nurse. In Brigstock High Street stands a house called "Conway" after a Nurse Conway who had officiated at a very difficult birth there with a successful conclusion.'

'If anyone was sick in Barby, the doctor came from the neighbouring village of Crick. A lady in the village acted as a messenger should anyone need the doctor. Messages were displayed in her window and as the doctor passed, he would look in. Prescriptions and medicines were left at her home for people to collect.'

'We had no doctor at Creaton so in times of illness one had to contact the surgery at Brixworth or Guilsborough. Then the doctor came to the house. When necessary medicines would be left at the post office. If it was just a cold on the chest it was more probable a home treatment of goose grease rubbed on the chest would be in order, and possibly, if lemons were available, a hot lemon and honey drink – still very effective!'

THE HOSPITAL

'My first memory in the 1920s is going to the local hospital in Kettering, then a cottage hospital, at the age of two in order to have a cyst removed from my eye. I wore a very large pair of red felt ankle strap slippers and socks which were too small for me. Local doctors did most of the operations, although consultants came from Leicester. Mother and my sister and I paid into the National Deposit Friendly Society, from which a form had to be obtained before we went to the doctor.'

The visit by the Duke and Duchess of York to Manfield Hospital.

MANFIELD HOSPITAL IN THE 1940s

'A great fuss was made when the Duke and Duchess of York (later George VI and Queen Elizabeth) visited the hospital and I remember as a very young child squirming my way through the legs to catch a glimpse of them and my father in a top hat.

On Blue Bird Day a collection was made for the hospital – I was too young to be allowed to go on the pub crawl in the evening but I understand it was a very good source of income! Fundraising was a very important part of the life of a voluntary hospital before 1948 and the advent of the National Health Service.

We once had a visit from the Australian cricket team, including the legendary Don Bradman, and the cricket bat they all signed had pride of place in the board room for many years. We had visits from many celebrities and on the lawn we had an annual firework display, the best in Northampton in those days.

What sticks in my mind most were the Christmas morning visits of the Mayors of Northampton. They used to visit every charitable institution in the town between breakfast and lunch and I had to get ready very early to go with my father to meet the Mayor on his first visit of the day to Templemore, later to be known as the John

Greenwood Shipman Home, in Dallington. Then home to open our presents and wait for the mayoral party to arrive at the hospital for the last visit of the morning. With the surgeons waiting to operate on the turkeys instead of the patients, lunch could often be delayed for two or three hours. It depended whether the Mayor was one who breezed into each establishment with a cheery wave and handed his bag of oranges and pennies to one of the staff to distribute or whether he insisted on handing them out himself and having a word with every patient or resident!'

SELF HELP

'Several older Helmdon people remember the Benefit Society. It was registered on 5th July 1884 and dissolved at the outbreak of the First World War. The object of the society was "to raise funds by entrance fees, subscriptions, fines, donations and interest on capital, for the relief of members, and for the funeral expenses of the wife of a member." Once a year, a club dinner or Feast Day was held "but no portion of the expenses was to come out of the Society's funds".

The Whit Friday Feast Day was the highlight of the year. The men paraded through the village, each carrying a stave about eight feet long. The band was playing ahead of them, but it never played while

The Wicken Sick Aid Club here celebrate 100 years in existence in 1939. Paying into clubs such as this secured an income for many families when the breadwinner was unable to work through illness.

BALANCE SHEET

OF THE

HELMDON BENEFIT SOCIETY

For the year ending December 31st, 1909.

(as sent to the Chief Registrar).

BENEFIT FUND.

RECEIPTS.	£	s.	d.	EXPENSES.	£	s.	d.
Contributions for Sickness	67	10	0	213 5-6th wks. full pay to 32 members	85	10	8
„ sums at death	13	14	6	289 wks. half pay to 13 members	57	16	0
„ Medical Aid	4	6	0	Sums at death to 2 members	10	0	0
„ Infirmary	2	15	6	„ „ 2 members' wives	5	0	0
Interest	11	13	4	Infirmary (for letters)	2	2	0
Advanced by Secretary	3	13	6	Repaid Secretary	7	15	4
				Medical Aid	4	6	0
	103	12	10		172	10	0
Amount of Benefit Fund at beginning of year	408	5	10	Amount of Benefit Fund at end of year	339	8	8
	£511	18	8		£511	18	8

MANAGEMENT FUND.

	£	s.	d.		£	s.	d.
Contributions of Members	1	14	4	Salary of Secretary	2	0	0
Fines	0	2	4	Printing and Stationery	1	7	0
Entrance Fees	0	17	6	Postage	0	13	2
	2	14	2	Valuation	0	18	6
Amount of Management Fund at beginning of year	6	17	2	Altering Rules	0	5	0
					5	3	8
				Amount of Management Fund at end of year	4	7	8
	£9	11	4		£9	11	4

SUMMARY OF THE ABOVE.

	£	s.	d.		£	s.	d.
Amount of Benefit Fund	339	8	8	Amount in P.O. Saving's Bank	343	16	4
„ Management Fund	4	7	8				
	£343	16	4		£343	16	4

HARRY EDDEN, ⎫
                      ⎬ Auditors.
HENRY HOWARD, ⎭

THOS. HERBERT GOODWIN,

Secretary & Treasurer.

they were walking over the bridge. They all went to church but the children had to stay outside as the church was always full of men.'

'To help the sick at Wicken, a club called the Sick Aid Club had been running for 100 years up to the Second World War. Their club day was held at Whitsun, with a church service followed by a dinner in the school. Afterwards there were children's and adults' sports with the New Bradwell Silver Band in attendance.'

'The Stanion Friendly Society was established in August 1861 and continued during the inter-war years of the 1920s and 1930s.

The Club met in the Lord Cardigan Arms, the home of Edward Spencer, who was Father of the Club. The stewards were Eli and Harry Bell. Meetings took place four times a year, on the second Thursday of the months of May, August, November and February. Every member paid five shillings per quarter, and three pence extra was paid on the August night in each year, for the Stewards' services.

Membership was limited to those under the age of 35 years, unless an extra sum was paid 'to the box', the amount of each sum to be left to the discretion of a majority of the members. In addition, no member was admitted if he were 'disaffected to government or troubled with the king's evil, or any other distemper, which may render him incapable of getting his living'. The use of the name 'king's evil' at such a late date is interesting. It seems to have been tuberculosis, and it was thought at one time that it could be healed by the touch of the King. James I had no faith in its healing powers as early as 1603, although the practice was retained by Charles I and Charles II in the later 17th century. To have it named as such in the 19th century is surprising.

The 'box' contained the property of the Society, and was in the care of the Father of the Club; any surplus cash was placed in the Stamford, Spalding & Boston Bank, Kettering, to gain interest.

Members who became sick or lame were allowed nine shillings per week during their illness, when funds were below £50; if above, more could be allowed, to be determined by a majority of members at the August meeting. However, no allowance was made if the illness were occasioned by quarrelling or venereal disease.

If a member died after being a member for a year and a day, £1 was allowed for his funeral; £2 if a member for two years and a day . . . and so on, up to a maximum of £6, to be disposed of as his friends thought proper. If a member's wife died, the allowance was halved.

Forfeits were taken in some circumstances – for example, six pence if 'disguised in liquor', or cursing, swearing, or promoting gaming; two pence if laying wagers, swearing an oath, or 'calling any brother member out of their names'. In extreme cases, a member could be expelled.

Friendly Societies of this type must have been of great value to those on low wages, where death of the wage-earner, or prolonged illness, or absence from work could have catastrophic results. Later, the need for them declined as people took out insurance policies.

Mr Hector worked for his grandfather, who was a carpenter. By 1936, an ordinary funeral cost £7, one with an oak coffin £12, and usually expenses were paid by an insurance policy; one shilling per week was usually paid as a premium on the life of a child. A 'parish funeral' was regarded as a disgrace and to be dreaded, cost ten shillings and was paid for by Kettering Council.

The principle established by such Friendly Societies, of payment when in work as an insurance against the effects of ill-health or injury, laid the foundations of the National Health Service, and it was its introduction which made most of their valuable work no longer necessary.'

'In those days there was no health insurance as we know it today and when the breadwinner became unwell, it meant hardship for all the family. Societies known as the Sick and Divide Clubs were formed. Each of the pubs in Easton on the Hill had its own club. There were three at this time, the Slaters Arms (now The Cavalier), the Blue Bell and the Engine. At the end of the year any extra funds were shared out between the members. This came as a welcome contribution towards the Christmas fare.'

'At Harlestone there was a Friendly Society known as the Odd Fellows, which provided sick pay to its members – the membership being very high. A man from the village of Brington came round the cottages every Sunday without fail to pay out members who were ill and collect subs.'

HOME REMEDIES

'Northampton General Hospital was our nearest hospital at Deanshanger, but they did rely on public support so various fetes and egg collections took place. Our doctor came from Stony Stratford but in the early days doctors visited on horseback. People paid into the dispensary for their medicines. Some people made their own cough mixture, one pennyworth of laudanum, paregoric, aniseed, peppermint and a stick of "Spanish" etc worked wonders. Ointment was made from the house leek. Mrs Green was our link with Stony Stratford, setting off with a huge basket and walking the two miles each way to collect medicines and do errands for a penny ha'penny, singing all the way.'

'I remember being given brimstone and treacle every Saturday morning, regular doses of cod liver oil, and also a paste made with aniseed and water. Camphorated oil or goose grease were cures for bad chests and flannel was worn as a preventive.'

SCARLET FEVER AND DIPHTHERIA

'In 1928, when suffering from scarlet fever, I was taken by horse-drawn ambulance to the county isolation hospital, which was situated between Hardingstone and Hackleton on the Newport Pagnell Road. The house was at the end of a long drive. Behind the house in the next field were two disused railway carriages that at one time had been used a a smallpox hospital. When almost fit to go home another girl, the only other patient at the hospital, and I, being nosy, went across the fields and into the carriages. There were beds and tables, chairs, cushions, mattresses and pillows, all half eaten away by rats and mice.'

'In 1934 in Cold Ashby there was a scarlet fever epidemic, which was contracted by young and old alike. Few people managed to escape this unpleasant disease. Many were taken into the care of the Staverton isolation hospital some 16 miles away.'

'Childhood memories recall that measles and whooping cough were serious illnesses, but even worse was diphtheria. If you mentioned a sore throat when that was about, you were whipped off to the isolation hospital and allowed to take only two toys. Tuberculosis was also still a threat and two children died from it at Welton in the 1920s.'

'In November 1916 I was four years old, quite poorly and had developed a sore throat. The doctor was called – he was not sure, but later my parents were informed it was diphtheria!'
    I do not know all the details but the "brown bottomed" cab that collected patients for the isolation hospital at Staverton came to fetch me but it was kept waiting whilst my father tried to find the doctor. Telephones were non-existent then and my father returned, realising I would have to go to the hospital. As I was the only child, it would

have been possible to isolate me in the house in accordance with regulations but only with the doctor's consent.

The next thing I remember is being wrapped up in a blanket and taken out to the waiting cab. I know I was crying and my parents were too – four years old, first time away from them, also diphtheria was a killer – would they see me again?

The doctor called about half an hour after I had gone!

However, children are resilient and Mr Wallace was a big man who held me close in his arms and comforted me, so that I soon left off crying and talked with him.

I remember very little of the hospital but my recollections are of the sleeping conditions. One night I was in a cot which was pushed up near a window and my feet could be put flat against the bottom bars so, obviously, it was much too small for me. Another night, I was with a boy from the village and another I was with my cousin aged six, another night with an older woman and, I think, a small child.

On one Sunday, my parents hired Mr Stock from the village to bring them in his cab (which was totally black) over to Staverton to see me. We all seemed to be in an upstairs room looking out of the window and down at my parents (and others) standing outside in the cold damp weather.

My mother (dressed in black because her youngest brother, head of Barby village school, had recently been killed in the war) dropped her handkerchief. We were all motioning for her to pick it up but to no avail. This led to me crying and my parents turned away, which made it worse.

Eventually, after about four or five weeks, I came home and Mother immediately discovered I had head lice. However, I can remember my mother getting quassia chips from the chemist, which were used in water for the daily washing of the hair. I have no idea how long the quassia chips/toothcomb treatment went on but, again, when I was older, Mother told me she had reported the matter of head lice – to whom I do not know. But, for her pains, she had to go before a Board – because, apparently, she had reported "authority".

During the period I was away, the Church District Visitor, ie the lady who delivered the church magazines, asked our nextdoor neighbour if she would take the magazine and give it to my parents. Such was the scare of getting diphtheria!'

DEATH IN THE COMMUNITY

'If it was a death everybody knew if it was a man or a woman by the Death Bell and roughly who it was, one toll for each year of their lives. An old superstition at Grafton Underwood was that if the ground was open for a woman over the weekend, there would be three more to follow.'

'Kitty's father was the village undertaker at Denford and she has records of £15 being the price of an oak coffin, with two shillings being paid to the bearers. She recalls that there used to be a beautiful hand hearse which was used for funerals. As with most villages in the early part of the century, Denford had its layer-out. Kitty can remember going with her father when he went to measure bodies for their coffins and also delivering coffins. One in particular was delivered to Ringstead using a horse, a hunter, that was a little unwilling to pull uphill unless it got a good gallop up beforehand!'

'When a death occurred at Clipston, the family called in the person who was known to be willing to do the laying out and the body usually stayed in the home until the funeral. Black was expected to be worn and anyone not possessing hat, coat and gloves for the service, would borrow them from someone else.'

'When I was a small child, sometimes if we heard the church bell during the week Mother would say "Someone has died in the village", and she would know by the length of the pauses if it was man, woman or child. In June 1924 I went to my cousin's grandmother's funeral at Holcot. We had assembled at the home and about half an hour before the service was due to begin, four village men (the bearers) came with a very antiquated wooden bier on solid rubber tyres to collect the coffin. When all was ready we followed in procession up the village street, each carrying a floral tribute or two, to the church.'

'When somebody at Easton on the Hill died, it was customary to toll the church bell for about quarter of an hour, three bells for a man, two for a woman and one for a child. Then on the day of the funeral the village bier was brought from the church to the house of the deceased by the four bearers of the coffin. These men then went into a neighbour's house to partake of bread, cheese and beer. The passing bell was tolled to let them know when it was time to assemble for refreshments. Then the coffin was placed on the bier, with mourners arranged two by two behind it. The procession slowly wended its way to the church, the mournful bell still tolling. It must have been a rough ride for the person inside the coffin. The iron wheels of the bier rattled noisily and shakily on the rough road to the church and cemetery for interment.'

GOING TO GOD

'In the 1950s I was teaching at Nether Heyford school. We had children from church and chapel attending school and our tradition was an Ascension Day service. My little infants who always behaved so well in church could now be free and they always picked buttercups and brought them to me and we had to find lots of jars to hold them all. Once a little boy found a bee. He said "Mrs Warr, did God make bees?" "Yes," I said. "Well, I don't like God", he replied.

One particular incident that sticks in my mind is of the child who asked "What happens at a funeral?" I prayed for guidance and said, "Well, that poor old lady who was so ill has gone to God; the part that mattered had, and the body that was buried was like an old dress that we throw away." In the school rebuilding programme, when a grate was removed we discovered lots of birds' skeletons, which were thrown on a heap of rubble. At playtime there were cries of "Mrs Warr, come quickly, some birds have gone to God with the parts that mattered".'

CHILDHOOD
&
SCHOOLDAYS

DAYS OF FUN AND FREEDOM

⊸⊝⊸

Whether it was in town or in a country village, the abiding memory of childhood before the Second World War is of days filled with fun and freedom. The fun may still be there for today's children, but sadly the freedom to wander in safety may now be something denied to younger generations.

OUTINGS FROM OUNDLE

'My memories of Northamptonshire begin at the age of four years in my home town of Oundle, which is 30 miles from the County Town of Northampton. Consequently, we seemed to be very remote from the happenings in the "top end" of the county.

I remember going, on Good Friday, to Biggin Woods and picking primroses ready for Easter. We went via Biggin Grange, and looked forward to a glass of lemonade given to us by the wife of one of the farm workers on our return journey. At other times of the year, we found Lords and Ladies, Spotted Orchids, Old Man's Beard and, in the winter, spindleberries.

When I learned to ride a bike, I was "off". On fine Saturdays, with a girl schoolfriend and her father, we discovered the beautiful villages round about – Wadenhoe, Stoke Doyle, Pilton, Aldwincle, Titchmarsh and Lilford, to name but a few. Sometimes, we struck off in another direction and found the two Benefields, Lower and Upper Deene and Deenethorpe, Brigstock, Lowick, Bulwick, returning via Southwick and Glapthorn.

On winter Sunday mornings, we went for a walk whilst our respective mothers prepared lunch – lovely roast beef and Yorkshire pudding cooked in a side oven. We were always prepared for anything that might "turn up" such as mushrooms, sticks to light the fire, blackberries etc. We knew where the wild pear tree was between Tansor Wold and Elmington and where all the crabapples could be found.

On hot Saturday mornings, we could be found with some lemonade, bread and cheese and a sweet or two, paddling in the brook down the Stoke Road. It was clean and unpolluted and we were not afraid of anyone in those days. Sometimes we found a little stream down the Barnwell Road, where the Country Park is now situated. It ran swiftly, was very shallow, and had a lovely gravelled bottom. We bathed and had a wonderful time.

Sunday afternoons found us in Sunday school and, in winter, after tea, church with Granny and Grandad. In the summer, we would walk "round the square", starting off along the Barnwell Road, past the Manor, along the Armston Road, past Red Lodge and home along the Polebrook Road – quite a step. We never seemed to be tired!

If we were very energetic we would go to Stoke Doyle, on to Pilton, over the Lynch Bridge at Lilford and home along the main Thrapston to Oundle Road. As I look back, I realise that we were not allowed to "play" on Sundays, or to make a noise and shout in the street. We wore our Sunday outfits and covered our dresses up with a starchy white pinafore at dinner and teatime.

The streets of the town were very quiet and safe, and we could bowl our hoops and spin our tops in the gutter or on the pavement. We played marbles in the street, and skipped according to the season and the current craze. There was a grocer's shop on the corner of our road where we were sent with a jamjar for a pound of treacle which ran slowly out of a container when the tap was turned. It was halfway between black treacle and the golden syrup we buy now, and was delicious!

We lived in an agricultural area and had no knowledge of the hardship and unemployment due to the aftermath of war that was suffered by the people in the large cities and up north. Our entertainments were simple, but very enjoyable. Twice a year we had a visit from Allen's Theatre, a travelling group who put on two shows a week, changing the programme on Thursdays; for example, *Maria Marten* Monday, Tuesday and Wednesday and *Uncle Tom's Cabin* on Thursday, Friday and Saturday. We were allowed to go to the Saturday matinee and sat on a form for sixpence! Also, in October and March, we had the fairs, sometimes Hollands and sometimes Thurstons. How sick I was in the swing boats!

When I was in my teens a great happening took place. My mother announced that certain ladies were going to form a Women's Institute and she was going to join. I can hear her now humming *Glad Hearts Adventuring* as she went about her work. The WI Choir was entering for the local Music Festival, which is still going strong, and so, I'm pleased to say, is the Women's Institute.'

NEVER ANY FEAR

'I was born in the 1920s in Higham Ferrers when recession was well underway. My father and his brothers owned a boot and shoe factory in neighbouring Rushden but after the First World War army boots weren't much of a saleable item so the factory closed down. The building and machinery were still there and it was a great place to play in. My father met his brothers in the office to deal with bills and payments and he would take me with him to play with cousins. I rode on the back of his bicycle, one knee on the back mudguard and one on a metal step on the wheel. He used to take my sister to have her hair singed in this way. She had a plait and the singeing was supposed to strengthen your hair.

The factory was a wonderful place for hide and seek, scooting on the trolleys and searching out metal labels, shoelaces, shoe boxes for dolls' beds and coloured leather remnants. I hoped one day to find real treasure. From the office to the stockroom was a beautiful wrought iron spiral staircase and poking about up there I found my fortune, an Oxo tin full of farthings which my uncles allowed me to keep. For the next few weeks I bought two aniseed balls a day from the school tuck shop.

Although well under ten, we were never taken to school or met out. We were allowed much more freedom in those days despite much stricter discipline. Sunday was God's Day and three visits to Sunday school and church was routine. Dinner was cooked at the local bakehouse for sixpence and the only recreation was a country walk to find specimens to look at under the microscope. The only reading was an encylopaedia and I was put off for years from enjoying them. I didn't in the least want to know about any of its fascinating information.

We were allowed to roam about the fields nearby and I spent many happy hours paddling in the brook and gathering watercress. There was a nearby rubbish tip which yielded treasures to be taken to our favourite field called the Hilly Holly. This was a delightfully uneven field because of local quarrying some years before. It was the perfect place to play "houses", each hollow a different house for "visiting" when mothers and fathers was suggested. There were trees to be climbed and the boys could fight wars and ambush each other for hours. This field yielded some beautiful wild flowers, the "totty" grass which could never be held still, eggs and bacon, bluebells, clover, cowslips and violets. There was never any fear and no-one ever thought the hollows might conceal anything nasty. Our parents allowed us to be there knowing we would be perfectly safe. I feel very sad that my children or today's children can never have that security. The Second World War put an end to the Hilly Holly as it was levelled and turned into allotments.'

A VILLAGE YEAR THROUGH A CHILD'S EYES

'Memories of the 1940s come flooding back as I remember my

childhood village with its tiny population of under 200 people – a close knit community with a caring spirit. The young looking after the old and the old sharing their home-grown produce with each other. I can see the cottage gardens with rambling roses around the doors, lavender hedges bordering the paths, hollyhocks and foxgloves reaching up the walls and purple clematis with flowers as big as saucers clinging to shaking trellis.

Many village folk kept chickens. Some had roosters, bantams, guinea fowls and the like wandering freely onto the narrow roads. Some villagers kept their own pig which was fattened in a sty at the bottom of the garden alongside the privy.

Our neighbours had a smallholding, and as was common in most villages, were related to my family in a distant way and quickly adopted as "uncle" and "auntie" by me. I made every excuse to visit them and help collect the eggs, round up the geese, chickens and ducks, throw them corn, and help give water to the day old chicks which struggled together under the heat lamp suspended above them. I helped Uncle call in the few cows and watched him tether them in their stalls for milking. His old green beret pushed hard against their sides as he squatted beside them on his milking stool, aiming the streams of hot milk into the shining galvanised buckets. He would carefully carry the milk over to the cottage for his wife to store and cool it in large bowls in the dairy, cold slabs of stone forming shelves around this shaded room. Another enamel bowl contained thick cream which had been skimmed off in readiness for Auntie to make her butter. The skimmed milk helped to feed the pigs which squealed at feeding times.

As I walked towards the yard, a pungent smell of boiled peelings and left over vegetables filled the air. The meal house had large bins of meal in it and I always remember the huge cobwebs which draped the dusty windows. Here the feeds were prepared, mash for the hens and swill for the pigs. As the buckets splashed their contents over the sty wall, pigs raced to put their snouts into the troughs, uttering contented grunts between each slurp. In the next sty, I stared in amazement at an enormous sow suckling a litter of silky pink piglets which scampered all over her.

Although his work is over now, a small pony had for years pulled a trap around the village, delivering fresh milk, eggs and cream to the locals. The milk was ladled from churns into shining clean jugs presented at the doors of the cottages. They sold pats of butter, too, endorsed with a cow on either side, their own special logo.

The year is 1947 and this tiny village is about to be lost beneath several feet of snow. Work ground to a halt and the men of the village took spades and dug a tunnel down the centre of the road, children huriedly fetched their sledges and these were used to carry shopping. The village school kept open for a handful of children, some of whom came from other areas on foot, as the buses had no chance of surviving the twelve foot drifts along the hedgerows. I remember small bottles of school milk in crates being warmed in front of open fires in the infants' classrooms. Everyone ate cheese sandwiches for lunch, as the hot meals usually delivered for lunch in huge containers had no hope of reaching us. I also remember the smell of sulphur from the coke burning on the school boiler in an effort to keep the radiators warm. The older children made slides in the playground, while the younger ones looked on enviously. This winter, which was to be remembered for many years, lasted for weeks.

When the spring arrived, one of the highlights for the village children was the arrival of the little lambs. We watched them skipping and dancing, and we collected catkins, pussy willow and primroses from the woods, not forgetting the violets which grew in profusion along the banks beneath the hedges. We used to take horse chestnut "sticky buds" into school and watch them with interest as their long green fingers uncurled into giant hands.

The weather was always warm and sunny, or so it seemed, and my birthdays were always a garden event with masses of children. After tea, we would run into an adjoining field, through the clap-gate and over a stile to play rounders or cricket. Hoops were bowled, marbles were fought over and five stones was played. Skipping games and hopscotch were also firm favourites.

Then the summer would arrive and the haymaking, followed soon after by the harvest. Women and children would go gleaning. Pieces of wheat from around the edge of the field would be cut with carpet scissors and stuffed awkwardly into sacks. Ears of corn would help feed the chickens which we kept at the top of our garden. Gradually, as each field was harvested, our legs became more and more scratched by the stubble left behind.

As the autumn approached and the conkers ripened and cracked in their shells, the children fought each other to get the biggest or the best conker for themselves. Serious games of conkers were played in the playground. We were lucky that we had several fine horse chestnut trees in the village and it was always a race to get there first.

Then thoughts turned to Guy Fawkes, bonfires on the village green, roasting chestnuts and potatoes, and the whirring of the catherine wheels. The farmer in the village tidied his hedges, mended his fences and chopped down trees for winter logs. Again, mothers and children took sacks and filled them to bursting with the

114

chips of wood which had fallen at the base of the tree. All these helped to save burning coal in the fires.

Produce in abundance filled the tiny church for Harvest Festival and the voices of the packed congregation rang out over the fields. The choir of twelve girls in their robes of scarlet led the singing. I had just joined the choir at this stage, and proudly I wore bows of red ribbon on my plaits and sang my loudest.

Sundays and the church played an enormous part in the lives of all the locals. Almost everyone had to walk the mile there and back as very few poeple had cars. There were three services during the day and we choir girls always met up before we set off on our journey but we never seemed to notice how far it was as we all joined hands across the road, laughing and joking. It all seemed fun and everyone seemed to be happy. Sunday afternoon was special for me because I was allowed to walk the half mile to the end of the village to the sweet shop. Here I spent my two ounces of sweet ration on a bar of chocolate. I probably ate it all before I got home again.

I would spend the six weeks of school holidays with the local kids and my cousin who was three years younger. We often watched the blacksmith shoeing the horses, our faces glowing with the heat from his furnace and turning our noses up at the smell of burning hoof. We watched the sheep shearing and dipping. The farmer didn't seem to mind that we sat all along his fences, just watching. We tried to catch sticklebacks in the brook and earlier in spring would carry great bowls full of tadpoles in huge jellied masses and stuff them into jamjars. It is no wonder so few managed to turn into frogs. Then there was birdnesting, but we rarely found a deserted nest so that we could go home with the treasure. Sometimes we would walk to the canal and watch the barges creep slowly under the bridge and into the locks. We would run up the towpath and try to help the lock-keeper push open the locks.

We would play for hours in a broken tree and imagine it was our own special house. This particular tree is still standing nearly 50 years later. Life was such fun when I was seven.'

THE GAMES WE PLAYED

Games were always outdoor ones, in the fields or in the streets of town and village in the days when nothing more dangerous than horse-drawn traffic was to be expected – and little enough of that in most places. To time-honoured rules, hopscotch, marbles, skipping, hoops and tops could be found wherever groups of children gathered.

THE FAG CARD FEAST

'I don't know if the "fag-card" feast was common to all villages, or singular to wollaston but it was always an annual event to be looked forward to in the height of summer, after the retreat of the real fair. The fair or "feast", as it was always known as its arrival marked the Feast Day of the church, was in June and was thoroughly enjoyed by all the children and, our appetite whetted, we used to erect our own feast on the corner of the street. Every competitive game in the home was dragged out; there were no "rides" involved in *our* feast, of course, but great fun was to be had with marbles, darts, rolling balls and whatever we could find to have "goes" on. The currency used was cigarette cards or "fag-cards". Most of our fathers smoked Woodbines or Goldflake and every packet contained a picture-card inside with a host of information on the reverse side of it. These were great collectors items and the more we had the more we could "spend" (and win) at the Fag-card Feast.'

PLAYING IN THE STREET

'Some of the games we used to play I don't even see anymore. I loved it when "whip and top" time came round, usually in the spring. We used to colour the tops with chalks to make them pretty as they spun round, and the difficulty we had in trying to get them spinning. Once they got going they lasted for ages. Some of the boys could just spin them off in their fingers, I could never do that. When the nights grew lighter we used to have skipping sessions. A couple of the mothers would come out into the street with a thick rope, and, we all skipped together, in and out of the twirling rope as we fancied.'

'Hopscotch was a favourite game at Lois Weedon and Weston but there were many variations. The game has changed little from when we were children. We would either throw a ball or a big stone, which we called a dobber, into the squares. Another game we played was "Tip-cat". We used a small straight stick about six inches long, which was pointed at each end. (The boys were good at carving the sticks). The roads were not metalled, as they are today, so we would make a hole in the road, the size of a bird's nest, and lay the stick across the hole. With a big stick we would knock it off the hole and whilst still in the air, hit it as hard as we could. The stick which went furthest was the winner.

Marbles made from coloured clay were put in a circle, a large glass marble, called a bolster, was thrown into the circle and the one who knocked the most marbles from the circle was the winner. Iron hoops were used for bowling along the road. These iron hoops were decorated with flowers on May Day.

We did not have many toys. I had a doll, with a china head, which opened its eyes and my friend had a fisherman doll, which cost sixpence ha'penny.'

'In the days before the advent of TV, children at Braybrooke played outdoor games in sequence according to the season; hopscotch, hoops, tic tac, whip and top, returning to "Ipsy kick the tin" in the autumn. As the nights got dark, the favourite hiding place was in the bushes of the Rectory Drive.'

'We used to have skipping ropes and stood on each side of the road at Middleton Cheney to turn the rope. We could play in the street, there was no traffic then. We also had hoops, wooden hoops for the girls, iron ones for the boys. We bought the hoops in Banbury but we called them "bowlers" (pronounced as in "owl"). At Maytime we would dress the hoops with flowers and sit a doll in the middle, just for fun, we didn't parade them or anything.'

'Mostly we played in the street with two boy cousins next door and other children who lived nearby in Kettering. We played rounders, whip and top, and "Catty" when we hit a short stick with a longer one, aiming to get it into the air. If a vehicle came we got out of the way. We girls skipped, with individual ropes, and also we begged ropes tied round orange boxes from the greengrocer; with these we held the rope between two girls, while the rest skipped as we twirled it to various rhymes. We played marbles in the gutter, with small clay marbles and the covered "glarneys" which were larger, made

117

of glass with wonderful patterns inside. In winter, we made slides down every hill and slope.

The baker came with a horse-drawn cart, in which we sometimes had a ride, with an occasional "ice bun". There was keen rivalry among neighbours for any horse droppings.'

'We used to make our own fun at Brigstock. We'd go fox-hunting. On moonlight nights, we'd be off round the fields, up Dust Hill and back to Hall Hill. One boy would be the fox and they'd say "Have you found him?" And we used to "Tally Ho!". I'd be about ten or eleven then in 1921 or 1922. There might be about 20 of us. They'd say "You can be fox tonight" and off he'd go. We'd give him ten minutes' start. There were no fears then.

We used to tap on people's windows with a button on a length of cotton. We got up to all sorts of tricks. The boys used to throw inkwells at the master in school. Oh, the boys in school used to be terrible. One put cardboard in his trousers because he was always in trouble. But with all that, we had to respect old people.

In the summer, the children walked over the fields to Stanion. We all set off with a truck and our mother packed us up with bread and jam and lemonade crystals and we used to come home at dusk. We made peashooters out of the rushes in Harpurs Brook.

We went conkering in the park and the owner from the Manor used to come with his dogs and chase us out. Some of the boys would climb up in the trees and wait quietly till he'd gone. We used to hang net curtains on his bushes and play "Mothers and Fathers", but he'd come and chase us away.'

'I used to play "house" with a friend in my Grandad's field at Denton and I remember playing with our dolls and making dirt pies. We also played hopscotch, rounders, hoops and whip and top. We used to pick up scraps of coloured paper from the bills that were pasted up in the village on a workshop wall and on a door at the top of School Lane. We would put these on the top of our spinning tops, which made them look pretty when they were spinning. We also used to skip and play marbles. We used to go up the fields, sticking and blackberrying.'

COUNTRY PLEASURES

'On a Saturday morning at Harrington, or in the holidays, we would take a pony and float (a box-like cart) and take hay to the sheep and cattle. We also collected wood and sticks from under the trees and in the farm fields. When we had a cart full we would stack it in a small outhouse.

We played a lot of hide and seek, climbing trees and hiding in the hayloft etc. We learned to play tennis by hitting a ball against the barn wall. We also did a lot of birdnesting, not often taking eggs because we only wanted one of each kind and would swap eggs with other children. We knew where to find a nightingale's nest, the long-tail tits, green woodpecker, owl etc, and we also knew all the wildflowers – wild orchids, wood sorrel, violets, marsh marigold and cowslips. For May Day we picked primroses and bluebells for the May garland. We made a book of pressed flowers and in 1928, when we had a camera, we took photos of trees and made an album of them.

I remember my brother buying ten Woodbine cigarettes in 1925 for fivepence, and we took them into the fields and smoked some, with much coughing.

My brother had a steam engine which had a funnel-like attachment with a small ball going up and down in the steam. We girls could not understand what he saw in this. In 1927 he was making his own wirelesses with hairs or cat's whiskers. He climbed a large fir tree to fix an aerial from the living room window, coming down to tell us that the tree was full of earwigs.'

'In the summer at Welton we wandered freely over the fields and liked to "help" with the haymaking. The men got very thirsty and kept bottles of cold tea in the shade of the hedge. During the war when we had double summer time people were still working in the fields at ten o'clock at night. Children also went "scrumping", they didn't think of it as stealing – it was just a game, which involved being chased by a grown-up. Most of the houses were thatched and the paths at the side of the village street were cobbled – so someone always had sore knees in those short trousers!'

'Out of school at Great Addington, the children used to net sparrows for sparrow pie, help take cows to graze, play in the spinney and toboggan down Springfield on a tin tray. They would fight to open field gates for the farmers on horseback who threw pennies to them.'

SWEETS, TREATS AND CHORES

⊖

The trip to the sweetshop was a weekly treat for many children, their pennies or ha'pennies buying a variety of goodies to be remembered with affection in later years. Pocket money had to be earned, however, and there were always chores to be done around the house or on the farm.

DOWN TO THE SWEETSHOP

'There were two sweetshops in Grendon village and one of these was a great favourite, selling all manner of goodies such as liquorice whips, sherbet dabs, marshmallow ships, gobstoppers and marvellous chocolate drops. In the back of the shop the father of the family did shoe repairs and they also supplied the village newspapers, the newspaper round being done by the daughter before school. The other sweetshop was on a corner in the middle of the village where the local youths would congregate of an evening, kept in check by the local village bobby who lived in Bozeat and cycled everywhere.'

'The post office and general stores at Sywell in the 1920s was situated at the end of the village street. It was kept by a Miss Eady and it was a great treat to visit her to spend our weekly pocket money of about two or three pence. We purchased sweets, kali and liquorice sticks, and we got a wonderfully large peppermint sweet called a gobstopper for just one penny.'

'Mrs Welch kept a shop in her house at Whilton and sold almost everything. Blocks of Sharps toffee and banana split were broken with a small hammer before being weighed. Children called in to buy their sweets for a penny or a halfpenny. The children would run errands for people out of a sense of duty, they were sometimes rewarded but did not expect it.'

'My Aunt Clara kept the village post office and general stores at East Farndon in the 1940s. Being the war years, food was rationed and sweets were on coupons, so living in a shop gave us no advantage over other children. We had just two ounces of dolly mixtures a week and divided them into seven small heaps, wrapping each heap in a piece of newspaper so that we had a few sweets for each day.'

SEASONAL TREATS

'Every summer in the 1920s the schoolchildren from Duddington were invited to the Squire's house. How we looked forward to those treats at the Manor. Tea was laid out on long tables and after tea we played on the lawns.

There was a Girl Guide group in the village and Miss Barbara Goddard from the Manor was our leader. The old stone cottage at the bottom of Todd's Hill was our Guide house and is still standing. In the winter we used to sledge down this hill, which went right down to the water's edge of the river Welland. If we reached the water on our sledge a great cheer went up. In the summer down there, we had our special "paddling place".'

'With the exception of the very few who had governesses, children at Hargrave all attended the small village school, run by one teacher, from the age of about three to eleven or 13. This provided nursery care to the relief of families with more children arriving, but it is not surprising that some did not learn much about the three Rs before they left. But outside of school they got a lot of informal education, fundamental to their development. They understood the adult world of work, seeing so much going on around them on the farms and in the foundry which opened to the street near the school. They had companionship and the whole village as playground for hopscotch, etc, the village stream and ponds for paddling and fishing, and in the fields everything for their collections of pressed flowers, birds eggs and butterflies. At harvest time games were created amongst the stooked sheaves of corn. Winter was wonderful, when the rectory moat as well as the ponds provided skating with adults. Children had entree into homes with new babies or dead people laid out and visited both with wide-eyed interest and enthusiasm. "Touch the dead person and you will never fear death", and they did, just as they kissed the new baby. They understood life and death.

There was little pocket money for children but the three shops sold sweets. Ice cream was made in the village in the mid 1920s, soon to be followed by the "Wally-Wally" (Wall's) man on his tricycle with its large iced container.'

THE MERRY COMRADES

'In the 1940s, there were very few organised activities for Sywell children. However, there were two highlights in our year. The first was May Day (celebrated on an agreed Saturday in May — May Day

There were very few organised clubs and activities for children in the 1950s. At Sywell the 'Merry Comrades' ran activities to raise money for the local hospital funds.

was not a Bank Holiday then). The second was a visit to the theatre to see a pantomime.

We all belonged to the "Merry Comrades" led by "Auntie Dick" of the *Mercury and Herald*. The aim was to raise money by running fund raising activities and by collecting "a foot of pennies"; a pound in value of "bun" pennies or "ship" halfpennies; or maybe silver milk bottle tops. The money was used to provide radios and later, televisions in our local hospitals.

On the evening before May Day we collected as many flowers as possible from our gardens. These were used to make the garland, trim the "throne" and make posies for all the girls. The girls' mothers really made an effort and always managed to produce a pretty party dress, usually long. The boys wore their grey school shorts and blazer or a suit – always short trousers, of course. (Thank goodness, jeans and trainers did not exist for us!) On Saturday morning we all congregated on the village green for the crowning ceremony, usually attended by "Auntie Dick". We then wound our way, in procession, around the village singing traditional May Day songs and collecting money. I seem to remember even then May Days were cold and we would finish the journey in our winter coats. We went home for dinner but in the afternoon we went back to the green and played party games and had a party tea (provided by our Mums) in the school.

If at the end of the year our group had raised £1 for each child we all became "captains". Actually, I think it was arranged for us all to become a "captain", but it gave us an incentive to work together as "Merry Comrades". Anyone who managed to raise an extra £1 themselves became a "star captain".

During the Christmas holidays all "captains" and "star captains" were taken on a coach to Northampton to a matinee performance of the pantomime. Originally this was at the New Theatre in Abington Street (Primark now occupies the site) but, after its closure, at "The Rep" (The Royal). The whole theatre was invaded by "Merry Comrades" for about three afternoons. "Auntie Dick" always seemed to be there and I guess she must have known all the punch lines and the words of all the silly panto songs we screeched in "fortisimo". At the end of the show the "star captains" were allowed on stage with the cast for a commemorative photograph – if you were lucky it appeared in the *Mercury and Herald*.

Unfortunately, "Auntie Dick" passed away many years ago, but I am sure that many local children of my generation remember and thank her for those good times of comradeship. God Bless you, Auntie Dick, there is no doubt in my mind where you are now – perhaps you are organising whist drives and raffles there!'

CHORES TO DO

'We young ones all had chores to do, fetching coal, chopping sticks etc. When I was twelve in 1919, I had to walk to Weedon (about two and a half miles) every Saturday to fetch the papers from W.H. Smith. I often got a lift on the milk cart. I had to bring the papers back to Everdon, then deliver them and collect the money for them. I got two shillings and sixpence for this when I was 14.

'The children at Cold Ashby earned pocket money after school by doing chores. They fetched water from the well or from the few pumps situated around the village, though the well water was thought to taste better. One child had the job of pumping water into a tank at the vicarage where there was an indoor tap. Fetching milk from the smallholding, morning and night for various neighbours, getting in the coal and sticks for the fire, blacking the grate, cleaning out the hens, running errands, scrubbing the lavatory seat, and many other household tasks – all earned them between a penny and threepence a week. There was a Scout troup for the boys and they often went on long bike rides to places like Stratford on Avon and Ampthill in Bedfordshire.'

123

'I was one of a large family living at Denford. There were three boys, three girls and then three more boys and I was the eldest girl. We all had our jobs to do at home. The girls helped with the cooking and the cleaning and the boys helped with the gardening. There was no regular pocket money but I used to earn sixpence each week by delivering the locally made pork pies around the village. I also used to take a young boy out for a walk in a pushchair on a Saturday for sixpence a week. I can remember walking along one of the lanes in Denford, past where my granny lived and an uncle next door to her, to get watercress from near the well.'

'I came as a young child for a weekend to Denford, and there were great pans of milk standing in the dairy at Talbot House, the home of my great-uncle and his sister. The milk was a penny a pint and the cream was skimmed off and butter made. I remember dipping my finger in the cream and my tall, stern aunt, standing up a few steps in the house, looking down at me reprovingly. I must have been under five years old at the time.

My family were smallholders, keeping cattle, sheep and hens. One of my jobs was to feed and let out the hens every morning up Brickhill Lane. I would cycle up there in the evening to shut them up again, leaving my cycle there and running across the fields to play tennis on a court behind a bunglow on the Thrapston Road. Although we think things were more leisurely years ago, life was quite busy, and even the youngsters had daily tasks to do.

I would take the cows down to the meadows each day, to the church meadow beyond the last bridge at Denford and swim across the river and back again. My grandfather supplied the village with meat and his brother supplied it with milk. There were a lot of cows at that time and the state of the streets and Meadow Lane in particular used to bear witness to their daily walks!'

THE BEST DAYS OF OUR LIVES?

Though discipline was strict, schooldays are in general remembered with affection and gratitude. A child's school life might start when he or she was three years old and continue until their 14th birthday, though it was not unusual for children to leave even earlier if they had a job waiting for them. Only for the few did the opportunity exist for education beyond the village school, and the scholarship exam loomed large over many a child's last year at school.

OFF TO SCHOOL

'The earliest memories of Helmdon come from Mrs Holloway, aged 91 years. She remembers her husband's grandfather telling her about the dame school, which existed in the village before the present school was built in 1872. The dame school stood in the place now occupied by the war memorial. It cost a penny a week to go to the school and as old Mrs Humphrey had six daughters, she could only afford to send the girls, her son had to stay at home and help do the work. He never went to school and couldn't read or write. When the dame school was knocked down, the site was used to break up stones to go on the road.

Miss Barnes seems to be the head teacher remembered by most people. She was head from 1918 to 1947. People remembered how red her face and neck went when she used the cane. They remember George Turnham pulling his hand away so her cane knocked over the ink well. Subsequent generations of children remembered the big ink stain on teacher's desk. Miss Barnes told Mrs Holloway that during the war she wanted a vegetable garden at school to teach the children gardening. When she requested a plot of land for this purpose from school governor Sidney Bartlett, he said that gardening was nothing to do with school, "let their dads larn 'em".

During the war the evacuees came and brought their own teacher. The children boarded with village families and the teacher lived at Falcutt.

Every year, the children had a party given by Mrs Lees of Falcutt House. There was a Christmas tree and every child had a present and an orange.

When the hunt met in the village, the children had time off from school to go and watch. Canon Bartlett, with his dog Bingo, used to pay the occasional visit to check the register and Mr Viccars was the school attendance officer who kept an eye on the truants.'

'For many years Miss Eales was the headmistress and another teacher, Miss Jones, who cycled up from Furnace Lane, Heyford, taught the infants. Mrs Clements, of Lime Kiln Farm can remember cycling to school with Miss Jones. The influence of Miss Eales in the village was remarked upon and she was admired for her efforts in getting children to grammar school. One villager who started school at the age of four, in the late 1920s, said she loved school.'

Although the normal leaving age was 14, Mr Cherry told us he left at twelve and a half during the First World War and got a job. (It was also possible in other parts of the country to leave before 14 years of age if there was a job waiting.)

In 1915 there was a "stern teacher" called Mrs Vann. School hours were: 9 am to 12 noon, and 1 pm to 4 pm with a break of a quarter of an hour morning and afternoon – no school milk in those days. Pen and ink were provided: there were double desks or "even three or four and the seats were attached". Pupils took their lunch to school or went home.

In about 1920, the school cleaner was paid two shillings a week. She had to be in school by 6.30 in the morning to light the stove. At about the same time, it was remembered that Mr Crawley (the rector) came to the playground at playtime and threw a handful of coins to the children. Old Mr Crawley used to give shoes to needy children and said that "the girls should wear pinafores for school".

From the First World War period and earlier, a number of farmers had sent their children to boarding school, and one farmer told us that during the 1930s he was taught by a governess in the mornings, and then went to private school at nine years old.

As an interesting footnote, Mrs Leeson told us that around 1890 her father had been required to pay one penny per day to go to the village school.'

'At Litchborough in about 1916 there were many more children in the village. Families were larger, and there were several rows of cottages which have since been demolished. The school which they attended was closed in 1976; it is now a private house, but the bell which summoned children to their lessons still hangs in the belfry. There were upwards of 50 children in two classes which were divided by a curtain, and many were the holes poked in that curtain to spy upon the other children. At playtime they were strictly segregated – girls into one playground and boys into the other. Being a Church school, it was visited by the rector for scripture lessons twice a week, and the children all trooped to church for a service on Ash Wednesday. On May Day a maypole was set up in the playground and the May Queen reigned supreme.'

'I went to Denford school in the 1930s. The school had just one room and a cloakroom with a washbasin in the corner, which is still there. There was an open fire, surrounded by a guard on which gloves dried on snowy days. There was a large sand tray at one end, I remember clearly, and we used to make desert scenes with camels and palm trees. At the other end, there was a clockwork train which ran on a circular track. Children went there between the ages of four and eight. The younger ones used to have a sleep in the afternoon on mats. At eight years old, children either cycled or walked to Thrapston school, a mile and a half away.'

'I started school when I was four and went to the village school at Denford until I was eight, when I went to Thrapston. We had to walk into Thrapston in the mornings but could catch a bus home – that cost a penny. If it was a nice day, we would sometimes run home across the fields and save our pennies! On a Tuesday we would perhaps get a lift with a farmer from Ringstead who used to come through with his horse and trap to market. I can remember the road at the ford flooding quite often and, on one particular schoolday, the water was much too deep to walk through and we were taken across in a horse and cart.'

'The school at Cold Ashby was a hive of activity with around 40 pupils. There were two teachers, one for the older children and one for the little ones. Plays were performed by the children throughout the year, with a Nativity at Christmas. Much excitement filled the school on these occasions, with costumes made from crepe paper and oddments of material. Hand bells were the musical accompaniment to the choir and all the children had lots to learn and do. At the end of each school year, the children with the best attendance received a guinea from the governors. A day off was granted on hunt day so the children could follow the hounds.'

'You left the village school at Everdon at 14 usually, but you could leave at eleven years old. The headmaster, my grandfather, was very keen on cricket. He was always bowling at us so we should get in the village cricket team. It was mixed boys and girls in class but we always played separately – the girls with the infants. We boys had gardening one afternoon a week while the girls had needlework. They could all knit or sew when they left.'

'I, like the rest of the farmers' children at Sywell in the 1920s, had to walk to school, taking a packed lunch which we consumed on the village green during the summer. In winter we were allowed to eat inside, all crowding round the large stove, where we also boiled water to make mugs of cocoa.

The school consisted of just one large room, with the boys entrance at one end and the girls at the other. The schoolmistress taught everyone, from the age of five to 14. We did not have individual desks, but sat next to each other on quite long benches. The younger

In village schools, children from 5 to 14 years were often taught in one large room. This is the entire population of Sywell School in 1923.

ones used slates and slate pencils, but as we got older we were allowed to have a real pen and ink. Woe betide anyone who made a blot in their copybook!'

'In the playgrounds at Grendon boys and girls were separated at playtime by a high wall and frequent cries of "Throw the ball over" were to be heard. We betide anyone who ran on to the allotment ground adjacent to the school for a lost ball. At the least, a ruler across the palm of the offender's hand was the punishment.

The cane was in frequent use at this time for boys caught smoking in the lavatories. The headmistress, Miss James, would haul them over a desk by the back of the pants without any trouble. One cheeky boy whipped round, snatched the cane and broke it in two; he was sent home and promptly given the strap by his father, landlord of the Half Moon pub at the time.

The boys at the school learned gardening skills on part of the allotment, next to the school. This was discontinued after the retirement of the headmaster, when his place was taken by a headmistress, who drove a bullnosed Morris, regularly turning the corner by the church by driving over the pavement curb.

Fortunately there were few cars in the village, about four at the most, so seasonal games were played in the road. Whips and tops spun along with leather laces, hoops, football, hopscotch, everything in its season. Skipping ropes were put across the road! Later on when cars became more numerous, taking car numbers became a favourite pastime.'

'The school at Barby, which was close to the church, had two teachers, teaching approximately 50 pupils between the ages of five and 14. The rector said prayers in the school every day. He also supplied the school children with milk from his own Jersey cows on his farm. The girls at the school were taught spinning and weaving. Loose wool that was found in the fields was collected, then spun and woven by the children.'

'As with all schools at the time, at Easton on the Hill priority was given to the three Rs. The children were divided into age groups which were then sub-divided into activity stages as follows:-

Stages 1/2, First years
Sand trays (for drawing and writing in) followed by slate and slate pencils.

Stages 3/4, Second years
Chalk on blackboard followed by crayons

Stages 5/6, 10 – 14 years
Pencils and finally pens

Each day began with assembly at which the singing of hymns would, on one day of the week, be accompanied by the National Anthem. After assembly and registration, each group would go to their respective classroom. Silence was the order of the day, and swift punishment, in the form of a cane or ruler, would come down upon anyone brave enough to disobey the rules.

Very few outdoor activities were included in the timetable. There was gardening for the boys and rounders for the girls, when the weather was fine. Rounders was played in teams of four, each distinguished by the coloured ribbons worn by the players.

The headmistress took the second class for needlework. This was always enjoyable. Our parents paid for the materials, and we learned to crochet mats, knit on a few needles and make pillow cases with button holes. During our final two years at school, we undertook more advanced work such as embroidery drawn on handkerchiefs, raffia and canework. We also learned to use the treadle sewing machine.

The routine of the school year included special events, such as St George's Day. On this day we would parade through the village carrying the Union Jack and singing patriotic songs. May Day was equally important and particularly enjoyable for us. We would carry a garland of flowers, picked from our own gardens, and visit every house in the village. This proved to be quite a long journey for one so young.'

'My earliest memories are of halcyon sunny days playing in the fields around the farm with my brother and the farmer's children. Before the tender age of five years we had to be able to ride a "fairy" cycle in order to ride the mile through the park to Overstone county primary school. At that time village schools did not provide school lunches or lunchtime supervisors and children had to leave the school for midday break. As it was too far for us to go home, we went to my aunt who lived near the school and provided lunches for several children.

On hot days we took our desks into the playground to do our lessons, and we were allowed to wear just our vests and knickers. The summers then always seemed to be long and hot and the winters cold and icy – in the mornings it was quite normal to "huff" on the bedroom window and scrape away the intricate patterns that Jack Frost had painted on the inside! As there wasn't any central heating we had to wear several layers of clothes to keep warm. (Do *you* remember the embarrassment of stripping off your woolly vest and liberty bodice for showers at secondary school?).'

SCHOOLDAYS IN FLORE

'My memory of my first day at Flore school, after Easter in 1931, when I was four years old, is very clear. I was taken to the door of the infants room by my mother. I wore a green dress, sprigged with mauve flowers, with elbow-length puffed sleeves.

We had long desks with fixed benches, each seating four children. We had slates and chalk for writing, and learned sums with an abacus, china beads and counters. Reading-books with pictures of Ned and Tom in knickerbockers and caps, and Fan in calf-length dress with wide sash and boots, must have been bought before the First World War. However, as, by the age of six, I was reading all the children's classics fluently and voraciously, teaching cannot have been seriously affected by the antiquity of the books. We measured and made little paper baskets and modelled Moses in the bullrushes in plasticine.

Moving up to Class II in another room and an excessively strict teacher brought opportunities to learn about Eskimos and Red Indians, to draw feathers and jamjars, and to learn by heart passages from St John's Gospel. We learned spelling rules and had plenty of practice in applying them; recited our tables and practised copperplate handwriting, drawing hand up lightly on the upstroke and pressing hard for the downstroke to produce "thick and thin". At eight, I was darning and hand-sewing the run-and-fell seams of a pink flannel nightdress, being well punched in the back for the crooked application of the breast pocket, which had to be unpicked three times before it was passed as satisfactory.

Learning extracts and painting scenes from *A Midsummer Night's Dream*, admiring a picture of Richard I in a cigarette card series of Kings and Queens of England stuck up on the wall for us to learn in sequence; reciting Wordsworth's *Daffodils*; growing mustard and cress on blotting paper; struggling with fractions and decimals; writing letters and compositions in readiness for "The Scholarship" – all were enjoyable experiences for me.

Our headmaster, a talented musician, trained us in three-part singing and entered us successfully in a Music Festival in Northampton. We ran in the South Northants Sports, I less successfully.

I left Flore school in 1937, having won a scholarship to Northampton High School. In 1934, I suffered the painful death of a much-loved father, which casts a dark shadow on those halcyon days, but my education at both schools, despite odd incidents I prefer to forget, is still a joy to remember.'

THE COMING WAR

'As a very young child growing up in Kettering before the Second World War, one of my earliest memories is of riding on the baker's horse-drawn cart. This was a treat which the baker gave to my sister and me every Friday. When we reached the top of the hill about 250 yards from our house, he would give us an apple pie and then set us on our way to run home down the hill.

I started school when I was four and a half and, in the classroom, there was an open fire surrounded by a large fire-guard with a brass rim on top. This was very useful for drying wet clothes on rainy days. On very cold days, our one-third-of-a-pint bottles of milk were thawed around this same fire. Every morning, we had an assembly and the headmistress, who wore black-buttoned boots, inspected our handkerchiefs and those children without one would be given a square of rag. After everyone had returned to their classrooms, the First Class, known as "The Babies" were taken into the hall to play with wooden blocks. These were about 2″ × 2″ × 12″ as far as I remember and we made co-operative models of local places of interest such as the Pleasure Park opposite the school or a local shoe factory or even Wicksteed Park. The toilets at this school were on the opposite side of the playground so a visit there meant a long walk or run. We did not choose to go there very often.

At the age of eleven, I attended the High School for Girls and, to my great joy, I was allowed to ride the one and a half miles on my bicycle. The journey took me across the town and the one set of traffic lights. I used to cycle home for lunch and then return for the afternoon session.

We were quite proud to wear our school uniforms and woe betide anyone caught out without her hat or gloves. I well remember the headmistress making a great pronouncement one day that we need no longer wear gloves with our blazers. That was a great concession. Even greater was the change from black stockings to fawn lisle. The younger girls wore knee-length socks. We wore black velour hats in winter and panamas in summer. The latter were dropped in the war years, as panamas became unobtainable, never to return.

Wartime brought other changes. Our school day began at 10.30 am and ended at 3.15 pm with an hour's break for lunch, which many more girls took at school as the break was too short for them to get home and back again. As we grew older, we had some lessons earlier in the morning in various halls in the town. The school which was evacuated on us used the school premises from 8.30 am until 10.15 am and from 3.30 pm until 5.30 pm. As the evacuee girls were all billeted in the town and many of our girls lived in the country, this arrangement worked fairly well. I think that the evacuees had extra lessons elsewhere as well. The changeover times were very hectic and I am sure the staff had many headaches trying to get one set of girls out and another set in during the 15 minutes allotted.

The boys who shared the other half of the building had a better arrangement as the Kettering boys were taught in the morning and the evacuee boys attended in the afternoon. In all, four schools shared the one building, now the council offices.

In pre-war days, we had to wear white dresses on Speech Day and for carol services but these were discarded as impractical as part of our war effort and we appeared in our box-pleated gymslips. Later in the war years, these were changed for a much neater pinafore dress. We wore red jerseys and black knickers for our gymnastic lessons. At Christmastime, these same red jerseys were worn by four small girls dressed as pages and carrying holly garlands on sticks when they escorted the long line of girls processing into the school hall to the strains of "O Come all Ye Faithful". They also carried the Boar's Head which was brought into the service with great ceremony every year. The fifth form, dressed in red cassocks and carrying torches in jam jars, became wassailers, keeping up a long tradition.

132

Our lives were not badly affected by the war and we grew up in a happy and contented atmosphere where we could work and play together.'

GAMES IN THE PLAYGROUND

'Games in the playground at Stowe in the past are still played today: ring o'roses, tig, hopscotch, hide and seek, marbles, jackstones or fives, skipping, "what's the time Mr Wolf?" and football, though with the change in little girls' hairstyles, the game of "pulling ribbons from pigtails" is not as common as it perhaps once was! Earlier in the century, there were spinning tops and bowling the hoop and "riding my skicycle (scooter) down the school hill".

The school playground used to be gravel and had to be weeded. At one period, in the summer months, there would be games outside on a Friday, and dancing indoors in the winter. A maypole in the playground was also mentioned.'

'There were two classes at Whilton school. Heating was by means of an open fire. During the dinner break some of the boys occasionally had a game of Hare and Hounds. Two boys would go ahead and after a while the rest would chase and try to catch them. This chase took place over the fields, resulting in the boys being late for the afternoon session and having muddy boots – punishment was given!'

THE CLOTHES WE WORE

'I vividly remember wearing black sateen bell-bottom knickers and a red long jumper for gym. One day I forgot the knickers, and my mother gave them to the friendly regular postman to take into school when he returned to Kettering after his local deliveries. He duly brought them in and handed them over, saying "You've left your knickers at home", much to my embarrassment! Gym slips and white blouses were the everyday schol uniform. Cooking at school was done in little white hats and smocks. Hats had to be worn for school, a black velour one in winter and a panama with a band round in the summer. If you were seen getting off the bus without your hat on, you were in trouble. Hats were also always worn to church.'

'Before the Second World War at Welton, boys wore short trousers in all weathers and boots, not shoes. Many girls wore boots too, which needed a button hook to do them up. They were not, of course, worn because they were fashionable but because they didn't wear out so quickly. There was a high fence between the boys and girls playgrounds and they were not allowed to mix at playtime. Children stayed at the school until they were 14. By the time they left they were too big for the chairs – and they stuck to them when they stood up! The school bell, a hand held one, was given to the school by Eric Fleming's father, who had picked it up on the retreat from Mons in the First World War.'

SIR AND MISS

'Before the advent of the combine harvester, corn was cut by a machine which also bound it into sheaves which were then stooked to dry and in due time carted into the rickyard and built into a cornrick. There it stayed until the contractor with a threshing machine came round to each farm in turn to thresh the corn from the straw. Of course this method attracted many mice and rats.

When threshing days came along we boys had great fun on our way to school helping to catch these vermin, contriving to slip some field mice into convenient pockets and taking them into school with us. When all was quiet a mouse would be set down on the floor to frighten our headmistress.

She was terrified and clambered on to her desk, long black skirt wrapped around her legs tightly for safety. We boys were ordered to catch the mouse – which we did, willingly and with much noise and scuffling, only to let another one free a few moments later. Remember that there was just one large schoolroom, divided by a partition to separate the infants from the "Big Uns".

The headteacher was certainly not green and soon realized what was happening and duly reported the matter to the governors, most of whom were the local farmers. My grandfather was one of them.

In due course I was severly reprimanded by grandfather who was a strict disciplinarian and was sent to bed.

Later in the evening I heard hearty laughter coming from downstairs. Grandfather was telling the tale to some visitors who had popped in for a chat.'

'At school at Brigstock we had those flat rulers and if you didn't behave you had that across the back of your hand. And when we went to school, the first thing the teacher said was "All of you show your handkerchiefs" and our mother always used to pin one on my dress. Well, we had to wear a pinafore and we had this handkerchief pinned on there so we didn't lose it. We all had to blow our noses first thing, and if you hadn't got a handkerchief, the teacher used to come round with pieces of newspaper. She made sure everybody had something. Even before we had a prayer or anything, we had to use our handkerchiefs.

The master used to stand with his back to the stove. He had a cane. On a Monday morning, he was always in a bad mood because he'd been out drinking the night before.

We had that old bleached calico to sew with making pillowcases and aprons. We had to buy them. The boys used to garden in the school garden.

On my first day in school (c1920), my mother warned me "Be careful of the horses and carts".'

'The infants school teacher at Great Addington was a Mrs Pearson, who started her apprenticeship at the age of 18 in 1912 and remained at the school until her retirement in about 1960. Mrs Pearson lived in Ringstead and would cycle to school every day, holding up her umbrella on rainy days, only to return yet again on Sundays to play the church organ.'

SWIMMING LESSONS

'In the 1920s lessons took place for Duston children in the pool by Kingsthorpe Mill, under the bridge over the river Nene. The instructor walked across the bridge whilst the poor little child, held by a string from a rod attached to an uncomfortable leather or canvas belt around their abdomen, was expected to move in the cold water with swimming motions.

Later, schools took their swimming classes at Phipps Brewery swimming bath at the bottom of Bridge Street near the level crossing. These baths at least had warmer water and were enclosed. After the swimming lesson, huge square plain biscuits could be purchased for twopence – they did taste good, but were known as ship's biscuits.'

SENT TO BOARDING SCHOOL

'When I was about 14 it was decided that I should go away to boarding school. The one chosen was the girls grammar school at Thame in Oxfordshire. It was not a very big school by today's standards, with about 100 girls and 40 boarders. The school was rather Victorian in outlook and the actual building, built in the 19th century as a boys school, was rather spartan with small four-bedded dormitories and no running water, just a wash basin with a jug of cold water. We were not allowed out into the town and always went for walks in a crocodile, be it before lessons started, to church or on a Sunday afternoon. We had very little free time and during the week, lessons and homework filled the day. On Saturday morning there was "mending", when holes in stockings had to be darned or buttons sewn on. Then there would be games in the afternoon if fine, either amongst ourselves or against neighbouring teams. Sunday started with writing letters home, then church, in the afternoon a long walk and then, after tea, church again. It was a strict regime, but we had a lot of fun one way or another.'

PAYING FOR THE PRIVILEGE

'Madge, one of ten children, started her school life at Brigstock school in Latham Street but followed two of her sisters to Kettering High School in 1921. Her father had to pay for this privilege and as there was no public transport the girls were taken to Kettering on Monday mornings on the milk delivery van. They lived with family friends during the week, returning home after school on Fridays on a wooden bus built in Brigstock by Mr Tom Smith.'

HOW MANY SPOKES HAD AN UMBRELLA?

'In the junior school I remember large classes, over 50, but the teachers seemed to have no trouble with discipline. I learned to knit on four needles, and we had access to many books. Before changing a book, we had to tell the teacher its content.

At this school rumours were rife about the scholarship exam. Mother told me some of the questions likely to be asked of those "called up" for an interview. What was Queen Elizabeth's wedding dress made of? Answer "She never married, so did not have one". Also, how many spokes has an umbrella? Answer "I don't know, but next time I open one I will count them." When I was "called up" to Northampton, because the High School was run by the County Council, I cannot recall any of the questions I was actually asked!'

TAKING THE SCHOLARSHIP

'As would be expected, in a small village with fewer than 300 inhabitants, Chacombe school in 1929 had only two classrooms, the Little Room for the infants and the Big Room for the older children. I was a nine year old pupil.

One March morning, the class was quietly engaged in arithmetic, with Mr Perry sitting at his desk, marking books as pupils came up, one by one, when the door burst open dramatically and the children looked up to see a boy standing there.

"Who are you, boy? Why didn't you knock?" asked Mr Perry, in his direct manner.

"Please sir, I'm Robin Young. Mr Barker says are any of your children taking the scholarship, because it's started."

All the children knew Robin Young. His father farmed Grange Farm, in Chacombe parish, just off the Middleton Cheney road. He cycled to Middleton Cheney school because it was nearer for him than Chacombe.

Mr Perry knew that Mr Barker was Head of Middleton Cheney school and quickly assessed the situation. He had been told nothing about the scholarship and our little school had no telephone, but he knew the routine.

"All of Standard Five, take your rulers and two pencils each and RUN."

A voice from the back of the class spoke slowly and quietly, as the Standard Five children, including myself, went quickly to the front to take two sharpened pencils from the efficiently – kept box on Mr Perry's desk.

"Please sir, I have a weak heart, and I am not allowed to run."

It was John French, the cleverest boy in Standard Five. Mr Perry turned to Robin Young who was still waiting.

"You're on your bicycle, of course, Robin. Can you take John on your back wheel carrier?"

"Yes sir." Robin was big and strong for his 13 years.

"Right. Off you all go then, and good luck."

So, on that sunny spring morning, at 9.30 am, seven children ran as fast as they could to Middleton Cheney, past an amazed pair of hedgecutters eating their breakfast by the roadside, past fields of green winter corn, where skylarks sang and soared, to the crossroads, where we glanced quickly to right and left to ensure that no main road traffic would exterminate us, past the first Middleton Cheney houses, where housewives peered through lace curtains wondering where the fire might be . . . until at last we reached Middleton Cheney school, so much larger than our own, standing in a big, asphalted, high-fenced playground.

In the playground stood Mr Barker, papers in hand, looking grave. Robin and John French had already arrived and John stood, unruffled as always, with a distinct advantage over the other seven, who were all completely out of breath.

"I shall have to telephone Northampton to see if you can start now and have extra time," said Mr Barker. "You will be one hour late in starting, if permitted." I was glad of the pause to get my breath back whilst Mr Barker went to phone. He came back and said, "Come with me. You will be allowed one extra hour."

The children clattered through the strangely quiet, unfamiliar school, to a large room, where the Middleton Cheney scholarship children sat at individual desks, well apart from each other. Eight empty desks were indicated and the children tiptoed to their seats, glad to release tightly held, hot pencils and rulers. I found the Arithmetic very difficult, but I enjoyed the English papers.

All this happened about a month before my tenth birthday on 5th April. When the scholarship results became known, there were problems. John French had passed outright and that was very good, because no-one from Chacombe school had passed the scholarship since Mrs Fisher's daughter, Eileen, had done so, many years before.

There were two "promotion marks" which meant that the candidates had to go to Brackley High School to take an intelligence test, because their written papers had not been quite up to scholarship standard. The problem was that one of the two children, Mary Snelson, was too old, being already eleven and the other, myself was too young, being only nine years old when the examination was held. Somehow or other, the problem was sorted out and, one summer's day, Mary and I, with our mothers, found ourselves travelling the road to Middleton Cheney, walking this time, to catch the bus to Brackley. We had to take our school exercise books with us. On the bus, Mary and I sat together. I was looking, ruefully, through my Arithmetic book with its predominance of crosses over ticks, when Mary picked up my Composition book, with its large round writing.

"I think that one is a bit better," I said.

"Oo-ooh, look at them blots!" said Mary, and my heart sank: my morale was very low. Mary's books were neat and her writing was small and good to look at.

Brackley High School was just inside the town, approached by a gravelled drive, off the broad Banbury Road. Past the bicycle shed, past the copse with its slender trees we went and into the covered quadrangle, which was prettily decorated with hanging baskets full of well-trained scarlet geraniums, white alyssum and blue lobelia. Mary and I were aware that numerous eyes were on us, as we passed the hushed classrooms.

In the quadrangle, Victoria Cave, Head Girl, made herself known to us. I was instantly and permanently impressed. In her navy blue gymslip, white tussore silk blouse and emerald green girdle, denoting that she belonged to a school sports team, and wearing House Captain's, Prefect's and Head Girl's badges, Victoria represented all the schoolgirl heroines I had ever read about in stories.

Victoria waited until twelve children had arrived, then we were all taken to the Science laboratory where the intelligence tests were to be held. I was interested in the smell of chemicals and the bunsen burners, and liked sitting on a high stool beside a solid wooden bench. I rather enjoyed the tests which had puzzles to solve, words to fill in, number sequences to continue and so on.

When it was all over, the boys and girls had a break while individual interviews took place in the headmistress' study. I was befriended by a girl called Pamela Bartlett, whose father was headmaster of the village school at Syresham.

The interview was a disaster, as far as I was concerned. Victoria took me up a wide flight of steps, then I was on my own, going up a narrow flight of steps, with instructions from Victoria, "Knock and then wait until someone says 'Come in'." So far, so good, but once inside, I saw not one lady, but the headmistress and two men, sitting one on either side of her, behind her large, well polished desk.

Miss Kate Whitehead was a handsome, dignified, small, rather plump, grey-haired lady, fashionably dressed in pleasing grey and white. Descended from Elizabeth Fry, the prison reformer, she had the same indomitable spirit and all the qualities needed to make a successful headmistress.

"Shut the door, please," she said, in her pleasant, well-modulated voice.

Already nervous, I was shaken still further by two things, as I entered. Firstly, the presence of the two men beside Miss Whitehead, whom I had presumed would be alone and horror of horrors, my own exercise books, blots and all, resting beneath the headmistress' hand, on her desk.

"Yes sir," I said, realizing my mistake immediately.

The rest of the interview is lost for ever in the mists of time. I remember being taken all over the school and around the grounds by Victoria, but not the journey home.

A few weeks later news came to Chacombe school that both Mary Snelson and I had "passed the scholarship" and would attend Brackley High School from September, 1930. Elated, I ran home to give my mother the news. Much later, she told me that she had felt quiet satisfaction that I would have the chance to rise above present circumstances of poverty and the educational limitations of staying on at the village school until the age of 14, with no higher education to follow.'

THE WORLD
OF WORK

BOOTS AND SHOES

Northamptonshire's footwear industry acquired a worldwide reputation for quality and reliability, and a large number of its inhabitants were employed making boots and shoes, either in factories or in 'shops' in their own homes, which were often built specially to carry out shoework in. Living next door to a 'thumper' must have tried the patience at times, but many towns and villages depended on the trade for their livelihood and that regular tapping at least meant that money was coming in.

CENTURIES OF SHOEMAKING

'From early times Northamptonshire was renowned for its leather work, probably because there were plenty of oak trees whose bark was used for tanning. It also had excellent meadows for cattle which produced hides of good quality. The development of the footwear trade in Walgrave was no different from that carried out in the majority of Northamptonshire villages.

In the Militia List of 1777 we have a record of Thomas Perkins, cordwainer. In 1841 the population of Walgrave was 593 with 34 men in the boot industry. Ten years later 10% of the population of Walgrave was so employed, working in "shops". By 1881 there were 101 people employed in the cottage industry. Until 1890 the shoe work was all done at home.

Many cottages had a "shop" probably not more than eight ft square at the bottom of the garden or attached to the house. Master craftsmen trained their apprentices in the use of a variety of arts; the mixing of pitch and tallow for waxing the stitching thread, preparing the dexter pot and putting rows of sprigs in the outer soles to extend their wear. Other skills followed until the craft was learned.

Leather was collected from the nearest town by a factor. The workers in their shops made the boots, entirely by hand, and at the end of the week received payment for the finished boots. They then picked up a fresh supply of material.

It was in 1890 that the first factory was built in the yard of The Chestnuts in Church Lane. In a small factory there was one machine, a press worked by foot and used to cut heavy leather for soles and uppers. The actual shoemaking was still done at home and the uppers were made by women. The boot and shoe trade was one of the last to be affected by the industrial revolution.

In 1890 a small group of craftsmen started a Co-operative Society. They purchased their materials direct from suppliers and then despatched the finished goods to all parts of the country. The society closed in 1906. In 1899 Mr Stephen Walker opened the three storey red brick factory in Old Road. Machinery came into the village. The hand-sewn men still worked at The Chestnuts and closing and "stabbing" was done by the women in their homes. Wages were low – sixpence an hour – and a pair of boots made entirely of leather cost about twelve shillings.

Prosperity came to the factory and therefore to Walgrave during the Boer War 1898–1902. Boots were made for the War Office, the Navy, the Crown Colonies, the Home Office and the Post Office. Contracts were awarded half yearly. If no contract was received there was no work for six months. All the boots were handmade. In the late 19th century brick terraced cottages were built and given the names Spion Kop and Klondyke Cottages, and Crispen Cottages. There were over 60 shops with about 100 people working there. Work in shops continued into the 1930s.

When an order was completed and inspected, the boots were packed in wicker hampers, labelled and despatched to exotic and far away places such as Barbados, Antigua, Jamaica or the Leeward Islands, the first part of their journey being by dray to Lamport station. All boots were stamped – Stephen Walker – and stories are told of soldiers from Walgrave serving in foreign parts recognising the Walgrave boot by its characteristic workmanship.

Boots were made for the First World War and during the Second World War work was still for the forces. In 1951 the factory was sold to George Webb who added two extensions, men's shoes were now made for civilian wear. The factory was taken over by another group and in 1980 closed completely with the loss of nearly 100 jobs.

Signs of the boot industry can still be seen around the village. Early stone and brick shops are used as garden stores or sheds, the Victorian red brick cottages with their attached shops were converted into kitchens or bathrooms, and the red brick chapel schoolrooms complete with partition folding doors and concert platform in the upper room, were attached to the Baptist chapel where Stephen Walker was a Deacon. There is a double decker shop at the Royal Oak, used as a store and for model aeroplane makers. The factory at The Chestnuts has been converted into an unusual dwelling place with an up and over door leading to a garage where once the carts stood. The factory, since 1982 the home of the Regent Belt company, employed 100 people making and exporting belts and luxury leather goods around the world. The outer building is just as it was when it was built, well proportioned with attractive use of brick, arched windows letting in light and the hoist still in position. Inside is one very worn ladder stair to the top floor and on the third floor rafters are six inch nails from which boots, awaiting sale during a recession, were hung. Stephen Walker's house was kept as much as possible in its Victorian grandeur, as the office complete with word-processors and computers. His billiard room in the attic was a leather goods display area.

Still the smell of leather pervades both factory and office, and snippets of leather find their way into the road where boxes of crafts are loaded into vans and lorries.

On 17 April 1992 work at the factory ceased. It has been transferred to the Long Buckby branch. Will this be the final demise of the centuries old leather trade in Walgrave?'

BEWARE THE 'THUMPERS'

'In the early 1900s, when transport was just a carrier's cart to Northampton and Rushden, men and women were glad to make a living working at home in Yardley Hastings. Shoe work was a thriving industry and today's senior citizens remember how the carrier would bring the leather and uppers to the workers, who used back rooms, workshops and even front rooms, if work was plentiful.

Women and girls were employed to make lifts, which were five pieces of coarse leather cut in different shapes to form each layer, then pasted together and cut to the required lift, that is, the heel. Other girls, as young as nine years of age, used to push a handcart to Bozeat for work, twice a week!

Some men used to make complete shoes and were nicknamed "thumpers" by neighbours hearing the persistent banging. Others completed uppers. Rushden factories were the main suppliers for the leather delivered by the carriers.

A small factory near the Red Lion was also a workshop, as was the Working Men's Club. The latter closed in 1914. In the 1930s, work was still continued by a shoemaker in a shop near his home; up to the early 1970s he was able to take up full time shoe-making. His skilled work was in great demand by a West End store, as well as by makers who specialised in surgical boots and shoes. Until 1949, even shoe repairs were carried out in a small shop in Chase Park Road. Those were the days! Or were they?'

WHAT'S A 'BOTTOM SCOURER'?

'In the old shoe-making industry there were many odd names and terms, ranging from "clicking" to "closing" and "rough-stuff" to "bottom-scouring".

The shoe starts its life in the "rough-stuff" room. The soles are cut out from "bends" and the insoles from "bellies". The uppers are cut from a skin in the "clicking" room and thence into the "lasting" room, where the upper is attached to the sole on the "pull-over" machine and then on to varying stages where words such as "welt-sewing", "rough-pounding" and, of course, "bottom-scouring" were heard. Finally, on into the "closing" room and "finishing" room, where the various pieces of leather emerge as a recognisable shoe.

In the early days much of the closing was done by the women on a machine at home and houses in my childhood often smelt of leather. The left-over leather from the cut-out shapes was all carefully collected into sacks of "leather-bits" and was used as fuel in the old-fashioned copper usually built into a corner of the kitchen (the forerunner of the washing machine) and was the only hot water system for the bath, either taken in the kitchen also, or in the old tin bath which was hauled from an out-house and placed in front of the living-room fire.

One of the customs of old fashioned shoe-making that always horrified me was the way that the men always kept their tacks, known as "sprigs", in their mouths and, as they hammered, the tongue ejected a sprig at just the right moment and so continuity was maintained. These tacks came in small sacks, about one foot by nine inches, called sprig bags and were carefully saved and used for all sorts of storage.

Of course, in many shoe towns and villages people's lives were ruled by the hooter which was sounded in the morning and at lunch time to summon the men to work and they were seen scurrying, so that they could clock-in on time, because a minute late meant losing a "quarter" – no such thing as flexi-time in those days.'

WORKING IN THE FACTORY

'I left school at 14 in 1936 and started work in a shoe factory office at Northampton for ten shillings per week. I gave my mother about seven shillings of this, the remainder was mine for clothes and fares etc. We could, however, buy a lipstick for sixpence have our hair Marcel waved for a shilling and purchase a bottle of "Evening in Paris" for about the same. I was taught basic book keeping, for typing I went to night school. Interior communications in this factory were primitive, being a phone with a wind up handle on the wall which you shouted down, so it was easier to send me as the "goffer". I grew to admire the skills of the clickers, men who cut out the top leather of the shoe; their room was at the top of the building with a glass roof for maximum light, but very cold in winter, stifling in summer. The women sat at long benches machining uppers, they were allowed to sing at their work as long as they didn't stop machining. The lower the floor the heavier the machinery, and in the skin room where presses cut out sole leather and the making room where everything was joined together, noise assaulted one's ears and everyone shouted or used sign language. Later I worked in a last factory and here the quiet of the kilns where wood lay in sweet smelling piles maturing at controlled temperatures ready for use, contrasted with the noise of wood sawing machines. Heels were made too, and so we always knew ahead what height would be the fashion. One day the machines were suddenly shut off, and a cry went up "There's a woman been scalped". The office manager as first aid man, no industrial nurses then, had to run at the double, I have always remembered this and hate to see long hair near machinery.

I was married during the war and became a "country girl", beset as everyone was by the difficulties of trying to set up home with dockets for this and units for that. We went to live at Collingtree where we farmed. Feedstuffs were rationed, so our pigs were fed on "Tottenham Pudding", steamed waste from Army camps and hotels which arrived black and malodorous in sacks and had to be chopped up with a spade. We also kept a small goat herd, which I'm sorry to say were notorious for escaping and terrorising the village. One lady late one foggy winter night met our "Billy" at the lychgate of the cemetery . . . oh, dear.'

OUTWORKERS

'In the 1930s a lot of houses at Denford had their own shoe "shop" (workshop) where outwork was done on boots and shoes. The work was delivered by horse and cart from Raunds. Mr J.R. Groom, who used to live in the High Street, is remembered as having lasts on his workbench. He was a member of a large, long standing Denford family and there is a saying that there used to be "more grooms than horses in the village" at one time!'

'I was born in a long narrow house in a typical Northamptonshire cobbling village. The house had been custom built by my grandparents to do shoe-work at home. When I passed the "scholarship"

146

at eleven and graduated to the local high school and started to bring friends home who had come from different backgrounds, they were intrigued to hear our kitchen called the "back-shop", the breakfast room the "middle-shop" and our living room the "kitchen". The "shops" were, of course, where the shoe-work was done, one for each of my grandparents, my grandfather doing hand stitching and my grandmother doing the "closing". Up to the day that my mother moved out at the age of 83, having been born and lived in the same house, we always referred to the rooms by their original working names.'

'Many of the men in Harpole worked in the village making shoes. They made the first set of football boots for the famous Tottenham Hotspur Club.'

'There were anxious times for the villagers when a new contract was being applied for, until it was actually signed. An amusing feature of those days was Shoemakers Monday, when some would don bowler hats and clean aprons and visit their local pub, imbibing perhaps more than they should. One elderly shoemaker was a favourite with the young boys of the early 1940s who were wont to stand with noses pressed to his workshop window. He would call them in and make whips from pieces of leather with wax extensions, which the boys then attached to sticks to play whip and top, the tops being purchased at the village shop, which sold almost everything.'

VILLAGE SHOE FACTORIES

'Arnolds Boot Factory started here in Everdon. At first, the boots were taken to be sold in Daventry and later it moved to Northampton. William Arnold used to come back to Everdon when the Feast was here. He would throw pennies for the children to scramble after.'

'There were five factories in Irchester in the early 1920s and factory workers from outside walked to work bringing their food for the day wrapped in a cloth or handkerchief, plus a bottle of cold tea. To alleviate the effects of the leather dust both men and women from the shoe factories took snuff. The usual amount purchased was a quarter of an ounce, costing tenpence. Needless to say, special scales were required to weigh such a small quantity.'

'In the 1950s there were seven shoe factories at Irthlingborough, the largest being Wearer Shoes, later David Scott Shoes. This was the last to close, as the gradual decline of the industry saw them shut down one by one.'

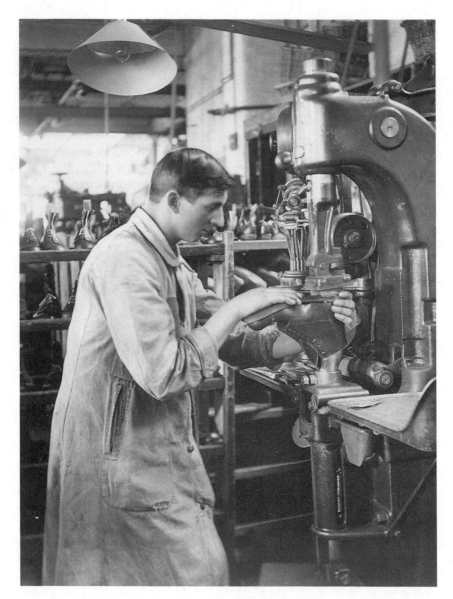

ON THE FARM

Agriculture was another major employer, the farm labourers working long and hard for meagre wages. It is tempting to look back on farming and to see only the joys of haymaking and harvest time, or the majestic working horses pulling the plough, but, between the world wars, one little girl from Overstone was warned by her father when they set off for a seaside holiday, not to say that they were farmers as in some people's eyes farmers 'were the scum of the earth'. It took another war to bring the farmer back to favour as he once again faced the task of feeding Britain.

WORKERS ON THE FARM

'I can remember when the farms at Yardley Gobion employed a great many villagers. Many of the farmhouses employed young girls as maids whose jobs included cleaning, doing the open fires, black-leading the ranges and doing the wash in outside wash-houses. Other jobs on the farms included milk maids, herdsmen, farm labourers and field workers. At Elms Farm they made butter in the dairy. The farms offered employment all year round because, apart from the steam engine and the introduction of a tractor, all work was done by men and horses. The Elms had a tack room, a saddle room, stables and sheds for the carts. I can recall high carts, spring carts, goat carts and a governess cart. The heavy horses pulled the larger carts and waggons, the plough, binder, drill and threshing box.

The farmers and their wives would go by horse and cart, loaded with eggs, butter, rabbits and cockerels, to sell at James' in the Drapery or Kingham's in Abington Street, Northampton. Cattle were walked from Yardley Gobion to Courteenhall where they rested in a field overnight, before being driven to the cattle market at Northampton.'

MEETING BEFORE WORK

'About 6 am at Everdon, the farm labourers would all meet up at the church steps, then some would go off to Snorscombe and others to Westcombe Farm in the opposite direction.'

Farms employed so many men in the days before they became mechanised. Women were employed too – in the farmhouse and the dairy.

WINTER'S WORK

'A farmworker's life is so different these days. Once the farm horses did most of the work and my husband remembers he had in the summer to catch his horses in the field at 6 am and get them ready for a day's work. In the winter they were kept in and this meant a lot of hard work keeping them fed and warm.

While the ploughing and other jobs such as hedgecutting and fencing were going on, my husband took his lunch and very often he didn't get a drink all day as his bottle of tea would get frozen. He was pleased when later on Thermos flasks came in.'

'My father and his brother worked for my grandfather at Denford who had a thresher (engine, drum and jack) and after the harvest, they went round the farms, threshing. During the winter months when they weren't threshing, they had a wood business, making hurdles and things from the wood they had collected in the spring and summer, and selling firewood. Some of the hurdles were used to make pens for the sheep dipping.'

HARVEST TIME

'Most men in Arthingworth village still worked as farm labourers in the 1950s. By working overtime in the harvest, they could earn £12 15 shillings a week. The women helped with the potato picking.'

THUMB BITS AND TIED HOUSES

'During the school holidays at our Sywell farm in the 1920s it was absolute bliss for us as children, with the haymaking, harvesting, sheep shearing etc. The farm labourers brought their lunch with them. It consisted mainly of thick chunks of bread and cheese, which I believe were referred to as "thumb bits", and they also had billy cans in which was tea and sugar. Mother boiled water for them and "mashed" the tea at eleven o'clock and again at three o'clock when they took a break. They usually consumed this in the cowshed, where I loved to join them.

We owned the tied cottages where our farmhands lived. Each one had a barn, with a loft, for storing the harvest produce, a brick-built pigsty (most of the tenants kept a pig and they had access to the pig-swill from the farm) and a long piece of garden at the back where the vegetables were grown, plus a pretty flower garden at the front, the scent of which I can still recall. They are all now privately owned.'

CHANGING TIMES

'The average weekly earnings on the farms around Harlestone in the 1930s were 15 shillings a week. Food was very cheap – beer was twopence a pint, tobacco three pence an ounce and the cottage rents were around ninepence to a shilling a week.'

'Farming at Braybrooke has completely changed from the 1930s. Prior to the Second World War only one farmer grew corn. His fields were a mile and a half from the village and one day some local lads who were disturbed while talking to the housemaids, hid in his hen house. The unsuspecting waggoner hitched the horse to the front and towed the hut to the cornfields for the hens to feed on the stubble.

As most of the fields were grass and used for fattening cattle, these were bought at market, principally at Northampton. They were walked by drovers, the journey taking two days. I often went with my father to Harrington to accompany them the last few miles.

Haymaking was a great time, taking weeks especially if it was a

151

wet summer. When the hay was being carted home, a ride on top of the load, with the cart swaying as the horse plodded over the rough ground, was enjoyed by children and workers. During the war all the fields with the exception of those too rough or hilly were ploughed to grow food. A rotation of wheat, oats, beans, barley and flax were grown. Hedges were uprooted to make larger fields, ponds filled in and spinneys removed. Harvesting was a tedious job dependent on fine weather. Corn was cut by a binder, people stooked the sheaves to allow them to dry, then they were carted to stacks. Later, in the winter, there was the visit of the threshing drum when corn was beaten from the straw and rats came tumbling from off the stacks to be caught by the dogs. Flax was pulled by hand and often children had a day off from school to help. The labour force was augmented by Italian and later German prisoners of war. By this time the horse had been replaced by tractors.'

'Some of the earliest memories about the land at Stowe come from the period up to and including the First World War. Miss Sylvia Starmer, whose grandfather, father and uncles farmed in Stowe, remembered her father "had three or four carthorses and a pony to drive . . .". The crops were "grass for sheep and cattle, wheat, oats, barley, turnips, swedes, potatoes and mangolds." Someone else recalls that £1 per week would then be earned for farm labouring.

Moving to the 1920s, Mr Lucas grew 60 acres of potatoes and there would be a man hoeing in the fields all summer.

A wage of £1.15.0d a week was earned by Mr H.W.T. Dickens' father who tolled every day of the week, starting at 6.00 in the morning and returning for breakfast at about 8.30. He "often ploughed all day with a single furrow plough – a lot of hard work, approximately one acre a day – very tiring. He worked numerous hours overtime for which my grandfather usually doled out one shilling (no not one shilling an hour, just one shilling). He did have concessions – we kept 300 hens in a field. We also had wood from fallen trees and I pinched his walnuts. Sometimes we got a ride to town in his 1924 bull-nosed Morris Cowley." Mr Dickens recalled a funny episode when his grandfather last drove the car and thought he was driving a horse and cab! He wasn't able to stop the vehicle and in his anxiety shouted "Whoa! Whoa!".

In the Second World War years, farms were beginning to become mechanised. However, at this time Mr Lucas senior, at the Manor, still had about 15 working horses for ploughing, and indeed at one time he bred Shire horses. Mr Hillyard was the last person to buy one from him. In the 1940s, a herd of pedigree Shorthorn cattle was kept at the Manor. Milking was done partly by hand, partly by machine.

In September 1945, Mr Lucas sold the farm and the cattle and moved to Rectory cottage, now the Dower House. Mr Briscoe bought the Manor together with 283 acres.

Following the introduction of tractors and balers, the combine harvester came in. Mr George Hillyard remembered the first one came to Stowe in 1943 and all the village turned out to see "this mechanical monster". The number of work horses became fewer and only light cobs were retained for use when feeding stock, etc.'

'All the farms at Gayton were mixed farming with cows, sheep, pigs and poultry, and all had horses working the ground, the first tractor coming to Gayton in about 1935. All had some arable land and the threshing was done by a gang who went from farm to farm with a threshing box and steam traction engine. Cattle were driven to Northampton on market days and it was not unusual for the early workers' buses at seven and eight o'clock to drive through a flock of sheep or herd of cattle on the road going to market. When they met at a crossroads, the drovers had to be careful to keep their herds close together to avoid mixing the animals up, which could result in chaos.

One farmer in the village, who owned four or five fields towards Banbury Lane, used to ride his bicycle up the old rutted lane, with two buckets of milk hanging from a yoke across his shoulders, then deliver milk to houses in the village. Some of the farmers sold their milk and eggs at the door, together with butter they had made. Customers collected their milk morning and evening in enamel cans with a handle and lid. People could also buy fertile eggs to put under a broody hen to hatch for their own back garden.'

'I can remember when all the work on our farm at Loddington was done by horses. The ploughing was done by two shires walking in the furrow with a man behind with the plough. The drilling, harrowing and rolling were all done with horses and, of course, the harvesting. The binder for cutting the corn was pulled by three strong horses abreast with a man seated on the binder to use the levers for regulating the height of the cutting etc.

I can well remember one day standing well out of harm's way with an aunt watching as they were finishing cutting a field. My father was standing at one corner with his gun waiting for the rabbits, and sometimes the odd fox, to run out, and when the man on the binder saw his gun poised he would stop the horses and wait for the bang before going on – the horses didn't take a scrap of notice.

A few years later a tractor took over the role of the three horses. If a field was nearly finished being cut in an evening and there was a possibility of any rabbits being in it, most of the young teenagers from the village would come in hopes of catching a free meal. I was always sent home at this point as I might have got hurt with the sticks flying in all directions.

After the corn was cut, the sheaves had to be put in stooks and later were carried to the stack yard to be put into ricks, which were thatched until it was threshed during the winter.

Oats were always cut first, when they were slightly under ripe, and remained in the stooks until the church bells had been rung on three Sundays, by which time they were considered to be ripe and fit to carry.

In the 1920s and early 1930s the threshing drum was moved about and driven by a traction engine, and then until the 1940s with a tractor. After that we had a trailer combine under the Lease Lend agreement with the United States. Threshing was a filthy business and my job was band cutter and feeder on the drum. I had a knife with a curved serrated blade attached to my right wrist, with which I picked up the sheaves as they were passed to me. I got hold of the string with my other hand and with a jerk of my wrist cut the band and the sheaf went down the canvas elevator into the drum, while I retained the strings. As the straw was going to be fed to cattle it would be harmful to them if the strings had gone through. Now we have one of the large self propelled sophisticated combines that does the cutting and threshing all in one go.'

'I came to live at Denford Ash, about a mile from Denford, in 1951 after I was married and have been living and working on a small farm there for the last 40 years. There have never been two days alike and therefore not time to get bored. There have been many changes, and not all for the better. There were four dairy farms in and around the village when we came, but dairy farms are few and far between now. There was no milk tanker in the early 1950s and churns were filled and put out for collection. The milk lorry has managed to get through to us every day in over 40 years. If, in the winter, it couldn't get through from Denford, it would come round to us via Raunds.

I have been told that in 1947, the really bad winter, nothing could get through because the hedges were high then and the snow had drifted against them. My predecessor took an old horse with milk churns lashed to a gate behind it and went through the fields to get the milk down to the end of the lane and had to do so for quite a time.

I recall in those early years, not long after the Second World War, the excitement of the threshing contractor arriving in the early morning and the rush to get cows milked and calves fed, sandwiches made (with still-rationed cheese) and gallons of tea made with the sugar allocation.'

WASHING THE SHEEP

'Farm workers would wash the sheep in the brook at Whilton Mill. One man would stand in a barrel in the water and push the sheep under the water with a long pole so that the sheep went completely under the water. The wool was considered to be more valuable if it had been washed.'

THE MOLECATCHER

'The molecatcher travelled miles around the villages around Grendon in the 1920s. He was also the gravedigger and stoked the church boilers on a Saturday night.'

LACE WORKERS

⊸⊃

Though, by the beginning of the 20th century, the great days of the hand-made lace industry were over, there were still memories of the lace schools where so many children learned to make a living and it was possible for some years to see older women at their cottage doors making pillow lace, as they had done for decades.

THE LACE SCHOOL

'In the 19th century Spratton was the home of a thriving lace school. In a room twelve feet square with just two windows as many as 30 girls and sometimes a few boys would sit all day making pillow lace.

Upon arrival at Spratton Lace School the new girls had their hair plaited so that loose hairs could not fall onto the pillows and be woven into the lace.

In the summer they worked from six in the morning to six at night with a half hour off for breakfast, an hour for dinner and a half hour for tea.

They had to maintain a workspeed of sticking ten pins a minute,

155

that is 600 an hour or 6,000 each working day. A working week was five and a half days, Saturday being a half day off. To keep up speed and to count the pins they would sing chants or tells, each village having its own verses or favourites. At Spratton if a child fell short on pins they would sing:

"Polly or Betsy a pin for the poor,
Give one a pin and I'll ask no more."

Each child counted her own pins and had to shout out the time each 50th pin, racing each other through the day. If, at the end of the day, a child was five pins short they would have to stay a further hour. They were watched over by a mistress who wielded a cane for punishment.

In the winter when the days were dark they would work from eight to eight. As dusk fell they would cluster round candlestools. These were small four-legged stools with a hole in the middle and six holes round the edge. In the centre hole was placed a long stick with a candle holder on the top and holes drilled through it for pegs which allowed it to be adjusted for height. In the six surrounding holes were placed wooden sockets, rather like large egg-cups, into which were placed water-filled glass spheres which concentrated the light on the lace pillows of the girls who sat around, three to each glass, 18 to a candlestool. Each pillow was set at a different height to make the most of the feeble light.

Children at the Spratton school had to pay twopence a week (threepence in winter) for the tallow candles and in return kept all the money earned. Some of the more nimble-fingered children earned as much as sixpence a day, the money being paid monthly.

Lacemakers, generally, celebrated two holidays, St Catherine's Day, 25th November, for the patron saint of spinners or St Andrew's Day on 30th November. In Spratton Lace School on St Andrew's Day they acted out a strange little custom. The children would lock the mistress out of the workroom and, when she demanded admittance would sing:

"Pardon Mistress, Pardon Master,
Pardon for a pin.
If you'll not give a holiday,
We won't let you in."

The mistress after a pretence of anger and rage would give in and allow a half holiday.

Gradually the village lacemaking industry died away with the perfecting of machine made lace but in 1891 there was a revival of interest at Spratton where it was found that 25 women were still working lace, but, sadly, no children were learning the art. Parents did not encourage it because it prevented them from going into service.

At that time most people worked on the land or in the big houses. There was a brick factory in Spratton, owned by Blundells, but in 1930 the clay pits were filled in with rubbish from the village and the brick-making disappeared.'

SITTING AT THE COTTAGE DOOR

'I was born in Yardley Gobion in 1907 and a regular scene in the village was women sitting at their cottage doorsteps making lace. One I remember in particular is Annie Aitkens, who sat at the door of her cottage next to the church making pillow lace.'

'In the early 1930s there were still about half a dozen traditional lace makers left in Greens Norton working at their pillows. At the turn of the century nearly every cottage had its pillow, after all it was an additional source of income. One old lady remembered how, as a

Mrs Billings – W.I. Lace Tutor for many years

young girl, she had to work on her lace for an hour after school, before being allowed out to play. How she hated it!'

OTHER WAYS WE MADE A LIVING

⟨⟩

Quarrying was an important source of employment for North-amptonshire's men, and there were many other occupations, a few of which are mentioned below – from the reporter on the local newspaper to making pork pies!

IN THE QUARRIES

'A seam of ironstone close to the surface had been quarried both north and south of Brixworth village from early times, both Lunch Lane and the allotments on the Creaton Road giving clear signs of the removal of a ten foot seam. After the First World War, Brixworth became an important source of ironstone and quarries surrounded the village. Steam excavators worked at the seam and the overburden was moved manually by labourers with heavy wheelbarrows from one side of the working to the other.

Imagine wooden trestles 20 ft high supporting a single plank. A very good circus act would be to run along this plank with a heavily laden wheelbarrow above a stage and a safety net – the "stage" was a rock-strewn base of the working and no safety nets were provided. This performance, 80 times a day, was carried out by the labourers for a miniscule wage. The ironstone was loaded onto narrow gauge trains which were then pulled by locos to the railway line that had been built from Northampton to Market Harborough with mineral extraction in mind.'

'In the past at Nether Heyford there was plenty of work in the neighbourhood from small craftsmen such as ladder makers and a shoe factory in Church Lane. There was also a brickyard and the smelting of the iron ore quarried out of the hills just below Church Stowe and brought down by a little old engine "Puffing Billy" on a single track railway to the Heyford siding. From there it was despatched by boat on the Grand Union Canal. There were also lime pits on the other side of Watling Street.'

'My father used to quarry limestone at Stowe by hand and collect it with a horse and cart. He processed it in order to sell to farmers for the land. In the kiln, only recently demolished, there would be a layer of straw on the bottom grating, wood, coal and then slack, followed by layers of limestone, slack, limestone etc until the kiln was full. The family used to break up the large stones to cup size in order to fit them into the kiln. The top was sealed with chippings and dust from the crackings mixed with water. The kiln would be lit from the bottom. It then took three days to burn up to the top. Processing took from seven to ten days. After cooling, the lime was extracted by "knocking the bottom out". Mr Tom Faulkner then filled up his farmcart and sold the lime at six shillings and sixpence a cartload in Pattishall and Nether Heyford. Despite the health hazard of this enterprise (he had a nose-bleed every time he emptied the kiln) Mr Faulkner lived to be 96 years of age.

Quarrying on any scale has not taken place in living memory, although there was the intention to reopen the quarry in the late 1930s.

TIMBER WORKERS

'Hartwell was once a thriving centre of the timber industry. Historically centred in Salcey Forest, it was natural that timber figured largely in the lives of villagers. Some of the older buildings in the village were in the forest and probably housed forest rangers. There were also strong royal connections, the area being part of the Duke of Grafton's estate. Today, unfortunately, the timber businesses have all gone and the forest has receded. The motorway effectively cuts the village off from the forest and so the links are very tenuous. I can remember ladies talking about their fathers working in the forest itself on the wood and I have seen photographs of men working in pits sawing tree trunks, one man in the pit, the other on top working a two-handed saw. Sadly these memories are lost as older members of the village community die and take their knowledge with them.'

'In the 1920s the "Drug" carts travelled through Duddington from the timber yards owned by the firm of Miles of Stamford. These large carts were pulled by magnificent heavy horses. Often the huge log trunks of oak had been felled in Kings Cliffe Forest and were chained together on these long carts for delivery to Stamford. The hills at Duddington and Collyweston posed a problem and to overcome it two extra horses were hitched to the first cart and when it reached the top of the hill they were unhitched and taken back to the bottom of the hill to be hitched to the second cart and so on. When you think of a large number of carts in convoy, it must have taken a very long time. Perhaps there was more time in those days. Life seemed so much simpler.'

BOATS AND ROPES

'An interesting feature of Stoke Bruerne village was the rope walk situated behind the canalside cottages. Ropes were made by hand, of course, and a strip of land was set aside for this purpose. The strands of rope were anchored to a post while the twisting went on, the ropemaker backing further down the rope walk as his rope grew in length. Two rope makers are remembered today. One, Jack James, helped to start the waterways museum so popular with present day visitors. The other was Mr Amos, who was highly respected. He not only made ropes, he also had a shop, a general stores. This was situated where the Bruerne's Lock restaurant now is. He was the father of Stoke Bruerne's most famous daughter, Sister Mary Ward (as she later became). Mary Amos was unable to train as a nurse in this country as she had contracted tuberculosis. Although this cleared up completely, she was left with trouble in her leg. Undaunted, she went abroad to train under Edith Cavell in Belgium. On her return to Stoke Bruerne at the end of the First World War she married Charles Ward, who was now running her father's shop, and dedicated the next 40 years of her life to nursing the canal folk.'

'Braunston boat yard began in 1878, owned by William Nurser. By 1928 his sons Charles and Frank had taken over. Boat building was its main work and it had a high reputation for its paintwork – Frank Nurser had a clear Braunston style.'

AT THE 'BIG HOUSE'

'My uncle was the groom and chauffeur to the family who lived at the Hall at Great Houghton in the mid 1930s, and to sit in his warm and spotless tack room and to watch him dealing so expertly with the horses was pure joy to me. Occasionally I was given permission by the lady of the house to accompany my uncle when he went on errands in the pale blue Rolls Royce. Many times I went proudly with my uncle, who always looked so smart in his chauffeur's livery, to fetch home the two "young gentlemen" from their boarding school for the holidays.'

'When the children left school in Lois Weedon and Weston, most of the boys went on the land and the girls into service. Some would go to Dallington House, Northampton for a period of eight months to learn how to cook or train to become housemaids or parlour maids. The fee was five shillings a month.'

'To supplement the family income I remember that my mother had a sewing machine and would sew for other families. They would bring in an old pair of trousers and ask her to make a smaller pair for one of their boys. Mum would unpick the old pair and use the best parts of the material to sew a new pair. For this time consuming job she charged threepence.

I went to school when I was three and left when I was 13 and went to work at Lord's Farm at Middleton, looking after the children mostly. I only worked in the house, not outside, from seven in the morning until seven at night. There was another lady, older than me, and she did the heavier jobs, scrubbed the floor. Well, I was only 13. I think the farmers used to go to the school when they were looking for someone to work for them. I stayed there for about three years then I went into service at Croughton. I came back to Middleton in 1917 and worked at the rectory for Rev Brown until his wife died in 1920. Then the Rev Tuke came and he asked if I would work for him. I stayed with him and did the cooking, I've always enjoyed cooking. I left when I got married in 1925.'

'At the age of 14 Mother took me to answer an advertisement for a kitchen maid at a large house in the next village. It was slavery; up at 6.30 to blacklead a large range and scrub the kitchen floor before the cook came down. She wore awful glasses, which she looked over if angry. Wages were two shillings and sixpence a week. There were days when nothing went right.

The Colonel died and I married in the same year, being let a cottage on the estate provided I went up to work at sixpence per hour. War came, so the staff left. Only the old parlour maid stayed. When she died I took over, until my husband died.

Then I said I could not live in the house any longer and gave the lady at the age of 95 years a choice of coming to the little lodge, which was empty, with me, or else going to a nursing home. My job ended when she died in her 99th year; ending my 50 years of service.'

'Most of the menfolk at Greens Norton in the 1930s were farm labourers, although some were employed as grooms and stable lads by the local gentry (more commonly called the "Toffs"!) who were hunting folk, Greens Norton being in Grafton Hunt country. During the summer most of the horses were put out to grass and many of the stable workers laid off. However, there was always need for extra hands at harvest time. The big houses around also required domestics so village girls went into service.'

LOCAL REPORTER

'Early days in Northamptonshire journalism are recalled by my brother, who began work as a junior reporter on the *Chronicle and Echo* before the war, the first step in a career which was to culminate in his becoming an editor.

Reporters had to work incredibly long hours for unbelievably low pay in the 1930s. After "training" at head office (which meant being thrown in at the deep end) my brother was sent to Daventry where he was expected to live on 35 shillings a week, less National Insurance, out of which he had to pay his landlady 25 shillings for board and lodging. After paying his bus fares to Northampton for Sundays off, and giving a few shillings to Mother, there was nothing left for clothing, holidays or emergencies. How did he manage? The answer lay in that magic word expenses.

In addition to covering events in Daventry, my brother had to make a weekly round of a dozen villages and was allowed to charge his firm a penny a mile for use of cycle. Advertisements for district reporters in those days always stipulated "must be able to cycle".

A less regular, but nevertheless welcome, source of income was lineage. If a Staffordshire man, say, was fined at Daventry court, my brother would send a report to the *Staffordshire Sentinel,* and receive a penny a line. A rare, but more substantial windfall occurred if an item of national importance cropped up in the area and was phoned to Fleet Street.

How was news gathered? Quite simple, really; from a network of contacts. There were daily calls at the police station, to look for items of interest in the occurrence book, and weekly contacts with officials of many organisations whose activities make up the rich pattern of provincial life. Then there were weekly, monthly or annual sittings of bodies such as police courts, councils, football matches, flower shows, school sports and speech days.

But above all, there was the constant need to be on the alert for items ranging from the tragic to the comic and bizarre.'

THE BREWERY AND THE PIPE MAKERS

'The brewery at Litchborough was owned and run by Mr Bill Urquhart. It was situated on the corner of Northampton Road and Towcester Road, and the Litchborough Ale produced there was appreciated countrywide. Mr Urquhart was asked to travel to St Helena to teach his skills, and help the islanders to set up their own brewing industry in order to provide much needed employment. After his retirement, the brewery was closed down, and now the buildings have been developed into private homes.

Litchborough's other claim to fame was for the manufacture of briar pipes. This skill originated in 1876 when Thomas Martin was apprenticed to an Austrian pipemaker in Soho. Thomas, and later his son Richard, produced pipes with the registered name Blakemar in their home village of Blakesley. In 1960 the business moved to Litchborough, where the root called bruyere, which had to be at least 50 years old, imported from Mediterranean lands, was smoothed, polished, stained, burned and repolished to produce mirror-like bowls in an amazing variety of shapes. The land on which the briar pipes was made was gradually developed into a beautiful garden centre, where visitors could wander round lakes and shrubberies before making their purchases.'

THE FOUNDRY

'The foundry at Hargrave, which met its end soon after the Second World War, employed about 24 men – skilled engineers and carpenters and apprentices. It was well established in the 19th century as "Engineers, Iron and Brass Founders". The engineers were inventors and patentees, world renowned for their invention of the steel double plough. They invented a sinking platform for the production of cart wheels which proved a vital innovation in keeping the army on wheels in the First World War. Nearer home, they were also the local coffin makers.'

THE RUBBER FACTORY

'At Stanion before the Second World War, the leather tanning factory at White Cellars Yard, opposite the Lord Nelson, was turned into a factory making rubber door mats and was owned by Mr Russell. The mats were made out of old car, bus and lorry tyres, and they had machines to strip off the rubber. First, they had to inspect the tyres for stones, nails etc in the tread. The old, unwanted tyres were burned in the stone pit.'

SKINNING RABBITS

'At Easton men worked in farming, the building trades, for Burghley Estates, ironstone quarrying, or engineering at Blackstones. Men and

163

women worked at Lees (of Grantham) on Porters Lane, skinning rabbits for their furs and making gelatine from by-products. The smell was said to be awful.'

MAKING PORK PIES

'In the 1920s a large number of villagers at Irchester were employed by Parson's Pork Pies. As times were hard in those days, and especially during a hard winter, Mr Parson supplied free hot soup, and not just for the staff.'

GETTING ABOUT

It is not so long ago that if you wanted to go anywhere you used real horsepower if you were lucky, and you walked if you were not. As the century opened few had personal transport other than farmers and the well-to-do with their horse traps or carriages. Then gradually the bicycle became available – at great sacrifice to save or to purchase at about sixpence a week. Cars appeared first usually at the rectory or the manor house, but for the average family aspiration did not rise much above the motor cycle and sidecar for many years. Group outings, which were rare, brought in the horse-drawn brake and then the motor charabanc, and the train opened up even greater horizons.

BY HORSE OR BY FOOT

'At the beginning of the century, horses were the main form of transport. Dr Wright from Blakesley would ride across the fields to his patients at Litchborough, and some luckless member of the sick person's family would be pressed into service to hold the horse while the doctor was inside. Preachers for the Baptist chapel would come from Northampton in a hired pony and trap, and would sometimes have to enlist local assistance to control their contraption down the slippery hill to Farthingstone.'

'Market Harborough was the shopping mecca for all the local villages. At one time the four and a half miles from Clipston had to be traversed on foot along roads that were little more than rough tracks, with stones thrown down and left to be bedded down by horses, carts or pedestrians. Eventually a horse-drawn carriage was organised to convey villagers to the town but on the return journey, travellers were expected to disembark at the bottom of East Farndon hill and walk to the top because the load of people and their shopping was more than the horse could be expected to draw up the hill. The carriage became known (with typical country wit) as Black Maria.'

'I can remember going from Denford to visit my grandmother and walking with my brother while my mother pushed my younger brother in the pram, to Catworth, where we would spend a night or two. Then we would walk on to Hargrave to see my aunt and probably spend another night there before walking on home via Raunds – a round trip. We wore high boots, some buttoned up and some with laces, with nails in the soles as the roads were very rough. I also recall visiting relations in a hired pony and trap. It was dark sometimes by the time we came home and we had oil lamps on the trap. I used to like to see all the lights from Islip furnace when we were up the hill before getting back into Denford. The trap seated six, four at the back and two in the front.'

'People from Brigstock used to go into Kettering once a year before the First World War, by carrier. My mother took us to shop at Hooton's Sixpenny Bazaar for Christmas shopping. It was in Newland Street. Coming home, the carrier used to whip the horse and make it run and the children would scream. Sometimes, people hired a buggy to go into Kettering.'

ON YOUR BIKE

'Before there were batteries for our bicycle lamps, I had an acetylene lamp on my bike which had to be lit with matches when I got off the bus at Thrapston from school on a winter's evening, before cycling back to Denford. Most people had bikes in the 1930s and 1940s for transport, although lifts could sometimes be obtained into Thrapston. I remember, as a child, being allowed to straddle the pole at the back of a "pole waggon" owned by a sawyer and drawn by carthorses, as he made his way into Thrapston to fetch wood to make hurdles, but on the way back no rides were possible because of the timber load.'

'Most families owned a bicycle as a convenient way to get into

165

Northampton from Great Houghton, being only two and a half miles away. My aunt and uncle had a bike each, and I first learned to ride on my aunt's, which was far too big for me but standing on the pedals was much better than sitting anyway. She also had a motorbike which she rode for many years, in fact she was a bit of a daredevil for all her four ft eleven inches in height! She could turn her hand to most things and would try anything, but woe betide anyone who crossed her.'

'There were not many cars about at that time, but my friend's father had a motorbike and sidecar, and our two fathers spent many happy hours tinkering with it. In the winter of 1927/8 there was a very hard and heavy frost for some days, and we were taken in the sidecar to Stoke Bruerne to see the canal which had frozen over several feet thick. It was quite a sight to see, there were crowds of people skating and sliding, and someone had even got a car on the ice.

In the summer however, our two Mums got out the motorbike one day, and with my Mum on the pillion, and us two girls in the sidecar, we were taken for a ride round the country lanes. There was no driving test in those days, they hadn't been thought of, and with much screaming with laughter, and showing large expenses of silk stockings (and knickers!) we had a wonderful time. I realise now of course that our Mums could only have been in their late twenties.'

THE FIRST CARS

'I was twelve years old (1912) when I saw my first motor car. I watched as it came from the Brackley direction and went towards Banbury. I don't remember anyone at Middleton having one at that time.'

'When very young, I travelled with my mother and father to Great Houghton in a motor bike and sidecar but when a little older my mother would put me on a Midland red bus in charge of the conductor (one could do this with confidence in those days) and my aunt would meet me when the bus drew into the Mayorhold in Northampton. However, just before one of our trips we were greatly excited as my father bought a wonderful Austin 7 motor car in navy blue; it was the only one in the street where I lived and all the neighbours came out to give us a good send off. Of course no one had to take a driving test, it was just a matter of getting in and trying it out, so after a final polish and pumping up of tyres etc we were off. We chugged along very nicely for an hour or so, and then caught up with a lorry going even slower than us! My father was patient for a few miles and then decided to take the plunge and overtake. This was a mistake. As we accelerated, the little car began to literally bounce from side to side, both doors flew open and we all clung on, sitting silently waiting for whatever was to come. The car must have looked like a small version of Chitty Chitty Bang Bang preparing to take off! We shot across the grass verge and ended with the car's nose in the ditch and three bumped heads. You see, my father thought he was correct in pumping up the tyres as hard as he could – the hard way to learn a lesson!'

CATCHING THE BUS

'Public transport was, of course, very important with so few people being able to afford the luxury of their own car, and I remember well the little white charabanc-type buses that the Minney family of Yardley Hastings ran from there into Northampton, picking up passengers from Denton, Brafield-on-the-Green, Little and Great Houghton. By the time they arrived at out village, being nearest to the town, they were often full to capacity but the cheerful driver would shout "Stay put, I'll be back for you in a jiffy". The roads were not as smooth as today's and a ride in one of these buses was better than any fun fair ride, in fact, the floor boards did not appear to be attached to any other part of the bus.'

'The farmers at Braybrooke used horses and carts until the advent of the tractor in the 1930s. Two of the farmers had Clyno cars with canvas hood to put up when it rained. There was a bus with solid tyres which went into Market Harborough to the Tuesday market. It started from Barn End in the middle of the village. In the 1930s the United Counties started an excellent service stopping at the village green and the church. It was on the route from Kettering to Market Harborough and for many years the fare to Market Harborough was fivepence return for adults and twopence ha'penny for children. Although Desborough is roughly the same distance, that cost sevenpence as the bus went onto the A6 road.'

'Until the United Counties bus service started in the 1930s, shoppers wishing to go into Northampton from Gayton had to go on the carrier's cart. In 1923 there was a bus service run by Mr S. Kirton of Eastcote and later by Mr Arthur Roberts. If workers were a few minutes late after work (sometimes the employers would keep workers late to finish their tasks), the bus would wait for them. Unfortunately, Arthur's bus was burned out and he sold the goodwill to United Counties. Workmen's buses left Gayton at

6.30, 7 and 8 am and came back between 4.30 and 6 pm. Buses ran to Northampton twice on Sundays, four times on Wednesdays and six times on Saturdays. The last one left Northampton at 10.15 on Saturday night.'

'Harpole had two rival bus services in the 1920s, Nutts and Surridges, but the funny thing to me as a child was, you either went with Nutts or Surridges. We went with the Nutts and some of my friends went with the Surridges. This was based on what politics you supported.'

'At first if you wanted to travel anywhere a place could be booked with the carrier, but this had to be done a week in advance. There was a bus service from Lois Weedon to Banbury on market day (Thursday) which cost one shilling and sixpence. You could also get about by rail. People walked to Helmdon station to get a train to Banbury or to Moreton Pinkney to go to Northampton. If you father worked on the railways you got a free ticket.'

'Sammy Walters started the coach business in Helmdon. First he had a fish cart and later a fruit and vegetable cart drawn by a horse with one eye. Sammy used to scrub the cart out and put in wooden seats to take people out for the day. He later progressed to a motor bus. It was a 30 seater but during the Second World War so many people used to cram on it to go to Northampton or the cinema at Towcester, that Fred Holloway, the conductor, used to stand on the steps and hold the rails by the door to prevent people falling off. Fred used to take people's shopping lists to Northampton and do their shopping for them.'

'In the late 1930s the single bus fare to Kettering from Denton was tenpence and the return fare was one shiling and twopence. A double-decker open-topped bus used to run from Raunds to Kettering and back on a Friday at that time.'

THE CARRIER'S CART

⊂⊃

The horse-drawn carrier's cart was at one time the only link between town and country, for goods and for passengers. Before buses and trains provided easy transport, a trip to market or the delivery of materials for the village shoemaking business would both depend on the professional carrier, travelling his regular route and a familiar figure to all.

GOING TO NORTHAMPTON

'Very early recollections for me are during the First World War years when the transport from Northampton, from all the villages was the carrier's cart. This was a caravan-type of horse-drawn vehicle with seats all round inside and a long box on the front where the driver sat. This box was to contain all small parcels and perishable goods. A rack held by chains on the back was for heavier goods and even large blocks of ice from the cold storage in Northampton.

Coming along the road from Spratton, a halt was usually made at the bottom of Hungry Hill. This was so called because the carrier, his wife and passengers always had their lunch, or victuals as they were called, at this place whilst many of the passengers walked up the hill to help the poor old horse. Incidentally, hot bricks wrapped in flannel were feet warmers and stone jars filled with hot water were means of keeping warm during the winters. Hungry Hill seemed so much steeper in those days and, during the spring, clumps of violets could easily been seen in the hedgerows and spinney.

Passing along the road, the jovial carrier normally shouted out "Merry Tom Lane" as we passed. This lane was named after the first Lord Spencer's favourite hunter who was killed jumping the brook and was buried there wearing the saddle, stirrups and bridle. A stone was erected "To the Memory of Merry Tom" to which a local wit added "Ridden to death by foolish John". It was then removed.

Two cottages, brick built, down the lane were known as Damsel Barn Cottages; they have since been pulled down. There was also a bungalow type of house at the level crossing. A farmhouse for Merry Tom farm still stands, although this is in another parish.

To add to the excitement of the journey, rabbits seemed to be in profusion and often a fox with cubs could be seen playing around in a nearby field.

169

The horse-drawn carrier's cart, like this one in Banbury Lane, Litchborough, would not only take you to market in the towns, but alternatively would take your shopping order and return with it later that day.

Passing along by the Red House, which was owned by Mr John Drage, we came to the bottom of the lane leading to Brampton Hill where there was a large farmhouse and several cottages used by the farm workers. On the opposite side of the road was Spinney Hill farm, built in the valley close to the river, consisting of two very nice brick built houses.

Arriving at the school in the centre of Brampton village, quite a number of villagers would congregate there to give the carrier parcels or orders for shopping to get from Northampton. Many of these people whom we could call characters are still very vivid in my memory.

The butler, in his shirt sleeves and green baize apron, standing with empty wine and spirit cases to be taken for replenishment; a footman or hall boy (no doubt from Brampton House) with a truck holding a laundry basket and several boxes; the gardener, in his tweeds and round pork-pie hat, who lived in the very pretty thatched cottage next to the school at the top of the drive to Brampton House (the cottage has now been demolished) and many village folk. There was the woman who always had a man's cap on her head with curling pins creeping out underneath; the little old lady, dressed in black and white, with her sun-bonnet type hat; the farm labourers with their cord trousers hitched up under their knees

170

with small leather straps or thatching twine; the red-faced roadman who wore a panama-type of hat in the summer and a large old trilby in the winter when he was sweeping the road.

Somehow the village seemed so very busy at that particular time. The milkman with his milk churn on his two-wheel truck, the brass shining so brightly on the top of the churn; the butcher with his delivery cart; the man walking his stallion through the village and many of the women folk standing in groups at their cottage gates discussing local news and the weather.

In those days, the cattle were walked to Northampton Market by drovers who went through Brampton about eight in the morning. Pigs, sheep and poultry were taken in horse-drawn floats at about ten o'clock in time for the eleven o'clock market.

In the early days of the 1914 war, a drover was unfortunately drowned by the old toll gate when he was endeavouring to rescue two sheep which had got into the river. I seem to remember that the river Nene was much quicker flowing and had much more water in it in those days, no doubt this was before the reservoir at Hollowell was built.'

'When my husband, H.D. Knight was 14 years of age he assisted in the family carrier's business. Several days a week, after taking orders for shopping, he would leave Walgrave about 10 am, with horse and trolley, accompanied sometimes by several people wanting to go into the town; passing through Holcot, calling at gentry houses, pubs etc and ending the journey at the Stag's Head Inn in lower Abington Street – a journey lasting two and a half hours. After the horse was stabled, fed and watered, the next involvement was to take orders to various shops in the town, such as Kingham's, where they ground their own coffee – such an aroma emanated from there – then the Drapery shops, Adnitts, Shepherd and Manning, James Bros, Brice's, Fitness (an old established shirt firm), Kendall's (a notable shoe shop) and Cockerill's (fruit and veg)-all since disappeared. Orders were delivered to the Stag's Head, and the return journey would begin at 4pm arriving back at base between 7 and 8pm, delivering parcels etc on the way. On the return journey between Holcot and Walgrave, two steep hills were encountered, and if the load was exceptionally heavy, a passing cyclist was hailed (there were no phones in those days) to request from home the help of a chain horse, to finish those last one and a half miles.

If it was a clear frosty night, the clip clop of the horse's hooves could be heard plainly as soon as it left the yard. In those days, Harry Sale, a boot and shoe retailer of Sheep Street, Northampton, cycled to Holcot and Walgrave collecting weekly payments from the

171

villagers, and many pairs of footwear were collected from his shop and delivered to his customers at twopence per parcel.

Wines, spirits and tobacco for pubs and big houses, were collected from Poole's, Abington Square, and Lee's of York Road, two main tobacconists. They were long days for the carrier, starting at 6am by feeding and watering the horses. On returning, the work was not yet complete, until they were again unharnessed, fed and stabled. Whilst on the subject of Northampton journeys, there was a small private school for boys – about a dozen pupils – at Holcot, run by Miss Cohen (a much respected lady), and boys who arrived by train at Northampton railway station, were transported by horse and waggonette.

Another job involved taking boys to a Northampton hairdresser (or should it be barber?) accompanied by Miss Hudson (known affectionately as Miss Huddy) who was their French teacher. Sometimes a horse and cab would be required to take several ladies to the shops, and the carrier (now acting as coachman) waited outside in the Drapery – wearing a hard hat, and knees covered warmly by a rug. Another service was to Lamport railway station, a distance of four miles, making one trip in the morning and one in the afternoon.

Flour came from Silvertown, London by rail; also coal and cobbles for Walgrave Co-op Bakery. On one of these trips, on arriving back at Walgrave with a load of cobbles, the back board dropped down, cobbles rattled out, and the startled horse galloped off, leaving a trail of cobbles round the village. The startled animal was an ex-Army horse, believed to have been shell-shocked during the war. A writer of recent years, Mr Watkins Pitchford, sometimes known as B.B. (now deceased) wrote in his book *A Child Alone* of lying among the ivy on top of a wall at his Lamport rectory home and listening to the clip-clop of the carrier's horse; he little realised that the carrier was a youth of his own age, not a grown man as he thought.

At the age of 17 in 1922, the carrier's cart was superseded by a T. Ford one ton lorry with solid tyres, and instead of two journeys to Lamport station daily, more could be undertaken – on one occasion ten trips were made from Walgrave Hall Farm, transporting wheat in sacks weighing 18 stones (two and a half cwts) to the station. After two years the T Ford was replaced by a five ton Bedford lorry enabling longer journeys to be made, such as taking boots from Walgrave factory to the Crown agents, Mill Bank, London, to Didcot Army Store; and to Manchester.

The carrier – now lorry driver – spent his 21st birthday broken down on the road to Manchester, during the 1926 General Strike, with a load of ladies' underwear from the Brook Factory in

Northampton, when only food was being allowed through. But somehow he delivered his load and arrived home safely.'

In the 1920's 'Old' Jack Smith started a bus service at Creaton, taking people to and from Northampton and elsewhere. All the buses were called after flies – Butterfly, Dragonfly, Mayfly and Gadfly! On market days the back seats would be removed and lambs put in their place. No cattle lorries them! The buses eventually gave way to United Counties – who didn't take the lambs. Jack Smith's son 'young' Jack ran the carrier business for the local villages. Taking orders from the local shops for wholesale goods, and from individuals who wished for certain things to be collected, or bought for them, the carrier would go to Northampton or wherever, to deliver, collect, seek items ordered and deliver them, payment on receipt, though this was not always the case – some people couldn't or wouldn't pay. The business was sold in 1937 to Mr and Mrs Garrett for £150. It is from Mrs Garrett that I am indebted for information. She told me of carting coal for the village coal yard, from Brixworth station for two shillings and six pence per load; moving household effects for just £3 and then not being able to get any more of the money other than four shillings after eight weeks of asking – so that had to be written off as a bad debt. They had the business for nearly 20 years, transporting goods for nearby Red Cross hospitals during the war, fetching and delivering all around. The strangest request they had was during the war. In a very bad spell of weather the General Hospital in Northampton asked them to take a corpse back to Spratton. Well, the coffin had to go beside the bags of flour and other goods! Not an easy job, specially when payments were slow, or not forthcoming. And nothing at all if the order was unobtainable '

OUR RAILWAY

Affection for the trains which passed so regularly through the Northamptonshire countryside, and which gave employment to many men in the county, has lasted over the years, despite the Beeching "axe" of the 1960s which saw the demise of so many country lines. Trains were not only a means of transport, they were a source of entertainment in those pre-television days.

NIBBLE AND CLINK

'Helmdon was a village with two railway stations. The bottom LMS station opened in 1871 and closed in 1951. This was known as the "Nibble and Clink" line. The top Great Central and later LNER station opened in 1899 and closed in 1963. The viaduct on this line, which is now a great local landmark, was built before the embankment was built. Alan Watson's grandfather told him that all the village boys used to laugh because they didn't think a train could possibly get up to it. They didn't realise that the soil from the cuttings would be used to make an embankment so that the track would run across the valley.'

RAILWAY CHILDREN

'We were Railway Children. The Great Central Railway dominated our lives at Woodford in the 1930s, where clocks were of no importance as everyone knew the times of the trains and in those days they ran on time. We who were fortunate enough to win a scholarship travelled to school by train to Brackley or Towcester, though if you attended Towcester grammar school you had to walk a mile and a half to Byfield to depart from there, and in either case

The coming of the railway. Its efficient and frequent service linking towns and villages is still remembered with affection.

174

you had a good mile walk from the station when you reached the other end. This was before the days of plastic rainwear so if it was raining you sat in wet clothing for the rest of the day.

In Sidney Road there was the "Railway Barracks", which was a hostel housing men who had come to work on the railway, quite a number of them coming from Ireland and others from many parts of the country. Some of them are still with us in the village, having settled and married here. Unfortunately, in June 1957 this hostel was razed to the ground by fire and was never rebuilt. Thank goodness there were no casualties.

When the railway was finally closed in 1965 it was like a death blow to the village. Over 500 men lost their jobs where they had worked all their adult lives, but most managed to find work in surrounding towns. Now, nearly 30 years later, the village is starting to live again.'

THE MAIN TRANSPORT

'Ninety to 95 years ago, as there were hardly any vehicles on the road, the railway was used as the main form of transport. Irthlingborough station was on the main line between Northampton and Peterborough and it was the only station where the trains stopped together and exchanged their cargoes at this junction.

The railway ran a dray service, which would collect any parcels etc from local businesses and shops in the town and arrive back to the station in time for the 10 am trains to arrive.

Deliveries would be unloaded into the goods yard or transferred to the other train and the trains would then depart. The dray would make the deliveries to the shops and businesses through the day and at 4 pm would start collecting again to meet the 6 pm trains.

The horse pulling the dray would stop and drink at the natural gush which filled the trough at the bottom of Smiths Hill and the stream started at the back of Finedon Road and then went on down Station Road.'

'The North Western Railway running between Northampton and Peterborough, opened in 1845, supported the Ringstead and Addington station. Here daily papers were collected by children for pennies, crossing five fields and the river over slippery stepping stones and flimsy footbridges. Villagers also walked to Cranford station to catch the Kettering train. In 1934 the railway station burned down – it was rumoured to have been started deliberately to cover a deficiency in the book keeping! Adjacent to the station were two mill cottages, adjoining the site of an old corn mill. Here wines could be

175

purchased and boats hired on the river. When the river flooded, as it frequently did, and the meadows froze, skating parties were held.'

'In the 1920s, the train fare from Irchester station to London on a Saturday evening was five shillings return. No changing either; it was straight through.'

AT THE WINDOW

'Often in the evening hours of my childhood years during the 1930s and 1940s, I would sit with my father by a wide open window. This window was a sashed one and we flung it open as far as it would go. We sat side by side on an old ottoman in which blankets were stored and looked out on a view straight before us of the road to the railway station, some cottage back gardens, the Bog Meadow (with the little mound surrounded by railings where the famous spring water was tapped) and then running alongside this meadow, the main London/Birmingham railway line. We used this line to travel to shop in our market and postal town of Banbury in Oxfordshire. Our home was in Kings Sutton on the edge of the Northampton/Oxfordshire border.

At our upstairs window, we would sit in the twilight hours, not talking much, but just looking out. If lucky, we would see some creatures of the night venturing forth on their quest for food. A fox might trot down the road and over the garden walls to seek an easy chicken-coop; an owl would cry from some dark tree; bats would flitter in the air. There would be many prowling cats. We would shout a cheery "Goodnight" to the man going for his evening pint at the pub and sometimes we witnessed his return! "Goodnights" were exchanged with travellers returning home on a late train.

Our view changed with the seasons of the year. From the gardens in summer, especially after rain, the sweet smell from bean flowers would waft up to us and from sweet-peas glimmering palely on their tall canes. The Bog Meadow would be awash with buttercups, milk-ladies, ragged robins, and we could if we listened intently, hear the cows chewing their cud in the tall grasses.

In the autumn and winter, the river beyond the railway would burst over, flooding the fields on both sides of the line and the Bog Meadow would become a sheet of ice. The boys and girls and some adults would slide on the ice until quite dark and one year much to our delight, a couple danced very beautifully on their skates. The lights of passing trains reflected on the ice so that it appeared two trains were travelling along.

Our main interest sitting at our high seat, was to see the trains

176

going on their journey from London to Birmingham and vice versa. London, a magical city to me . . . Buckingham Palace and the Zoo, and Birmingham . . . a dirty city, the Bull Ring and football matches. We could see the fire aglow in the cabin of the steam engines and the fireman wielding his shovel.

On special evenings my father and I would sit at the window with a great feeling of expectancy. The Royal Train was due to pass through on its way from London to Birmingham; no doubt for their Majesties to grace some function in the Midlands during the next day. I do not recall how we obtained this information but probably my father heard of it on the wireless or from the *Daily Mail* newspaper. We would be at our window early to see the station master, signalmen, and I believe the village policeman go to the station to be on duty at this important time. We would sit in silence with our ears alert to hear the distant approach of the train and then it would steam slowly into view passing the station and draw carefully to a halt. An extremely long train and we would see its bright carriage lights and wonder how many people were needed to attend to the Royal wellbeing. The train would then back slowly past the station again and shunt off down the quiet Adderbury branch line. It would remain there for the night hours so that the King and Queen could rest and be prepared for the journey to Birmingham and their duties the next day.

When morning came, some villagers would walk to the fields bordering the Adderbury line and come back full of stories of glimpses of their Majesties at a window at breakfast time. Their many disbelievers scoffed at their tales, retorting sarcastically "eating their boiled eggs, no doubt, complete with their crowns on"!

In not so peaceful times, my father and I would look out of our window to see in the darkness the munitions trains passing through during the war. These convoys showed no lights because of the blackout and they bore their loads of tanks, armoured cars and guns with just the sound of the engine and wheels in the night. There were hospital trains too and we would imagine them full of wounded soldiers dressed in their distinctive bright blue suits and red ties travelling away from the horrors of the Front back home to safety.'

AFTER THE AXE

'After the Beeching closure of the Cambridge to Kettering railway line, a steel girder collapsed on the bridge over the disused line, after heavy rain and frosts, leaving a gap of 30 ft long by six ft wide and about 30 ft deep. I was the last driver, in a Land Rover, to cross the

177

bridge in the dark! The Denford Ash to Raunds road was closed for several months to vehicular traffic, but a precarious path was made for schoolchildren and their bicycles, otherwise there was a detour of several miles.

Before this collapse of the bridge, the children and I took advantage of climbing up and having a ride on the old steam engine, which helped to dismantle the line and cut it into lengths for disposal. There was a crane which lifted the cut sections of line, each about 10 to 15 ft long, into wagons behind the engine.'

WAR & PEACE

THE FIRST WORLD WAR

Northamptonshire's towns and villages sent their young men to the war in 1914, many of them never to return. For those at home, the war years were a time of hardship and sometimes of actual hunger and shortages, with the sight of guns and soldiers on the county's roads a constant reminder of what fathers, sons and brothers were facing overseas. When news came that it was, at last, over, the church bells, silent for so long, rang out again in joy.

DRIED PEAS AND BLACKBERRIES

'Four of the years whilst I was a child at Long Buckby were war years. Times were very hard, but because we lived in the country a bit of extra food came our way on occasions. When flour was available my mother baked her own bread and she made chocolate using cocoa butter. My brother was born in 1918 and my mother told me that when she was pregnant she was sometimes so hungry that she sucked dried peas.

On sunny September days we were told not to return to school in the afternoon but to go blackberrying. Our harvest was taken to school the next morning and we were paid a halfpenny a pound. Some of the mothers would join the children in order to earn a bit of money. The fruit was used to make jam for the soldiers.'

'During the First World War my Dad wasn't in the army but did some ploughing on the farm at Denford and wore a band with a red crown on to show that he was doing war work. My Uncle Fred did go in the army and he was wounded twice and had to come back to England and work on the farm. Living in the country during the war, food was not too bad. We kept hens and Grandad had pigs. My mother and we children went gleaning, which fed the hens, and we had an allotment where my Dad grew vegetables.'

ESCAPING FROM LONDON

'I was born in the inherited family home at Southwark, South London, in February 1914. During the First World War we were bombed out of a factory where we were sheltering. My brother, seven years older than myself, was badly shocked – so the three of us went for a holiday in Mears Ashby – a small village near Wellingborough, Northampton. The last part of the journey was by carrier's cart – this being the only transport. About three times per week the owner of the cart would travel into Wellingborough, collecting or delivering parcels and goods at a penny a time.

Food was far more plentiful in the village than in London, so we stayed there for ten weeks. My brother went to the village school; just two classes. In the middle of this time the potatoes needed harvesting and everyone just had to help. All the youngest children, myself included, were taken into the first class and my first memories were of sitting in a circle and being taught colours with small coloured balls.

We were then burgled at Southwark, so we had to return to sort things out. In 1918 there was no rationing, and food in London was very, very short. So off we went again to Mears Ashby and were able to get the same cottage. My mother was very capable and having helped many of the villagers with sewing, make-do-and-mend and letter writing, was made very welcome. I then went straight back to school and loved it. Nearly every day, in our spare time, we went "sticking" – this was walking through the fields and woods picking up any type of wood or twigs as paraffin and coal were almost unobtainable. A fire had to be lit even to boil a kettle – can you imagine it now? On our return we missed the spaciousness of the country.'

IN AID OF THE POW FUND

'On 12th October 1918 Higham Ferrers held a Market Day in aid of the Prisoners of War Fund. Sir Henry and Lady Randall performed the opening ceremony on the Market Square. All factories, shops, farmers and clubs gave a donation and an employees' collection and also had a stall or side show. The Mayor, Thomas Patenall, made an appeal for "the 12,000 brave fellows in our County Regiment who . . . while bravely defending us were captured by the enemy and are enduring cruelty, want and untold agony. Twenty-one of these are from our own Borough."

Stalls included china, confectionery, palmistry, flowers and vegetables, boots and shoes, fish and chips and refreshments. A concert was held in the Town Hall at intervals from 4.30 pm, price sixpence and threepence, and the day ended with dancing in the Band Club until 10.30 pm, tickets a shilling. The Market Square was illuminated until 10 pm and the magnificent sum of £741 9 shillings was raised.'

IT'S OVER!

'There was a man at Everdon called Walter Boughton, who had a great voice. When peace was declared, he was out in the fields behind where the council houses now are. He shouted out so that people could hear the news, then someone went and rang the church bells.'

'I was at school in Denford when the First World War broke out and remember the teacher telling us there were some nasty men trying to get here and I was convinced they were going to come up the river. The school at Denford closed during the war and we went to Thrapston to the "Top School". I can remember clearly being there on a Friday afternoon when the war ended – bells started ringing and buzzers were going and we got under our desks, quite frightened and not realising what was going on.'

PEACE CELEBRATIONS AND REMEMBRANCE

'At the end of the First World War my mother and I were living with my grandmother at Little Houghton while my father was fighting in what is now Iran, but was then called Mesopotamia.

I was only six, but I can recall the first Armistice Day quite well. I remember being told that I must be very quiet for two minutes at 11 am, the very first of so many two minute silences. I was told that even the trains stopped that first time.

In my grandmother's house there was a long passage where a row of bells hung, connected to the various rooms. These were real bells with clappers, and Clara, my grandmother's maid whom I loved dearly, had told me that when the war was over she would sweep them with her broom. The bells were far above the head of a six year old and I was very excited when she did so, on that first Armistice Day.

I also remember Peace Day some months later. There were sports on the lawns at Little Houghton House, where a cousin and I won the three-legged race easily, owing to much practice. All the children had commemorative mugs – mine disappeared long ago, but I remember that it was made of rather dingy earthenware with, I think, pictures of the King and Queen.

The war casualties were so terrible that even children had some idea of the tragedy of it all. Happily, my father returned safely.'

'At the Peace Celebrations of 19th July 1919 it was to be expected that cities and towns would include in their celebrations military parades; contemporary reports show that many villages, Stanion among them, celebrated much as they would the successful harvest – a thanksgiving service, food and entertainment. As the report on Stanion put it, "A nice lot of bunting gave quite a festive appearance to the village."

Sports were held on the field behind Mr Clarke's Home Farm (now the flats on the corner of the High Street and Cardigan Road); the ladies beat the men at cricket by eleven runs. The soldiers raced, and both men and women battled in tugs-of-war. This was a year when it rained on the wrong day and the outdoor events had to be held on the following Monday, but the meat tea, for all the villagers, was held on the Saturday. It must have gone on for hours, even allowing for the children having their jelly and playing around Mr Clarke's barn, watching their elders. At least one of the children was watching when a reveller found great difficulty coping with his jelly after all the celebrations.'

A LAND FIT FOR HEROES?

'These hard times in turn produced a tough, close-knit community in Brixworth and the benefits of survival included a kind of friendship less apparent today. Many large families, despite the harsh conditions, never reached the stage of starvation and poverty seen elsewhere. Mr Dickens, for instance, despite the loss of an arm in a quarry accident, could be seen daily on his bicycle with a large bucket of feed for his poultry which he kept on the Creaton Road allotments (he lived at the other end of the village), and his was typical of the fight for survival of many villagers.'

'Harlestone paid dearly in the Great War by losing 20 of its young men. Obviously, the village took a long time to recover from its terrible loss. A financial depression which began in the 1920s, being especially severe in agriculture, did not improve the employment situation as farming products had to take a severe drop in prices, which made farming hardly viable. The estate and farms were unable to take the boys from school as had been the practice for many years, so most began to cycle to town for work. The Duchess of Grafton arranged for soup to be given to children at least two days a week where families were in need. Many were very thankful for it.'

PRIDE AND POVERTY IN THE 1930s

⊖

This account of a child's visit to her grandmother is a poignant reminder of the many people who struggled to keep afloat in the hard times between the wars, and did so with pride and with dignity.

STAYING WITH GRANDMA

'The old green bus rattled along over the tarred and gravelled country roads carrying me away from Kettering. I was eight years old, and for the first time going alone to stay with my widowed grandmother who lived in Twywell. The shiny brown rexine which covered the bus seats smelled peculiar and stuck to my bare legs in the heat. I watched the beckoning, sunlit fields pass by outside and thought of the following days in excited anticipation. At last we arrived, the bus squeaked to a halt, and there was Granny waiting for me at the bus stop. The conductor helped me off the bus with my "luggage" and I gave Grandma the brown paper carrier bag full of groceries, but insisted on carrying my little blue case the short way home myself.

There was no mains electricity in Twywell in the 1930s, or gas either for that matter, but, being a child, the lack of mod. cons. did not concern me at all. It was much more fun to carry a candle up to bed than to merely flick a switch as I did at home. My Grandma had only her widow's pension of ten shillings a week to live on at this time, but the word "poverty" was never heard. It was just called "trying to make ends meet" in those days and people like my grandmother struggled with it silently. In any case, among the village society, cleanliness was rated more highly than means and a woman was judged by the whiteness of her washing, her well-scrubbed doorstep and, indoors, by her immaculate black-leaded range.

The stone cottage to which my grandma had moved after the last of her children had married, was situated in a terrace, tucked away up a yard, about halfway down the main street near the chapel. The rent was two shillings and sixpence a week, a quarter of her income. Each cottage had a nice strip of garden and a path which led to a row of barns along the bottom. These housed the bucket closets and the old coppers for boiling the washing; they were places to store wood

184

and coal and where one would also find the long galvanized baths which had to be carried up to the houses every week for bath night. By the middle of the 1930s, a few people in the village could boast a water closet and perhaps an outside tap, but these luxuries were quite rare and most families were still managing as they had for centuries, fetching water from the pump which stood on a square of cobbles near the chapel. A spring outside The Old Friar served the bottom end of Twywell, its water gushing in a never ending, sparkling stream out of a spout jutting from the old stone wall.

The back door was the only entrance into the cottage and led directly into the stone-flagged kitchen. This was about four feet by eight feet and furnished only by a scrubbed table with a white enamelled bowl on it and a similar pail beneath, carefully covered with a tea towel, containing the drinking water. There was a small disused fireplace over to the right at the narrow end, and shelves set out with pots and pans, pretty biscuit tins and tea-caddies. Pictures crowded the walls, and one in particular I remember very clearly – a very large gilt framed picture of two young women wearing simple white gowns covered by grey cloaks, kneeling in the snow in prayer. The text underneath read "In Thee we trust".

To the left of the entrance door was another which concealed the staircase, a cupboard for storing food, and straight ahead was the door to the living room which was, I suppose, about eleven feet square. Here the casement window was deeply recessed, showing the thickness of the walls and allowing for a little window-seat. Along the window-sill stood a profusion of plants grown from cuttings. My grandmother was a good gardener and clever with house plants which she watered with cold tea! Outside the window the meadow began immediately below and spread out on either side. In spring and summer, it was strewn with wild flowers and kept neat by cows and horses. There was, I remember, a magnificent elm tree growing in the middle of the pasture where the horses sheltered from the heat. The patchwork of hedges and fields stretched out uninterrupted to the skyline over towards the neighbouring village of Cranford. I remember being told that one day when it was very warm and the window was open "Big Charlie", the great white cart horse, came galloping near the houses and, seeing the plants, poked his head through the window and scattered them all to the floor, terrifying Grandma half to death.

The black iron range competed with the window for attention. Here was the heart of the cottage, providing heating and a hob for simmering, an oven for baking, and a trivet for heating flat irons. A kettle always stood on the range, the water in it always warm, so it did not take too long to boil for tea. In the evening it was cosy to sit on the couch, draped with its red crocheted shawl, my feet on the home-made rag rug, watching the hot embers glowing and listening to the plop of a cinder falling through into the ash basket.

The oil lamp stood on the table under a pretty, ornate wall clock, and shed its own warmth across the little room. Grandma would sit near the lamp so she could do her sewing. There was no wireless or gramophone but we always had a lot to talk about, and sometimes she would sing to me in her beautiful contralto voice. All too soon, it would be my bedtime; a candlestick was taken down from the mantelpiece, the candle lit, and by its light I climbed up the stairs.

The two bedrooms were innocent of any floor-covering, the floorboards scrubbed as clean as the kitchen table. There were little fur rugs at the side of the beds which were rather splendid in shining brass and black enamel. These, and all the furniture in the cottage, dated from Grandma's marriage in 1901. The dressing tables and washstands were of light polished oak with white china knobs on the drawers and further tastefully decorated with tiny painted leaves. The wallpaper was striped in a Regency design.

Grandmother did all her own decorating and white-washed the living-room ceiling every year. This was necessary because of the smoke from the fire. She would go to the summer sales in Thrapston and buy four or five rolls of wallpaper for sixpence a roll, pasting it to the wall with flour mixed with water. It required considerable skill as the walls were uneven, the paper very thin, and if the paste got on the face of the paper it left a dirty mark.

There were no arranged outings on these summer holidays. I would accompany Grandma to the post office to collect her pension, after which we would go to a little shop a few doors away. This was one of the few times she revealed she was worried by her plight. She looked at the items on the counter: matches, paraffin, candles, washing soap and half a pound of sugar in a blue bag and lamented that most of her money had gone, and only the sugar was edible.

We would go to the churchyard to trim the grass on my grandfather's grave and arrange fresh flowers. In 1922 he had been killed by a roof fall in the Islip ironstone mines, while carrying out his routine safety inspection, before the men began work. After digging his body from the debris, the miners placed him on a makeshift stretcher. They found his 16 year old son who worked nearby and together they carried him the several miles across the fields. In the late afternoon, the little cortège arrived in Twywell – they laid the stretcher in a washhouse and one of them went up to the house to break the news to my grandmother.

This was the terrible tragedy that changed my grandma's life from one of comparative comfort to a day-to-day struggle for survival.

Three children were still at school, the youngest only five years old. The eldest, who would become my mother, was 18 and away in service. She came home to look after her mother who was ill for some time with the shock of the bereavement. She found a job in a shoe shop in Thrapston and contributed most of the 14 shillings earned to support the family. Less than £100 was awarded in compensation, a shabby amount for a life, even for those days. This Grandma saved, and shared between the three sons when they left home.

My favourite holiday activity was "sticking". We used to walk along the hedgerows, picking up small twigs and their dead branches. I learned how to put my foot on the longer pieces and twist them upwards to break them into neat manageable lengths. We would bundle the sticks up and bring them home to use for firelighting. Sometimes we would find larger pieces of wood if any trees were being felled. That would be a red-letter day because a log could be used to eke out the bag of coal which cost half a week's money. Another bonus would be the mushrooms which could be found in numbers where the horses grazed. Even an egg or two might be discovered in the hedgebottom, laid by some straying hen. As it could not be known how long ago this had occurred, the eggs were carefully cracked into a cup first. If all was well, a pan was soon set sizzling over the fire for our well earned tea.

Food was always scarce, but Grandma grew potatoes in her garden, a row or two of peas and carrots. There were gooseberry bushes and an old apple tree. These helped out in the summer months, but it is certain that the winter was a time for tea-kettle broth, bubble and squeak and very little meat.

When the last day of the holiday came, preparations began for my parents' arrival. The fire was well stoked and the damper adjusted so the oven would heat up to do some baking. As it became hotter and hotter in the living room, Grandma looked doubtfully at the jelly she had made; even the kitchen was too warm to allow it to set. It was deemed necessary to get help from the little village shop opposite The Old Friar. This specialised in home-made ice cream during the summer months and the shopkeeper was used to people asking for ice to pack around trifles!

And so the two o'clock bus came, bringing my parents. They chatted, we had tea and the jelly was nearly set! After the washing-up was done, we walked once again across the beloved fields. I collected more flowers and watched daddy-long-legs dance in pools of sunlight. As it grew dusk, we returned slowly to the cottage, and made ready to catch the old green bus back to Kettering.

By the middle of the 1940s, the ironstone pits had encroached to the very edge of "Grandmother's" field. It was unsafe because of the blasting and the animals had to be removed. Thistles took over and, for many years, it became almost a wasteland. By the early 1950s, water and electricity were laid on and many cottages, including my grandmother's, were demolished. The pump was dismantled. For some years, the spring outside The Old Friar continued to flow. People came in their cars from the towns to fill bottles with the water to take home! But now, even that is no longer to be seen and the wall has been rebuilt.'

THE SECOND WORLD WAR

When war came once again, Northamptonshire this time faced bombing and sudden death on its own streets. Local people did their bit, ploughing or digging up land for food production and welcoming the many soldiers stationed at nearby bases. Prisoners of war, German and Italian, became a common sight working on the land.

GROWING FOR VICTORY

'During the Second World War fields that had always been grass had to be ploughed up to grow corn. Gone for ever were the cowslips and the little purple and pale mauve orchids that grew in profusion with the other wild flowers.

Tractors replaced the horses and to help with the extra work four land girls were allocated to our farm. One left after a while as· she did not enjoy good health and was not strong enough for the work. The other three were splendid girls who had worked in factories but quickly adjusted to the long hours and hard, often heavy work. They stayed until after the war and admitted years afterwards that they were some of the happiest days of their lives.

Every farmer had to grow a quota of potatoes and the school children were given a week's holiday in October to help harvest them. If the weather was bad the holiday was extended for a few days.

Everyone was "growing for victory", people grew vegetables instead of flowers and allotments were in great demand. Some people who had never had a spade in their hands took a piece of allotment and with advice and help from the "old hands" were very proud of their produce.

Housewives purchased Kilner jars and bottled everything they could in the way of fruit and vegetables and the children were sent out to pick blackberries. Sometimes one could get a little preserving sugar to make jam.

School dinners were introduced at this time as the women were all working, replacing the men who were in the forces and in munition factories.'

WELCOMING THE FIGHTING MEN

'War brought many new faces to Litchborough. First came the 13th Hussar Regiment who lived in the WI room and the Baptist schoolroom, and parked their tanks up on the Maidford Road at the top of Mell's Close. When they left their place was taken by prisoners of war.'

'In 1939 the railway marshalling yards at Woodford became even busier than usual, carrying freight for the war effort to all parts of Britain. Troop trains regularly passed through the station and we teenagers would congregate on the platform to see them pass and wave them on their way. In 1942 land girls, soldiers and airmen came to the village, the airmen being stationed at the newly built RAF station at Chipping Warden and the land girls and soldiers (4/7th Dragoon Guards) based in the village. The land girls were housed in a new hostel on the Byfield Road, now Hawkins Shoe Factory, and the soldiers were in billets in different parts of the village. They all mingled with the villagers, many of them marrying local lads and lasses.'

'The RAMC camped in Gas Lane, Easton (now Park Road) and later the Tank Corps parked their tanks behind the church, unofficially known as Tank Lane. Then the Polish paratroopers arrived prior to the Arnhem landing. The officers all stayed at Easton House, which had been requisitioned for the purpose. Dances at one shilling and sixpence, concerts and parties took place regularly at the Church Army hut, with troops and locals joining in the events. Plays and choral music were regular features.'

'Villagers at Greens Norton were surprised one morning to find tanks parked on the village green; they belonged to Canadian troops taking part in manoeuvres and the soldiers were camping in Kingthorn

Wood. There was also a prisoner of war camp in the village, firstly Italian prisoners and then Germans. The men were employed on local farms.'

'Grendon helped the war effort by collecting iron, aluminium, newspaper and cardboard for recycling. The Home Guard met weekly and mounted firewatchers on the church tower. Many old farm implements were stacked at road junctions to be used to block the roads if the Germans invaded. Camouflage nets were made by village women at nearby Wollaston, with transport supplied by one of the farmers' wives with their meagre petrol allowance. An Italian prisoner of war camp was established on the outskirts of the village and the men helped on local farms.

Grendon Hall was used by the forces as a training centre and during the latter part of the war by the Free French force to train members to be dropped to help the Maquis in occupied France. During that time only French was spoken at the Hall in order to deter and confuse anyone not connected with the work.'

'There was a memorable occasion at Benefield when the Americans stationed nearby gave a party in an aircraft hangar and Glenn Miller, the danceband leader, played for them.'

'Arthingworth was mainly used for troop retraining in the early years of the war and up to 1,000 men were stationed in the village at any one time. They arrived in convoys or marched in on foot from Kelmarsh station. Much of the training was concerned with the testing and use of tanks and there was a firing range westwards from Hall Field across the river. A curfew was enforced while training was in progress, and the children were also forbidden to go out on Sunday afternoons, when lorryloads of girls were brought from Derby to entertain the American troops.

Men from the USAAF station at Harrington used the Bull's Head pub in Arthingworth regularly and any black troops had to leave the pub if white troops arrived.

Various regiments were stationed in Arthingworth, including the Gloucesters and the King's Dragoon Guards. A Gurkha regiment kept its own sheep in Hall Farm and its shepherd was responsible for catching a sheep and slaughtering it to feed the men.

On one occasion, Field Marshall Montgomery came in his famous Rolls Royce.

Bill Voce, the former England fast bowler, was stationed at the Hall for a time and, during his stay, cricket matches were played between a team from his Guards Regiment and an Arthingworth eleven.'

BOMBS AND AIR RAIDS

'Many gardens were dug and vegetables planted, and people kept hens and pigs. Iron railings round houses and in the churchyard were taken for munitions. The young people of Braybrooke went into the services, others worked in the Land Army or in Market Harborough factories where they made parachutes, screws and parts for aeroplanes. Desborough airfield situated to the north-east was manned by British personnel. To the south Harrington airfield was manned by Americans. They had Flying Fortress bombers which made daytime raids. Many times I saw planes climb into the sky and circle until the formation was ready to set off on its long journey. Between the aerodrome and Braybrooke there was 223 Maintenance Unit. This was the bomb dump to supply the planes. Many 500 lb bombs were stacked along the roadsides, and at intervals prefabricated huts full of detonators. There were manned sentry boxes on the approach roads and farmers needed passes to get to their fields.

At night we heard the drone of Wellington and Handley Page Hampden bombers going on night raids. On moonlight nights we used to watch the dark shapes going across the sky. I remember seeing the glow in the west when Coventry was bombed. We sheltered under the table. The village Home Guard, assisted by two Special Constables, patrolled the railway line and rested in the platelayers hut. We had a stick of five bombs parallel to the line but no damage was done. The next morning the farm worker and his family in the nearby cottage moved back to Wales. One night an Avro Anson crashed in a spinney and a training Wellington bomber landed in a field.'

'At Irchester the Primitive Methodist chapel in Farndish Road was bombed in May 1940. Several houses on both sides of the road were damaged and nine people were killed.'

'On 15th November 1940 Evenley had a night to remember. It was just after the Blitz on Coventry when Evenley had a narrow escape. There was a dance at the hall and just after everyone had returned home a string of bombs were dropped from the Mixbury Road to the A43. One bomb fell in a garden near the school, another in a field where nine cows were killed and 15 injured. Damage to property was slight, just cracked windows and ceilings and some tiles shaken off the roof.'

'My friend and I were walking towards Long Street in Hartwell to

191

meet some local "fellas" when we heard a whistling noise. We both lay down in the middle of the road because a plane was overhead. Then there was a terrific bang – the bomb had fallen near Hartwell Park. Suddenly a lorry owned by Whatton's woodyard came along and one of the men who belonged to the Local Defence Volunteers asked "Where did it fall?" All I could manage to say was "Over there!".'

'During the war a plane carrying Canadian airmen crashed in Yardley Gobion and residents, forming a chain, worked through the night passing water buckets to help firemen fight the blaze. There is a plaque in the village church commemorating the young men who died in the crash.'

'At the bottom of our garden Father had erected the Anderson shelter we had been issued with. Mother made this as homely as possible and even put up a curtain to conceal the tin bucket in the corner . . . when nature made it essential that this was used everyone sang very loudly.
    My job in the event of an air raid was to collect the family dog, a harmless friendly mongrel, and put on his muzzle. He thought the whole idea great fun and better than spending the night in his lonely kennel.'

'The first flying bomb or Doodlebug to fall in Northamptonshire landed in the Manor House orchard, opposite Creaton church. No one, thankfully, was killed or injured, but there was structural damage to buildings, windows were blasted out and doors set askew. One poor man was blown out of his bath! It seems Lord Haw Haw later said on the radio that "it was meant for Creaton as Northampton would *never* be a target – German students had been treated well in the town pre-war"!'

'A Doodlebug dropped across the meadows near Millers Farm at Woodford one Christmas Eve, making my young son think that Father Christmas had come.'

GROWING UP IN WARTIME

'I was the first in the family to go to Wellingborough High School, which I loved. There were almost equal numbers of scholarship and fee paying girls. New friends were wealthier, they had cars and telephones. Father worked in a shoe factory and used a bicycle to get there.

In 1939 I passed my School Certificate, with Matriculation. Later in August, Mother took my sister to Felixstowe, as we had not had our usual fortnight's holiday, leaving me to look after Father. That week the evacuation of children from built up areas began; rumours reached us of the filthy children, who all wet the bed! Mother had offered to take two small boys in our house, to balance two girls. When they came to our road, we were allocated two sixth formers from Walthamstow High School, both 18 and young women. Several girls schools were sent to Kettering, too many to accommodate, so our girls and the rest of their school were sent to Wellingborough within a week. We shared our school with Dame Alice Owen's High School from Islington. We were rather nonplussed by these large girls, Father and I decided he would sleep in my sister's single bed while the girls shared the parental double bed.

One girl was a pianist, a joy to Father who loved singing. The night war broke out, we had a sing-song in the front room, and were interrupted by the unexpected return of mother and my sister. Mum was horrified to see light streaming from the unblacked windows. Mother had blacked out only the living room, it had not occurred to me to do anything towards a blackout.

When we returned to school, everything had changed. We started to learn new subjects, a real challenge. There was war fever in the air, we all felt that we should do something to help the war effort, Our much loved carol service, where we all wore "a plain white dress" and white stockings did not take its traditional form. Also, Father told me that he felt unable to keep me another two years.

Most of my friends had left school and at New Year I joined one in the Food Office. This was housed in the museum, next to the library, and had little equipment. Books and forms in cardboard boxes went on top of the glass cases of exhibits. Our job was to write ration books for each person in the borough, and also permits for local shops to purchase food. When rationing began, we had to count all the coupons brought in by the shopkeepers. Also, we had to keep the register up to date and change the address of those who moved in or within our district. Some were entitled to extra rations, pregnant women for example, and beekeepers had sugar to feed their bees. I remember the night Coventry was bombed, we were working late (no overtime pay – my wages were 17 shillings weekly). We wrote away to the ominous drone of wave after wave of enemy bombers overhead.

At first we also dealt with milk rationing, complicated because of the different categories of those entitled to extra rations, such as children, pregnant women, and various people with medical conditions. Later the Milk Office was set up in a building nearby.

During the last war, everyone on the home front did their bit for the war effort. Here the ladies of Great Haughton are preserving fruit.

As soon as the war began, the indoor baths were covered over, and we had only the outdoor pool, so that curtailed our swimming. The baths became a First Aid Post, and my father did duties there, as he had experience of ambulance work. Mother kept hens and rabbits during the war, so we noticed no real restrictions on food. As a grand gesture, I gave up sugar in tea and found it much more palatable.

In 1941 I went to Leicester Royal Infirmary to train as a nurse. Clothes rationing began that year, but we student nurses were able to order anything we liked from the lengthy catalogue from a Manchester warehouse, from which we ordered our uniforms, so we laid in stocks of plain underwear and black shoes and stockings, as well as pyjamas and dressing gowns.'

THE WI HELPS OUT

'After Dunkirk the army arrived and stayed under canvas in the field near Grafton Underwood church. The WI organised a canteen in the village hall where the troops could go and have tea and sandwiches, write letters and play cards and darts. The WI ladies became members of the WVS through this. The army stayed about two months and then were shipped off to the Middle East, and sadly many of them were killed out there. One or two of the soldiers were married while here and spent their honeymoon in the cottages. The aerodrome was built by Wimpey, a lot of the construction workers being Irish or gipsies. The RAF had it to start with and the villagers had the opportunity to go to the ENSA concerts if they wished. When the Americans arrived some of the girls from the village worked in the Red Cross and NAAFI.

The WI helped a lot with the war effort, sometimes collecting nettles, or rose hips for syrup. They would be sent a canning machine when tomatoes, pears and plums were ready and members spent a day at the village hall canning their produce.'

PRISONERS OF WAR

'Between Briggs Lodge and Denford village, where a local butcher now fattens bullocks, are the remains of a wartime German prisoner of war camp. The men worked on local farms and one of these men who worked on our farm has twice been back to the UK with his family and visited us and his old hut.'

Little Addington's Prisoner of War Camp. The Italian P.O.W.s worked under supervision on nearby farms where their cheeriness and singing won them many friends.

195

'There was a prisoner of war camp situated a mile down the road from us at East Farndon and sometimes these Italian, and later German, prisoners would walk in the fields. One day my friend and I were playing with our dolls when a young man sat down with us and started to show us photographs of his family. How different from today.'

'Little Addington had a prisoner of war camp which housed Italians, distinctive in their brown uniforms. They were responsible for building a sewer through the village and also helped in the fields. The leader of the camp was Eddie Sherwood who was a very keen gardener and the camp was one in which the prisoners could take just pride.'

'There was a POW camp at Wakefield near Potterspury. They were Italians and could be heard singing when they left the camp and drove down through Deanshanger to work.'

STRANGERS IN OUR MIDST

In 1939 the first evacuees began leaving the cities. Some of these poor little migrants stayed only a short time, preferring London with all its dangers to the unknown of the countryside, and some brought enormous problems to the families and organisations that took them in. Others never looked back, finding in Northamptonshire a quality of life which drew them back as adults.

FACING THE PROBLEMS

'Some years after the end of the war my mother received a document from the Queen thanking her for taking in evacuees. As an only child I welcomed the company of these strangers who had a funny way of speaking and no knowledge of the countryside. They had lived all their lives in an East End flat and their mother had, it seemed, always gone out to work. At the weekends she had done all the family washing in the basement, never hanging anything out in the fresh air to dry, no wonder their underclothing was such a dull grey colour.

But if I enjoyed the extension to my family my mother certainly did not. Imagine a very houseproud person who had her life well organised, with one child (who had stories tell) been housetrained and out of nappies at ten months, taking on two energetic, rowdy, undisciplined youngsters. We had a brother and sister from what was a very large family, the rest were housed close by.

Nowadays we understand stress and its effects but from the start Mother had to cope with bed wetting, which she had not been prepared for so had not put in any waterproofs. Wally the Boy came home from school regularly with an ominous 'Pants Full' ducky waddle and from an eight year old boy this was no joke. Mother had to clean up the mess and then, without the modern aids we take for granted, hand wash the trousers and pants ready for the next day. These children did not have a very extensive wardrobe so drying clothes round the living room fire (the only fire in the house) was a permanent feature and that unmistakable odour of soap and urine could never be disguised.

Sadly our evacuees did not stay with us as long as I would have liked; they preferred the life (or maybe death) in London to sleepy old Northampton.'

'In 1942, during a bombing raid, my home was destroyed and to escape the horror of all that destruction it was a relief to move to Great Houghton. During the war years the village became a different place. There were many evacuees from London, filling up homes as well as the small school at Little Houghton, the overspill having to have lessons in that village's parish hall. Great Houghton had not had a school for many years and so it meant we had to walk between the villages four times a day – no school dinners in those days! All food, of course, was rationed to a bare minimum and housewives became experts in making a little go as far as possible. It was amazing how fit and well we all seemed to be on such a meagre diet, however, it was probably a little easier in the country with the opportunity to grow some fruit and vegetables, and keep a few hens.

During these difficult years, the family at the Hall moved out leaving it free to be used as a hostel for children with special problems who could not be billeted in private homes. This provided employment for several village ladies as cooks, nurses, laundry workers and seamstresses etc. I well remember one child arriving already suffering from a particularly virulent form of ringworm which quickly spread from child to child at the hostel. This resulted in all having to have their heads shaved before undergoing hospital

I WISH TO MARK, BY THIS PERSONAL MESSAGE, my appreciation of the service you have rendered to your Country in 1939.

In the early days of the War you opened your door to strangers who were in need of shelter, & offered to share your home with them.

I know that to this unselfish task you have sacrificed much of your own comfort, & that it could not have been achieved without the loyal co-operation of all in your household.

By your sympathy you have earned the gratitude of those to whom you have shown hospitality, & by your readiness to serve you have helped the State in a work of great value.

Elizabeth R

Many children were evacuated from London to Northamptonshire to mixed reactions for both hosts and visitors. Those who had evacuees billeted on them received this message of thanks later by the young Queen Elizabeth.

electrical treatment. Cotton mob caps were made for each child to wear, boys and girls alike, but the happy conclusion was that most of the children's hair grew back with attractive waves and curls.'

LIFE WITH UNCLE CHARLIE

'When I first arrived in Barton Seagrave I had no idea where it was. All I knew was that I wanted to go home. It was a grey damp day – 1st September 1939. Yes, I was one of those in the crocodile of London children being evacuated – "Vacs" as we were known. After bus journeys, a train journey and lots of tears, my sister and I found ourselves in a strange room with strange ladies. We sat on the steps of Barton Seagrave school on Barton Hill waiting to be given a home. I remember a lady asking me "Would you like to come and live with me?"

"No!" I replied.

"I'll take you for a holiday in my caravan."

"No." (What was a caravan?)

She talked in such a funny voice. I now know it was perfectly spoken English. It was Mrs Kirby who was the wife of Exauad Kirby, Head of the English Department of Kettering Grammar School. He taught, and was the mentor, of H.E. Bates.

A teacher, who had travelled with us from London came and said "Come along, you are going to live with this gentleman and his wife"'. They were to become our beloved Uncle Charlie and Auntie Maude. They lived just above the school in a row of four stone cottages. Our cottage used to be the home of the head gardener at Barton Hall, the home of Lord Hood. Uncle Charlie was Barton's blacksmith – what stories he had to tell.

Our first outing with Uncle Charlie was on Sunday morning 3rd September 1939 to go down to the village shop to buy some "peps" (sweets) and to show us off to his niece who lived in one of Barton's then eight council houses. It was while there, I remember hearing war declared.

To us, as children, Barton was divided into three areas – The Village, Barton Hill and Warkton Lane. Warkton Lane was where all the rich people lived, including the bosses of Stewarts & Lloyds works at Corby, doctors and Dorothy Whipple the author. They all had cars. It was always the hope that as we walked for the bus to take us to Kettering, someone would give us a lift. I suppose it must be said that we who lived on the hill rather looked down on the village folk, while they called us "them snobs on the hill".

After being pushed from school to school in Kettering – Uncle Charlie who was a past Governor of Barton Seagrave school, used his charm which he had in abundance, to get my sister and me into the school on the hill. It was one large room which divided the infants from the juniors with a curtain. At the juniors' end was a big open fire with an enormous guard around. We used to put our half pint of milk near the fire to warm for breaktime.

The local children gave us such a hard time. They really resented us as we were the only two London children and most of them were born in Barton. I never could spell and on my first morning while doing a composition, I asked my partner (sharing one of those desks that the top didn't lift up – so the books were always falling on the floor) "How do you spell apple?". Immediately, her hand went up, "Please Miss, this London girl can't spell apple". We became friends later.

I remember how thrilled I was to be called out, after the register, to write in chalk on a little blackboard, how many children there were in school – 32 was the highest number I remember writing.

We settled down very well, until we had a big set-back. One morning, near Christmas, two American soldiers walked into the classroom. There is always a buzz isn't there, when a different face is seen in a classroom. Miss Hill, with a tap of her cane (which she used) brought the school to order. Then one of the soldiers spoke. He said "We understand there are two London evacuees here. Would they come out to the front." So my sister who was an infant stood up. The soldier said "We would like to give you these dolls as a present from the soldiers based at Grafton Underwood Station". I think our friendships dropped to zero for a little while after that!

The rector in 1939 was a wonderful gentleman, the Rev Harold Curtis. He was tall with a white walrus moustache. He was unmarried. He loved children. I can remember going to the rectory on Christmas Eve to take a present to him from Auntie Maude (the rectory wasn't as today where you just walk in, it was a great honour to be invited in). The maid showed us in and in the hall a huge fire was blazing. I'd never seen such a big fireplace. We waited, it seemed, for ages, then Rev Curtis came and chatted, and patted our heads and gave us sixpence each which when pocket money was two pence a week, seemed a lot of money. When he died, only close friends and all the children from Barton Seagrave went to his funeral. I can still vividly feel the sadness at school.

May Day, of course, is a unique tradition of village life. For some reason May Day celebrations ceased during wartime. One day a parcel arrived. My aunt had made my sister and me two lovely dolls. One was a sailor, the other a Red Cross nurse. Auntie Maude came up with an idea and said we could have our own May Day, so we dressed a garland made of two hoops and in the middle we put the·Red Cross doll. My sister was May Queen. She had a real piece of lace curtain for her veil and real flowers for her headdress. My friend and I were her attendants. Another friend carried the collecting box. We were so excited. It dawned a bitter cold day but we utterly refused to wear coats over a "first-time-on" summer dress. House to house we collected – everyone was most impressed. I can remember the letter arriving from the Red Cross thanking us. It seemed most important. I think we were put to bed with hot water bottles to get us warm, no hot bath to jump into!'

THE SWEETNESS OF VILLAGE LIFE

'My early life was spent in East London, the daughter of a railwayman, one of two children; not well off but happy in the only way of life we knew.

In 1940 we had the first real air raids and they were every bit as bad as they appear in newsreels. Father had dug out and installed an Anderson shelter where we spent quite a few hours, hoping the next bomb would not hit our house, and constantly worrying about our cat who would not take cover with the rest of us unless we caught him in time. At the end of about two weeks my mother decided we children must be sent to a safer place and registered our names with the relevant authorities.

Thus it was that my six year old brother and I found ourselves on a train each with a luggage label attached, carrying gas masks, a small suitcase and a shopping bag, heading we knew not where. It was September, days of mellow warmth, blackout at night. All place names had been painted out or removed because of the expected invasion by enemy forces. We were told to take food for the journey – sandwiches, cake, biscuits, nuts and raisins, and fruit, but no drinks. In 1940 there were no canned drinks and bottles would have been dangerous.

It was a nightmare journey changing from coach to train to buses, arriving at a strange place. Following a roll call, we were marched through the village and taken in by people who were able to do so, mostly in twos.

My brother and I were accepted by a kind and lovely lady, who lived with her brother and their mother. We were cared for so well, washed, fed and put together in a large, white feather bed. Left alone we wept. A heavy plane flew over and we instinctively cowered, but finally we slept as only children can.

The next morning I asked "Please can you tell me where we are? I promised to write to my Mummy." We were in Weedon, Northamptonshire.

I shall always remember the sweetness of village life as it was then. The peace and quiet, the soft air, the soft water, milk with cream halfway down the bottle. The farm animals, beautiful stately cows who walked through the village street to the milking sheds. Pigs living in an enclosure at the top of the village, chickens running about, and golden waving wheat almost as tall as my brother.

Our kind foster parents kept hens and we had fresh vegetables from the garden. They also kept bees and made wonderful honey. The hives stood in the orchard where the trees were laden with damsons. We settled down quite well, although I found the village school something of a come down. With so many extra pupils it must have been difficult for everyone.

One Sunday afternoon I went for a walk with my kind lady leaving my brother helping with the bees. To our astonishment we met my mother, on the point of collapse, having walked a long way round to reach the village from our little railway station, long since vanished. My father had packed her off to join her children, and without road signs she had completely lost her way. She soon recovered and was found a billet across the road. Father came down for a weekend visit and for a while we were happy again. It was not to last.

The bombs fell on Coventry, relatives descended on my kind lady, and my brother and I had to move on. This time we stayed with one of the village postmen and his wife, who also boarded two lady schoolteachers and provided lunch for two businessmen who worked locally. Their son, who was in the army, came home on leave bringing with him a girlfriend. The three bedroom council house was bursting at the seams, my brother caught measles and after that we moved again!

This time we were split up; I went to stay at the local newsagent's, owned by a young couple with two small children, while my brother went to a house where he was one of eight boys – two of their own, one thought to be a grandchild although we were never sure, and five evacuees. It was chaos, they all caught impetigo, and the five moved on. Mother was getting a bit desperate. She had also moved twice, the first time because a new baby was due and the second because the house was so overcrowded she could never manage to get a bath. My brother in his fourth billet was giving trouble and had to move yet again, I was being used as an unpaid nanny, and Father had had enough and went to see the Billeting Officer in charge, who requisitioned a cottage for Mother to rent, so that we did not have to return to the war zone. It was still only 1941.

My father in London worked a twelve hour day, firewatching at night. On alternate weekends he worked overtime and in between came to Weedon where he caught up on his sleep.

The cottage was infested with black beetles, had no back door and the only tap was outside at the back so that both clean and used water had to be passed through the window in buckets. Even so we were happy to be all together in our cottage if only we had not been worried that Father might not survive the air raids. That was the only period in her life that Mother smoked cigarettes.

Much more could be said about our sojourn in Weedon, but in July 1945 we returned to London. It was battle weary and we had years of shortages to face, but our little house still stood.

I never gave up returning to Weedon. The friend I made at school here and whose mother took in my mother at one stage, is still my close friend today. I was bridesmaid at her wedding and godmother to her first daughter. My own son spent many happy school holidays in Weedon, and when my husband was no longer with us we eventually came back to live here. For me it was a homecoming and I have never missed the city life.'

DAD'S ARMY

The Home Guard, immortalised to later generations as 'Dad's Army', has had to live down an enormous number of stories told at their expense – many of them absolutely true! What would England have done without them, though, as night after night they stood guard against the possibility of facing an invading German army.

THE VALIANT VOLUNTEERS

'In Harrington, about 25 valiant volunteers of all ages and occupations, armed with civilian gas masks, shotguns, sticks, wearing an LDV armband and with two rifles between them, prepared to capture any Nazi parachute invaders. If there was an enemy landing, the church bell was to be rung, all available men were to report immediately or, if in isolated lodges, await instructions. Sometimes haymaking, calving, milking or vital agricultural work caused a delay! If it was not a school day, I was often conscripted to deliver messages on my bike but, fortunately, the odd alert turned out to be a barrage balloon which had broken loose and I never had to confront the enemy singlehanded! Standing orders were "No Panic" and "No gossip with general public on duties, careless talk costs lives."

After three months, the uniforms arrived, but no boots yet. I recall a hilarious evening in our kitchen when my mother was co-opted to help take measurements. Some sizes were not available in the stores and needed a special order – sometimes a needle and thread were essential.

Nightly, two guard patrols manned the highest point at Wharf Lodge Farm. One defaulter, severely reprimanded, had tossed up whether to turn out on a bad night and tails had won to absolve him from duty! Two young volunteers, having been out courting late the previous night, lay slumbering under some straw when a visiting inspection officer reported nobody on duty. Another time, they suspected an enemy approaching and, issuing the challenge "Halt, who goes there?", terrified two local girls returning in the early hours. The section commander, checking patrols, heard sinister rustlings and coughs and, at the third challenge, prepared to fire – as an inquisitive bullock peered over the hedge.

Following the delivery of sufficient rifles, ammunition and equipment, more concentrated training was needed – target practice, field manoeuvres, mock battles with neighbouring villages (strategic points often The Bull's Head or Tollemache Arms), bayonet practice, use of hand grenades and Molotov cocktails, camouflage, and first aid lessons by the rector's wife.

What comradeship and fun there was and great community spirit until the stand down in December 1944. In those dark days, when Britain's freedom was threatened by enemy invasion, we were so thankful for the Home Guard, knowing that we could sleep safely in our beds and, if danger came, Dad's Army, now a proficient fighting force, would defend us with courage.'

'Denford had its own flourishing Home Guard, formerly called the Local Defence Volunteers. From where the railway bridge used to be near their post at Denford Ash, on a clear night they could see the searchlights and flash of the bombs falling on London.'

'Deanshanger had its Dad's Army. I remember one putting on his gasmask and trying to blow a whistle. Another time when marching round the village the order was given 'to "Left wheel" and they marched into the butcher's shop.'

'There was a Home Guard unit with a hut near Stowe Lodge. One man was given a rifle covered in grease, which was removed by pouring boiling water through it. The Home Guard was quite strong because many men in Stowe were exempt from call-up if they were over 25 and engaged in agricultural work. General Knapp (retired) was in overall charge.'

'The Home Guard at Duston was formed from the older men of the village. They had to climb tall towers and spend their night watches in pairs or fours up there, to look out for and report air raiders on their field phone. One night a stick of five bombs was dropped by a German plane. It fell across the overhead telephone and electricity wires on the line of pylons which stood across the fields at the back of the village farmyards. The senior Home Guard, Mr Hobly, who arrived in the field with his men and their buckets and syringe pumps, decided to demonstrate how to put the fire out. He put his foot in the bucket and started to pump the water out. However, unknown to him, the bomb had cut the overhead electric wire and it had fallen where he was working in the dark – he was electrocuted and was the first war casualty in our village.'

ON MANOEUVRES

'Much entertainment was provided for residents when the mature gentlemen of Great Houghton village formed a company of the Home Guard. They practised hard with broom handles and stirrup pumps and also how far they could throw a mock hand grenade. The best fun of all was when the Army "proper" came to engage them in manoeuvres. These took place in and around the village itself, so a trail of onlookers followed either to cheer the Home Guard on or to point out a hiding place of a sniper, but despite all this "help" the Army were the victors. The only time I remember the Home Guard being called out was when the RAF plane crashed in the centre of Northampton. One of the crew had been spotted bailing out just below the village near the river Nene as the plane limped, on fire, towards the town. The identity of the plane was not known and, of course, it could have been a German bomber, and so several Home Guardsmen went off to "capture" the parachutist, who was brought to one of the houses and given tea and sympathy.
   There were several prisoners-of-war brought in to help on the farms but the only one I can remember was an Italian whom everyone called "Joe", and who stayed on at Lime Farm after the war had ended and never did go back to Italy. He didn't talk much but had a big grin from ear to ear showing his large browny/green teeth.'

The church tower at Moulton was the scene of manoeuvres by the Home Guard which turned out to have hilarious consequences in the 'Dad's Army' tradition.

'Sunday manoeuvres were being held between the Moulton and Overstone platoons and Bob, being a churchman, was stationed on top of the church tower as lookout and instructed by his sergeant to keep well down out of sight and to scan with his fieldglasses the hedgerows to the north east, where movement had already been noted.

Bob duly watched the men crawling (and cursing) through the brambles, well aware that he was seeing his own mates, several of whom he could name. Visited by the sergeant he ventured to suggest that an attack might well come from the south east. Against orders he had peered in this direction and detected unknown men crawling through the hedge in Crowfield. Authority would have none of it and Bob was again left to his own devices for a long time. The enemy crept nearer until at last Bob could bear it no longer. Men were well on the way towards the village and he hurriedly carried out his written orders: he wrote a message describing the coming attack, wrapped it round a smooth pebble, tied it with string and tossed it down to his runner below who was to convey it to HQ in the nearby Artichoke Inn. Sadly the string slipped, the paper fluttered away pursued by the agitated runner, and by the time that it had been retrieved and delivered the enemy had emerged into the High Street, crossed the road, dashed through the yard of the Working Men's Club and seized the Moulton HQ.

Moulton was vanquished and the men, now best of friends, went in for a friendly drink. "What about me?" shouted Bob, still marooned on the tower. The reply was devastating. "You're dead and the church destroyed," he was told, "come on and have a pint."

One of our members saw this incident from a different angle. She still lives right up against Crowfield and remembers seeing the Overstone men creeping down the hedgerow among the nettles and brambles intent on surprise attack. Her parents owned a large and bumbling dog who saw them too and rushed over the wall intent on defending his territory – worrying the Sunday soldiers. It was his noisy attentions which drove them out of cover and into their frantic rush over the street and on to a glorious victory at the Artichoke HQ. Bruce the airdale inadvertently sided with the enemy and became an Overstone collaborater.'

OBSERVER CORPS

'There was an Observer Corps post outside Easton on the Hill. This was manned by a few locals who were too old for active service. They did a good job, being responsible for quite a few enemy aircraft being hit.

At the outset of war the men had to provide their own binoculars and warm clothing. The plotting device was in a field surrounded by sandbags, which the men would shelter behind on cold nights. Later a hut was provided, and the instrument properly set up. There was also warm clothing for the men – an RAF overcoat and a black beret.'

THE LAND ARMY GIRLS

⟶

Work on the land was a welcome alternative to the services for many women, and they entered into what was a hard and demanding job with energy and resource. Initial suspicion on the part of local farmers usually turned to acceptance and the Land Army girls were an essential part of the fight to keep Britain fed as imported food gradually disappeared from the table.

THE FIRST COURSE

'The first Land Army course was held at Moulton Agricultural Institute in early 1940. Four students took a week's tuition. One was a newly recruited Land Army girl, one the daughter of a county newspaper editor, one a horticultural tutor, and one a girl who wanted to make home-made butter – the family had a house cow! So they milked cows and did gardening and general farm duties, including the care of pigs. We never met again afterwards.'

THE DAY I JOINED UP

'The uniform inspired me!' The girl who lived opposite in Birmingham had joined, and she looked great. I wanted to be a Wren, but they had too many – so it had to be the Land Army, from the busy Midlands to Southwick via Northampton, where we met and were greeted in 1941. We were then transported to various hostels around the county, when eventually two of us were "dropped off" at Southwick. The forewoman thought it a good idea if we got "stuck in" straightaway, and marched us a mile along the road to a field where they were potato picking. We must have looked a sight – new uniforms complete with hat and nice clean shoes – no wonder the lads giggled at us for the rest of the afternoon. That was the first of our experiences!

On the whole the county people, farmers, labourers and lads, treated us kindly, but there were some who saw us as a threat to their menfolk, and so were not so kind. We took a lot of teasing and were given some rotten jobs. I was told to feed the bull one day, so fearlessly went into his yard, where he was supposed to be tied, only to find we were eye to eye! (Much laughter in the background from the lads needless to say.) The worst job for my conscience was when the dear old billy goat died, and the farmer's 15 year old son and I were destined to bury same. We duly dug the grave, and dragged Billy towards it, only to find we had forgotten about the horns, they wouldn't go in, so Jim thought if he jumped on it, it might help – needless to say, all spare wind blasted forth in an enormous bellow, and I did a four minute mile down the stack-yard!

We went from farm to farm, always three or four of us, helping through all the seasons, and we worked as hard and as long as the men. We learnt to milk, feed calves, plough, harrow, and all the jobs connected with the harvest. We watched the excitement of the rabbit shoot at the end of corn cutting – the rabbits were needed food in those days. We sat under hedges, and at the top of stacks we had helped to build, to have our cheese and piccalilli sandwiches at the lunch break, and if we had some good mates, we had a swig of their cold tea, and my, it was good . . . We got hot and sticky, we got really frozen picking up sugar beet, and dreaded the threshing days, especially barley, it got into every article of clothing. We used to spend the time praying that the thresher belt would break, so we could have a break, sometimes our prayers were answered. Then eventually we had bicycles so we could get back to the hostel much quicker, in winter often to find the water pipes frozen, and many the dark, cold, or wet night we had to use the village pump, form a chain, and bucket water back, for a wash. We learnt to live well together, girls from all backgrounds and different parts of the country. Lovely country dialects I had never heard before, and alas, don't often hear now. My first experience of a Northamptonshire accent was when we were going to work one morning, a wisp of a girl said, "Ooh, I ain't 'alf starved", so I commiserated and offered her one of my sandwiches, whereupon she burst out laughing and said, "Oh no, me duck, I'm frozen to death."

Slowly we became accepted by the community and often were treated to some extra rations, especially if there was a pig that had just met its end, or an egg, if they had a lot arrive! The farmers were mostly pleased to have us, we worked hard, and there was a tremendous sense of pleasure and pride seeing the results of our handiwork. There were hoed sugar beet, the lovely new potatoes, the field strewn with muck, all distributed by hand from little piles dumped around the field, the bullocks and heifers we had hand fed, and the lovely butter we made, and the cream we separated, both of which I am sure was illegal. No machines in those days, but a lovely sense of comradeship, and a feeling that you were doing your bit for King and Country.'

Land Army girls outside Mr Wilson's farm at Glapthorn. They came to Northamptonshire from as far as Leeds, London and Durham to do the farm work while the men were away fighting.

LIFE IN THE HOSTEL

'A group of Land Army girls came to Northamptonshire from Lancashire and Yorkshire by train. They were picked up at Thorpe station and finally arrived at the new Titchmarsh Hostel. Some were raw recruits and they came from all walks of life. They were dressed in breeches, brown shoes, fawn socks, cream shirts, green pullovers, a big brown overcoat and a wide brimmed hat. The green tie had "WLA" written all over it.

The hostel had bunk beds and was in a field close to the church. The vicar kept an eye on us as well as paying us our wages. From the hostel, farmers in the area collected us in groups or twos and threes to do all manner of farm work. The first farmer I went to, at Thorpe, said we were murdering his hedges.

After I had been at the hostel for six months, two of us were installed in a cottage in the village with a lady to look after us. We had no means of transport so the other girl, who had worked in a department store in Liverpool, sent home for two bikes. When they came they were just the frame and the wheels, no bell, pump or other accessories, but we were away!

One of the jobs I did was to take two white mares across fields to

Gidding to the blacksmith to be shod; that was great fun. We did threshing, stooking corn in the fields, picking potatoes, milking, and carting "muck" by horse and cart. So many villagers befriended us and the farmworkers were always willing to help us.

We met up with the other girls at the hostel from time to time, and of course met the airmen from Polebrook aerodrome. We also visited Ashton Wold, which was a convalescent home at that time for wounded and sick men from the forces, and they came to the village hall for dances and whist drives.

Land girls in their distinctive clothes could be seen everywhere around Northamptonshire villages during the war and there were many hostels housing girls like us.'

THE FAMILY HE LEFT BEHIND

After the war, widows and their families were left to cope as best they could on a small pension. The women worked at whatever was available, a fear always at the back of their minds that if they ceased to be able to support their children, the family would be split up. This poignant story is typical of many in those post war years.

'I was born in Daventry in 1941 and my brother in 1944. When I was three years old my father was killed in Belgium. I have only one memory of him – it was on the day my brother was born (at home, as it was in those days). He was standing by my mother, who was in bed, and beside them was my baby brother, lying in a wicker laundry basket.

We were lucky to be living with my widowed grandmother, so that my mother could go to work in a shoe factory when we both started school. In those days, her only income was her war widow's pension. She told me years afterwards that her one fear was that her children would be taken from her if she could not support us. Life must have been very hard for her and as I grew older and became more aware of things I became involved in the morning firelighting routine and the blackleading of the kitchen grate. I did all the shopping for my mother and grandmother.

I felt the "odd one out" at school. All the other children had a father and a mother, and their mothers always came on Parents

Afternoon to look at their work. My mother could not afford to take time off work to come, although she arranged for one of her friends to come to see my work – it wasn't like having Mum there. I so wanted to please my mother, she worked so hard and seemed to have no social life at all. I worked hard at school and passed the scholarship to go to the grammar school – she was so proud but, oh, the sacrifices she made to buy my school uniform.

Before she married, she had worked as a cook at Welton PLace, the country home of the Garrard family (the Crown jewellers). She was a wonderful cook and told us lovely stories of her days in service. To help make ends meet, she used to make and decorate Christmas cakes for our friends and neighbours. She also plucked and dressed chickens, geese and ducks at Christmas for many people in Daventry. I remember the smell of the chickens being singed on the gas cooker – then she floured them and wrapped them beautifully in a large sheet of greaseproof paper. I often delivered them for her. She charged one shilling.

When I was 17, my mother married a widower with four sons. I think she was happy – for me, things were never the same again. But I had four new brothers, whom I came to love deeply.

My mother died in 1966, aged 49. How I would love to have her here now, just to spoil her and give her some of the pleasures of life that we have come to take for granted through the sacrifices of women like her.'

HIGHDAYS
&
HOLIDAYS

MAKING OUR OWN
ENTERTAINMENT

⟨∋⟩

Before the days of television, which has seen the demise of so much outside entertainment, people were quite prepared to fill the little leisure time they had with a sing-song around the piano, amateur dramatics, listening to (or playing in) the village band, or, that high spot in the village week, attending a local dance and whist drive.

ROUND THE PIANO

'In the long winter evenings at Sywell in the 1920s we used to read, learn to knit and sew until it was bedtime. For entertainment families gathered together for a sing-song at various intervals. Mother played the piano, Dad the violin, one aunt was a singer and all the rest of us joined in. We had no wireless for several years, and then it was a "cat's whisker" type and we had to wear headphones to listen in.'

ENTERTAINMENT IN THE VILLAGE

'Farm labourers worked long days and long weeks. In the evenings at Hargrave most of them spent time in their gardens or allotments to provide whatever vegetables the family ate. They might then go to one of the pubs or to the men's reading room where they played cards, dominoes and darts. The pubs were lively with singing and music (piano, concertina, violin) which echoed round the village. Other activities were seasonal such as cricket or skating. There was always a tug-of-war team to compete with nearby village teams.'

'For recreation at Nether Heyford, apart from the pubs, there was the Jubilee Hall where the young folk, mostly men, came to play darts, skittles, rings, bagatelle and cards, and to do a little boxing. It was teetotal and dubbed "The Pussyfoot Club".'

'Between the wars, the WI in Brigstock was noted for its choral successes. The ladies met weekly with their own pianist and conductor. Competitions were held in Leicester, Peterborough, Oundle and Northampton, the journeys being made by hired bus. Whatever the venue, the dessert at lunchtime always seemed to be peaches and cream.

A library was run from the WI hall on Saturday evenings by one of the members. The books were delivered in large black cases from the County Library. This same lady organised the refreshments at the garden fetes which were usually held in the grounds of one or other of the large houses in the village. These were highlights in the village calendar and often had music provided by the Brigstock Silver Band. Flower shows were held at Mauntley House, which was later used as a hostel for the men working at the Corby steelworks before being demolished to make way for new housing.'

'At Whilton the scout troop held concerts and there were visits from the Long Buckby Co-op Concert Party. Occasionally the children of the village were taken by coal lorry to Long Buckby for sports and a tea party. Church Army captains came in a horse-drawn caravan and camped on the village green. They would stay for a week and give talks illustrated by lantern slides. The old laundry belonging to the rectory was converted into a club room and a billiards table from the rectory was moved in. The men from the village had their own billiards team.'

'Woodford was a busy village in the days of the railway; with men going on and coming off shift at all times of the day or night it was a village that never slept. Railway carriages were used as pavilions at the playing fields and there were cricket, football and tennis clubs, all very well supported. There were weekly whist drives and dances, first in the old tin hut which stood on the site of what is now the church car park, and events were also held in the Ex-Servicemen's Hall which has recently been demolished, leaving only nostalgic memories for those of us who grew up in the village. Once a year Hansons of Rugby and Leamingon Spa took over the hall for a week and sold pianos and sheet music. This culminated at the end of the week in a Grand Talent Contest where many of us entertained high hopes of attaining stardom, but few of us ever did. This was a real highlight in the village year.'

'The headmistress of the Duddington village school, Miss E. Abbott, was a marvellous English teacher. She arranged concert parties and wrote the material for plays and sketches which were performed in the school room. Before the village hall was built all the social events took place in the school. As there were only desks to sit on, the village people brought along their kitchen chairs for all the social events. The largest entertainment to be held was at the opening of the village hall. A special tableau was written by Miss Abbott and two performances were given to packed audiences.'

'One of the highlights of the year in Lois Weedon and Weston was the Red and White concert party which came from Woodford Halse. The concerts took place in the Parish Room, which was in the vicarage. Before the village hall was built in 1923, the chapel schoolroom and the school were also used for entertainments. The Parish Room also housed a library, which was run by the vicar's wife. The children would go round the village with a list of books, people would choose from the list, the children would go back to the vicarage, collect the books and deliver them.'

'The "village social" at Great Houghton was really something to look forward to, and was always well supported. These were held in a crumbling building which had been the old school but which was subsequently called "the Institute". Mrs Annie Roberts struggled up the lane to it (known then as "The Cracknuts" or Cracknuts Lane, but, sadly, since changed to Rectory Close) carrying buckets of water and fuel for the huge open fire, which had to be started in the afternoon to get the building warmed up. There would be piles of sandwiches and cakes to make and set out and many helpers would be involved. The music would come from a wind-up gramophone and a piano, and also renderings of his own compositions from Mr Frank Munroe on his harmonica. There would be lots of games and dancing and for one game a huge bag full of odd clothing, including old type underwear, of course, would be dragged in and this would be pushed and pulled around the circle, a bit like pass the parcel, until it was empty and most participants wearing some outlandish piece of apparel, causing great hilarity.'

DANCING AND WHIST DRIVES

'Madge remembers playing piano in the Latham Street schoolroom in Brigstock when her mother, the local organiser of the Nursing Association, held fund raising events. A whist drive was held in one room whilst in the larger of the two rooms dancing took place from 8 pm until 2 am. Madge was paid five shillings for her efforts and often at the end of the evening her fingernails were completely worn down. Madge also played the piano at the Brigstock Camp, which was used in the 1920s by the Ministry of Labour and Employment Training Department for the retraining of men from many parts of the British Isles.'

'We would dance in the malting house in Pitsford on holidays, when Mr Newman brought his fiddle, or on Whit Mondays when we had a band and the players had a barrel of beer between them.'

'Whist drives and dances were held in the school at Whilton. All the desks had to be moved out and put back again before school the next day. French chalk and boracic crystals were used to make the floor slippery. This often led to complaints from the headmistress.'

'I came to Benefield in 1935. My husband and I were both keen dancers and made every effort to attend the Glapthorn village dances. We lived at Westwood Lodge, which lay across two fields from the nearest road, so the way to go to dances was to put on our boots and push our bicycles across the fields. Reaching the road, we changed boots for shoes, left the boots under the hedge and cycled to Glapthorn post office, where we had friends. I could then change into my dance frock. Dancing to a local band often went on until two in the morning and then, reversing the procedure, we made our way home.'

'Up until the Second World War, there used to be a social in the village hall at Everdon every Thursday night. It cost sixpence. If you were a lad, you couldn't stand about, you had to dance. The older women would make you.'

STAGE LEFT..

'Before the Second World War the schoolrooms at Barby were the venue for all local activities, such as whist drives, dances, choral groups and drama groups. Then after the war a Nissen hut that had been used in the village for prisoners of war was acquired and became the village hall. The well known Barby Players drama group staged plays in the hall but one problem was that, to get on stage when performing, the cast had to climb through the windows – stage left, stage right.'

'Close to the site of "Widows Row" in Brigstock was the field where the travelling Gaff Theatre was sometimes held, and also the annual funfair. The actors of the Gaff performed a variety of plays, of which *Maria Marten, or Murder in the Red Barn* is well remembered.'

THE VILLAGE BAND

'Woodford had two brass bands in the village. The Methodist band was irreverently known as the "Bun and Monster" and the other one as the "Beer and Baccy".'

'The Litchborough village band would practise in a barn and play on the green on warm summer evenings. It was conducted by Mr Harry Darby who owned the village cycle shop. In the 1920s Rev Green wrote a *Song of Litchborough* which was sung at village concerts by Charles Thorneycroft and included verses about the band:

> We've recently resurrected our Band;
> They're alive, and the noise they make is grand –
> With cornet, tenor, euphonium,
> And Charlie White banging away on the drum!

> They've instruments needing much breath to be filling 'em,
> But there's Darby, Thorneycroft, Jacobs and Billingham,
> So plonk down your money, and keep up the Band,
> For harmony in the village is grand!'

'There was a Salvation Army barracks in Everdon and they had a band which used to play outside the church. There was also the village band, the Everdon Silver Band, which used to practise in the disused stable at the Old Rectory. It was nicknamed "The Beer and Bacca Band" and it used to parade at the Feast, on Bank Holidays, at the fete and on Boxing Day. People used to say:

> "Band's out again,
> So it will rain."

FILMS AND RADIO

⏥

Going to the pictures was a treat looked forward to all week by children and adults alike – and Northamptonshire even had its own brush with stardom when an epic film was made at Irthlingborough. At home, the radio, often beginning with the 'cat's whisker' and headphones, brought a new pleasure to evenings around the fire.

GOING TO THE PICTURES

'On Saturdays Watts cinema at Irthlingborough, now the Civic Hall, was always full. The front seats, mostly children, were at one time fivepence, then came the sevenpenny ones, then ninepence, and the dearer ones at the back were a shilling. When the first talkie film *Broadway Melody* was on, the people queued along the High Street and right up Board Street.'

'To go to Irthlingborough cinema on a Saturday evening from the Addingtons cost fivepence return bus fare, fourpence for the cinema, twopence for a piece of fish and a penny for chips – total one shilling for a night out. Wages then were approximately £2 a week.'

'At Woodford there was the old Hippodrome in South Street which was burned down and this was replaced by a picture house which proudly flaunted the name of The Savoy (this is now the church room). Programmes changed twice a week and the first film to be shown there was Greta Garbo in *Queen Christina*. Wednesdays and Fridays we children were allowed in for twopence, all in the front seats and much hilarity and jostling for what we considered the best view took place. The adults usually tried to avoid those evenings if possible.'

'I have very happy memories of Saturday morning pictures in the 1960s. We went to the Granada Cinema in Kettering High Street – a group of friends. It cost sixpence to get in and we used to love taking our favourite pop records with us as the first few to arrive every week with their particular record could go on stage and mime to it after the cartoons had been shown. I'll never forget miming to "Zabadak" by Dave Dee, Dozy, Beaky, Mick and Tich with a couple of friends while about 20 others danced behind. It was always a mad dash to the stage door during the cartoons to be in the first 20 or so to dance on the stage. After this there was a full length feature film, followed by an exciting serial which made you not want to miss the next episode.

On the way home I used to love calling into Boots and spending my two shilling and sixpence pocket money on my favourite books followed by a stop at the fish shop for a bag of shrimps – Saturdays were my favourite day of the week.'

THE LURE OF THE SILVER SCREEN

'In 1913, when *The Battle of Waterloo* was filmed in the area, the film company took up residence in the Horseshoe pub at Irthlingborough. The family who owned the Horseshoe at the time were called Inwood and were a very attractive family with dark, almost Italian looks. The Inwoods moved into a farmhouse in College Street, returning daily to take care of their film company guests. A certain Charles Weston, who was the producer, fell in love with the beautiful daughter Alice, and gave her a part in the film; her brother Jack also had a small part. When the film was completed, Charles Weston married Alice and took her back to America.'

THE CAT'S WHISKER

'My father was interested in the wireless in the 1920s. I wonder why they called them wireless – they had more wires than a grand piano, and they were big things, what with the cat's whisker, and the accumulators, which were almost as big as the set. We started off with headphones and then progressed to a large trumpet-shaped speaker. On top of that we had to have an aerial that stretched from the house all the way down the garden to the branch of a tree.'

'I can just remember our first wireless; it was a wooden box which opened, and several things plugged into various holes and both my parents sat very quietly wearing headphones because the sound came through very faintly! When I was about ten in the mid 1930s we had a proper wireless which ran on an accumulator (a glass container that held a certain kind of acid and had to be charged every week at a local garage). Great care had to be taken with these, because if you spilled any acid it would burn holes in clothing or upholstery in no time at all. We only had the wireless on for the news and important events, and we children had it for Children's Hour.'

GATHERED AROUND THE SET

'Mr Henry Wright proudly possessed the only wireless set in Great Addington in the 1920s and one night in 1925 he planned a wireless concert in the Board Room. An aerial was erected specially for the event and the villagers gathered for the concert, only to receive an apology that the broadcast had been cancelled due to the death of Queen Alexandra!'

THE SPORTING LIFE

Sports, competitive or otherwise, played a large part in leisure time in Northamptonshire and anything from ice skating and impromptu ice hockey matches to tennis and cricket was played with enthusiasm and passion. Football referees were not the most popular of people when the home team was losing!

WINTER GAMES

'The Coneygears was situated at the bottom of Spinney Road in Irthlingborough and all the fields and meadows in winter were flooded by the farmers by means of opening the river banks. Consequently, when the hard frosts arrived, the valley could be skated on. Hot chestnuts and hot potatoes were cooked there and the farmers would light up the area so that it looked just like a picture postcard.'

'It is hard today to imagine ice hockey being played at Litchborough, but apparently one hard winter, when Sunnybanks Pond at the bottom of Farthingstone Road (once known as Pond Lane) froze over, an impromptu ice hockey match was arranged.'

'During the hard winter of 1929 the lake at Welton was frozen for several weeks and skating parties were held and ice hockey played. A group of boys who were playing on the ice came across something wrapped in a London newspaper – they were horrified to find the body of a baby. The mystery was never solved.'

'When I was a schoolgirl I skated on the frozen river Nene for about a week. It was only the second time this had been possible in over a century, and it has not happened since. The weather was so severe that great ice flows went up and down until they gathered on the banks on the bends, and then the whole river between the bridges froze solidly. As most of the people were farmers they could not work, so hundreds of people came from great distances to enjoy the fun. The skates were not the beautiful white boots with attached skates that we see today, but were very crude bits of metal blades with wooden sides with a nasty bit of turned up steel to act as brakes. Every pair of granny's lace-up boots was rummaged from attics and barns, and leather straps went up in price! An ox was to have been roasted on the Saturday, but unfortunately a thaw set in, and so ended the fun.'

WATER SPORTS

'Fishing was a popular pastime at Wootton. Wootton Brook seems to have been a bigger stream than it is today and some older villagers remember catching pike and setting eel lines at night. Mr Martin hung eels out to dry in his back garden.'

'Denford was a great boating and fishing centre before Wicksteed Park existed. There used to be two boathouses in Denford and people came from miles around for a day out from Kettering, for holidays or even honeymoons. Teas were served there. There was a big floating landing stage outside one of the boathouses and on one occasion there were so many people on it getting on and off the boats that it capsized and tipped the whole lot in the water.'

'In the 1930s one of the local characters in Irthlingborough was Jim Horner. He would loan punts and boats out on the river just by the old bridge. This was much appreciated by the young people and it was very busy down there at weekends.'

CRICKET, TENNIS AND GOLF

'At Braybrooke in the 1920s there was for a short time a tennis court behind the Swan Inn. There was later a football team who played matches in the 1950s, but as most of the players were non residents its was disbanded. The outstanding success has been the cricket club founded prior to the First World War. In the 1920s they won the Oxendon Cup and each member received a gold medallion. They moved from the field in Oxendon Road to the Castle Grounds in 1946, and John Profumo, MP for Kettering opened the pavilion.'

'Cricket at Stowe IX Churches was played on Manor Farm field, though there was no proper team. The bats were made from a lump of wood. If you managed to hit the ball, you often wished you hadn't because it jarred your hands.'

'Gayton had a football team and a cricket team, some of the players were in both teams. Every Boxing Day, the married men played the single men at football, before converging on the two pubs just before noon. In the early part of the century there was also a golf course, founded in 1907. The site was a field called Great Grounds on the right hand side of Wrights Lane, then an unfenced road leading to Banbury Lane from the end of Milton Road.'

'In the 1920s Brampton was fortunate to have a tennis club with two courts, these being situated where the Spencer Arms car park now is. The cricket club was flourishing, having many notable fixtures, and they were fortunate to have the services of a very good secretary who was the village blacksmith. The ground was situated at the top of Golf Lane in Church Brampton. The annual cricket club whist drive and dance at the school room was one of the social events of the season.'

FOOTBALL

'I was in the village football team at Everdon in the 1920s. Once we were due to play an away match but my football boots were worn out. I cycled to Daventry to go to Willoughby's, the shoe shop. The only pair in my size were marked at ten shillings. I only had eight shillings but Mr Willoughby said "If that's all you've got, you can have them for that." I was so pleased and relieved to have another pair of boots.

School age boys used to play football in the road before school started in the mornings. There was no traffic to run you over, only the odd horse and cart. We couldn't play on the green as there were trees in the way.'

'Stanion Juniors were a good football team and one yar we never lost a match. Wally Land, who was blind, and his sister Mary, carried cans of tea up to the match, each time we played at home. The football pitch was across from the top of Little Lane, over two fields called Horse Copse, next to Stanion Wood.'

'During the 1920s, Yardley Hastings football team was well known in the neighbourhood for its fitness and skill on the field. Stories of winning the shield and the cup were always worth listening to, especially when, in one village, the ladies supporting the losers set upon the Yardley team with their umbrellas!

Transport to away games was provided by Harratt's van, which did service on week-days as the carrier's cart. There were no windows in it, except for one small one in the door at the rear. Passengers sat on forms on either side and, if you did not make the first eight inside, the floor was the next best seat. The van was an "Albion", a Rolls Royce of its kind, though by this time the engine had seen better days. At every hill, be it large or small, the cry was "Everybody out!" to push and shove the old van over the top and so ensure that they reach the field of play on time.

The same thing would happen on the run into Northampton with the villagers at "Clothing Club Time". Everybody knew that they would have to get out and push, but third-class riding was better than first-class walking. The prestige of having travelled in the van would provide a talking point for weeks afterwards.'

'Football referees were paid a premium to come to Harpole to officiate during the 1930s, and were dumped in the ditch or pond down Glassthorpe Lane if the decisions did not go down well with the home supporters.'

THE HUNT

'Passing the entrance to Brampton Grange, one was aware of the great activity with the hunting fraternity as long strings of horses were exercised by grooms or were being taken to the local meets of the Pytchley. Mr Bert Drage, a bachelor, lived at the Grange for many years and what he didn't know about hunting was not worth knowing. In 1953, when he was 88 years of age, he wrote a book of reminiscences. He farmed 350 acres and broke nearly every bone in his body whilst in the hunting field. He was also a staunch churchman, being churchwarden at Brampton for many years and he boasted that he never missed church on Sunday wherever he was.'

'One event in Barby which used to attract attention was when the Pytchley Hunt met at the rectory for the stirrup cup. Riding with the hounds at one time were the Prince of Wales (Edward VIII) and the Duke of York (George VI), who were staying in the area.'

'The Woodland Pytchley Hunt races used to be held at Dust Hill at Brigstock between the wars, before they moved to Dingley. The bookies used to get drunk and drop their money and the children picked it up.'

CANARY BREEDING

'From the early 1900s the breeding of canaries became a flourishing hobby in many parts of the country. Northamptonshire had many enthusiasts and societies were formed with the help of "Cage Birds", the official journal which advised on every aspect of keeping cage birds; breeding, feeding, showing, cages, sickness etc.

Shoemakers and those workers whose business was often carried on in their own premises were especially keen, and great interest and rivalry was shown in each others' birds. Sometimes the fancier had few canaries, even one or two, but the cage would be hung in the owner's workshop and as much pride and pleasure obtained as if there were 30 or more. Numbers varied and lean-to aviaries were built on a house wall, a spare room was used, or permanent brick buildings in the garden. Few birds were kept in the living rooms of the house.

My father was a great "bird-man", and from an early age at Long Buckby I remember the daily care and routine of his canaries that occupied most of his spare time.

A brick built aviary in the garden often housed upwards of 100 birds; mostly of the buff-coloured "Norwich" variety, these being his preference. This building, with one side completely window and another large one high on the side wall, was always kept locked, although the key was in the lock during the day. Incidentally, when the building was planned, it was said that size would not be rateable; judge Father's feelings when it was discovered that it was a foot over every way, a fact he did not forget!

The clear wall side was occupied by a fixed flight almost half the height of the wall, and held a great many birds flying freely and show cages were fixed above. We often went into the "bird-place" with Father and it was a great joy and feeling of responsibility when we were allowed to fill the drinking pots and seed containers. Also to wash them! The cleaning of the cages and flights went on non-stop; it was a time consuming job, requiring gentleness and quiet movements as the birds are so easily frightened. Strangers often unsettled them, particularly if they spoke loudly or waved and pointed at them; then the birds would fly blindly round the cage obviously distressed. Father would talk quietly to them and they would gradually calm down (This was one of the reasons the door was kept locked). *If* we were sent in, it was strict instructions not to make a noise or move clumsily. Even when Father was there, the entry of a stranger had quite an effect. The birds would immediately stop singing and there would be silence – complete and uncanny. Then one would whistle, a few tentative notes gradually taken up by the others until all were singing, a veritable outpouring of melody.

The feeding of the young canaries was an act and labour of love. A nest box of three or four babies, multiplied several times was a lengthy process. Every morning two or three hard boiled eggs, mashed with a smidgin of butter was well mixed with finely crushed Osborn biscuits (no other kind would do!) The resulting mixture was then fed to the hungry open-beaked youngsters on the end of a matchstick. Father was very expert and the hen birds looked on with quiet approval. A sick bird would sometimes be brought into the house for Mother to restore to health, not always successfully!

But Eli, an old friend and a great prize winner and "father" of winners, appeared to be beyond help in spite of the whisky with which Father tried to revive him. Sadly he was consigned to the chimney back of the living-room fire. Mother watched as the flames crept nearer to him and finally – ever optimistic – picked Eli up with the brass tongs and placed him in a small basket on the hearth. Sometime after she heard a faint "cheep", growing stronger as Eli slowly returned to life and a further span of roughly two years! Quite a veteran in the bird world and always a talking piece.

Bird shows were the highlights of the year, particularly during the winter when the fanciers displayed the results of the breeding season, offering some for sale and seeking new additions to improve their stock. We went with Father on such occasions to Leicester, Bedford, Rugby, Coventry, Birmingham and Northampton – very special treats indeed!

The birds had been sent on before and when we arrived at the Show Hall, Father hurried off to the Stewards table to find out where the birds had been placed and to pay any dues required. Sometimes it would be a large show – with rabbits, pigeons and poultry – or just canaries. How exciting it was! Caught up in the crowd of exhibitors and visitors, the noise and chatter and the thrill of seeing a First or Second and Third, or even Highly Commended card on our cages was bliss. And if the bird was sold for the asking price we were even more pleased! After the show we went to a cafe for tea – always the same – "large plates of ham for the adults, small ones for the children, and a selection of cakes". Mother did not always stay the whole afternoon, she liked to visit the shops and my sister and I greatly enjoyed our visits to the ladies and children's departments – a complete contrast to the Long Buckby shops.

But the highlight was the Country-wide Show at the Crystal Palace. What searchings and deliberations went on to find *the* exhibits. We once had a First and several Seconds in the Norwich Class and sold some; but there was great rejoicing when a fellow exhibitor and personal friend won the Cup for the Best Bird in the Show together with a substantial sum.

Yes, it was a wonderful hobby. Father spent many happy hours in the company of his canaries, feeding and cleaning, mixing a coloured feed so as to produce deeper hued plumage, planning the breeding pattern, entertaining visitors, who came to buy, borrow or lend, so as to improve the quality of their feathered friends.

For 60 years he maintained his aviary, always diminishing in numbers until the day came when even his familiar routine became too much. But the popularity of the canary had passed, few of the old fanciers had survived and the shows ceased. Budgies, parakeets and other tropical exotic varieties took over – a single specimen often the family pet.

My earliest memories are full of birds – undimmed through the years of the World Wars and the depression of the late 1920s and early 1930s, when the sale of a canary meant new boots or a dress for one or other of we four children. Never to be forgotten the occasions of the shows in the different towns, of steam engines and piercing whistles, of crowded and overheated showrooms, bowler-hatted and cloth capped men, ladies in large hats – excited children, laughter and chatter – rows and rows of birds in every shade of yellow, whistling, singing freely, and unrestrainedly. Yes – it was a deep and wonderful brotherhood of canary lovers.'

ROYAL OCCASIONS

<del></del>

Coronations and Jubilees were celebrated with gusto by towns and villages throughout the county, an excuse to get together for tea, sports and entertainment once again! At the 1953 Coronation of Elizabeth II, the new television sets which enabled people to actually watch the ceremony as it took place, proved as memorable as the day itself.

THE 1911 CORONATION

'In August 1911 a report on the Coronation festivities at Stowe IX Churches appeared in the Weedon Deanery Magazine. "As loyal folk we began the day by a service in the parish church and in the beautiful litany prayed as we should for King George V, his Queen and all the Royal Family. After service, all who were able to do so adjourned to Upper Stowe, where a quoit match and other athletic sports were indulged in. At one o'clock, a dinner was provided by the careful thought of the Coronation Committee, which was thoroughly enjoyed by men and boys of working age. After dinner, came more sports. At 4 pm, a meat tea was provided for the women and children and this, as the dinner, was done full justice to. Unfortunately, the rain somewhat dampened the ardour of some of the more elderly of our people, but the bonfire, notwithstanding the rain, which unfortunately came down a day too soon, did not prevent the merry blaze which brought to a close the Coronation Day of George V and Queen Mary.'

THE JUBILEE 1935 AND CORONATION 1937

'For the Silver-Jubilee of George V and Queen Mary, Overstone's celebrations started off with a service in the parish church. A national form of service was followed.

Overstone were lucky in the fact that Mr F. Gandy, a very generous man and proprietor of Overstone Solarium which had been opened shortly before, offered the facilities there for the village celebrations. Not many people had cars in those days, so a local farmer lent two waggons to transport the villagers. These were decorated with red, white and blue crepe paper and benches from the village hall were installed as seats. Many a laugh was caused as young and old were hauled into the waggons, included the newest arrival in its pram. The waggoners were dressed in traditional smocks and the farmer's son conducted the singing en route. On arrival everyone sat down for a meal. After the meal all the children received a commemorative cup and saucer. Then followed sports for all ages. I feel sure a barrel of beer was provided to quench thirsts.

Two years later, the 1937 celebrations for George VI's Coronation followed a similar pattern.

By 1953 for the Coronation of Elizabeth II, with the advent of television, arrangements were slightly different. The service was held on the preceding Sunday. Not everyone had television sets but those who had, invited people in to watch the ceremony and care was taken that everyone had the opportunity to watch. Then in the afternoon once again it was round to Overstone Solarium for a sit down meal. This time there was no need for waggons as there were enough cars available for transport. This time all the children had

Many towns and villages organised festivals to celebrate the Coronation of George VI in 1937, like this one at Moulton.

Coronation mugs. The weather was not very kind so the children's sports were curtailed.'

'If any important occasion arose in Roade village the local clubs and associations would get together and arrange quite a large scale entertainment. On the occasion of the Jubilee of George V and Queen Mary in May 1935, a whole week of events took place, the main one being a pageant on the actual day, 5th May. Each section of the community took part. I, of course, was part of the school section. The boys and girls put together a huge cross about six feet long and three feet wide, and filled it with spring flowers. It took four boys to carry it, followed by girls in white dresses, and it was layed at the foot of the war memorial. After a short address by the vicar, and singing of hymns and a blessing, the schoolchildren went back to the school to get ready for our section of the parade. We represented the British Empire. There were Australians, Canadians, Africans, Indians, Scottish, Irish and Welsh. Everyone represented something. Our mothers had been very busy! One little group was the League of Nations, carrying white doves of peace, and at the head of it all came John Bull leading a large white bulldog.

So there we were on this beautiful spring morning, with the breeze fluttering our banners. Henry VIII and his six wives, walking very stately and solemnly, followed by Elizabeth I, Sir Walter Raleigh, the Earl of Essex, Mary Queen of Scots, oh! and there was my aunt looking magnificent as "Bloody Mary" and our next door neighbour as James I and another of my aunts as Prince John. I remember her knitting the whole suit of chain-mail out of fine string and then spraying it with silver. The thing that stands out most in my mind of that whole parade was our vicar. There he was, I could hardly believe it, sitting on Old Bailey's farmhorse, which had been scrubbed and polished till it was pure white, and his Reverence dressed in a suit of armour (made no doubt of cardboard) with the shield of St George, and accompanied by "men at arm" (members of the WI). Every single thing had been made by themselves and they had covered practically every aspect of history up to that day.

In the dusk of a warm spring night, all the younger element and a lot of the older ones too, congregated around a huge bonfire that had been built in the recreation field. There were ooh's and ahhh's as the fireworks lit up the sky. The boys chased the girls round the bonfire and if they caught us, kissed us in the rosy glow. Little did we realise that within a few years, these lads would be gone to fight a war, some never to return (including the lad who was John Bull on that morning). On this spring night however, we hadn't a care in the world. We were young, and it was May 1935.'

'Stanion Parish Council Minutes record the 1935 Jubilee programme –

9.00 am   Thanksgiving Service.
10.00 am   A Jubilee Masque presented by the school children.
1.00 pm   Lunch for all residents of 60 and over.
4.00 pm   Tea for all the village children up to 14.
6.00 pm   Sports for all, with refreshments, on Mr Clarke's field.
10.00 pm   Scout's bonfire.

Mr David Gray, aged 90, the oldest inhabitant, presented all the school children with their mugs and entertained them with songs. After their lunch, the older villagers were also entertained in the school, but at four o'clock the children's hard-working mothers had the school ready to serve tea to their offspring. Meantime, a cricket match was in full swing on the field, until sports took over, and finally the bonfire. Mr Swingler's committee worked very hard and produced an action-packed day.

Just two years later, after the death of George V and the abdication of Edward VIII, George VI and Queen Elizabeth were crowned. Stanion dusted off the bunting, reconvened the committee, ordered the souvenir mugs donated by Mr Edward Lomas of Manor Farm, and retained the services of "Stanion's Grand Old Man" (David Gray again) to present them.

The children rehearsed their play and their mothers fashioned the costumes for the fancy dress parade, to be led in procession round the village by Stanion Jazz Band. The schoolchildren liked dressing up, but there was an additional spur to their efforts: a collection was always taken during the parade, later to be divided among them. £1 8s 0d went quite a long way in pennies at Wally Land's shop in Chapel Yard. And then there were prizes for the best costumes, or perhaps the most topical. Ronald Land, dressed as a nursemaid, pushed a pram in which the "quads" were howling and squealing – reflecting an event recently reported universally, to great amazement. Mary Pridmore and Harold Gray swept by as the King and Queen in their royal coach.

Of course, there was a meat tea for everyone, and a social evening in the schoolroom; no sports, it poured with rain in the afternoon. I remember that rain – it rained in Kent, too, where I sat at my desk dressed for sports, clutching a paper bag. Buns don't taste the same when they should have been consumed outside. But we did have a fancy dress parade led by a jazz band – it must have been quite a sight!'

'At Braybrooke George V's Jubilee started with a church service, followed by lunch for the adults, maypole dancing, sports and tea for the children. Each child received a cup and saucer. In the evening there was a social with village soloists singing *Little Brown Jug, Just a Song at Twilight, Three Old Maids of Lea* and *Green Grow the Rushes O*. The day concluded with a huge bonfire in Mill Hill, the highest point in the village.'

'To celebrate the 1935 Jubilee Yarwell held a race from Top Gate Lodge in the Seeds to the dovecote, games and a tea in the afternoon. The street was decorated with garlands.'

THE 1953 CORONATION

'I remember walking down the village street in Cotterstock to the post office on 6th February 1952 and hearing solemn wireless music coming from all the houses. This was the BBC'S tribute to George VI, who had died that morning.'

'We lived a mile and a half up a farm drive near Apethorpe in 1953 and had a very new TV set. On Coronation Day friends from the village walked up to watch and to enjoy sandwiches and sausage rolls.'

'At the Coronation of Elizabeth II, Braybrooke provided mugs for the children and a tea. Races were held in the castle grounds for young and old. The adults had a buffet supper which cost one shilling and sixpence a head – one sausage roll a penny ha'penny, one individual trifle fourpence, two sandwiches (meat) fourpence, two savouries threepence ha'penny, one cake twopence ha'penny and one cup of tea or coffee.'

'In the villages around Earls Barton, people decorated their houses, the winner getting a small prize. There were street parties for the children, each receiving a special mug, and teas for the adults, usually followed with sports and a dance at night.

I remember the Queen's Coronation very well. Except for a few news items on the TV I never did see it, because I had a baby daughter at 2.45am. I had a long and tiring labour and slept most of the following day. There was a big red and blue bow pinned to my breakfast tray and they gave me a small radio to listen to. I surfaced from time to time and remember once a very excited announcer yelling "They have climbed Everest and reached the top"; Edmund Hillery and Sherpa Ten Sing had planted a Union Jack on the summit. The Mayor and Mayoress of Wellingborough came to see me and also a newspaper reporter and photographer – all warmly wrapped up as it was a very cold rainy day.'

'On Coronation Day I remember, like everyone else, the cold. We crowded into a small room to watch our Queen crowned on one of Collingtree's three television sets. In the afternoon there were sports, and one of the first tasks of the new Collingtree WI was to organise tea for all the village.'

'The Coronation in 1953 provided an ideal opportunity for a colourful celebration and houses and streets in Cold Ashby were decked accordingly. The best dressed house was a fully fledged golden coach. Much fun was had trying to throw a streamer of red, white and blue flags from one house to the house opposite. The celebrations included a children's party with fruit salad being served from a milk churn. Fancy dress was great fun and everyone was encouraged to do a party piece, which the under tens did with relish as payment was a whole sixpence, a small fortune. Sports and games carried on well into the evening.'

MAY DAY

⟨⟩

One of the great highlights of the year in Northamptonshire was May Day, when the schoolchildren of every town and village chose a May Queen and decorated garlands with spring flowers before parading around the streets and dancing around the maypole.

MAY DAY AT PITSFORD

'Out of the girls of the top class at Pitsford school were chosen two "May Ladies" – who after much consultation with Mrs Nightingale (who had been cajoled into first teaching needlework and later the infants as well) as to whether they had white dresses, usually produced their own. Songs, meanwhile, were carefully rehearsed to the old harmonium – *Hearts of Oak, Rule Britannia, Now is the month of Maying* etc – all note and word perfect.

In the last week of April notes were sent to the "big" houses asking for the flowers for the May garland and when it would be convenient for the children to come and sing on 1st May. And what generous response was forthcoming, the children calling for the flowers at a given time. Clothes baskets of huge daffodils from Moulton Grange, baskets and baskets of spring flowers from the Wakes at Pitsford House and the various occupants of the Hall – and with what appreciation they were received by both children and adults alike, with appropriate remarks for some special flower – "this will go at the top", perhaps, of the beautiful but malodorous Crown Imperial. All the baths and every possible container from the school house were filled with water to hold the flowers. All the village contributed and no garden failed to have its small or large bunch of flowers – wallflowers, daffodils, polyanthus, early tulips (in an early spring), all were there and all equally gratefully received.

Then too came the dolls brought by the girls, and many an admiring, perchance jealous, eye cast on the motley assembly.

And what of the garland, two hoops interlaced and bound with moss, on which to lovingly tie the flowers. The "old girls", usually newly marrieds, were invited to help trim the garland, which was suspended in the infants room. The day before May Day the top class girls were busily employed bunching primroses, pansies etc which were handed to the trimmers. The dolls were paraded and one chosen for the centre pivot and tied on firmly, and the trimming

233

began in earnest, each working to balance with the other. Other dolls and golliwogs were added. White flowers were kept back for the May Ladies' white muslin mop caps.

Meanwhile out in the yard the top boys, under the eye of the Rev White, were actively decorating the "Jack-in-the-Green", a cane contruction (made by blind Mr Thompson) to be borne on the shoulders of a boy inside. Laurel, barberry and evergreens were tied on, with only the feet of the bearer to be visible underneath as he danced and bowed his way along.

May Day arrived. The children assembled, usually well wrapped up against the treachery of a cold May wind. The May Ladies in white and with white shawls, preceded the garland now borne on the shoulders of the two oldest girls. The Jack pranced alongside and the remainder of the school in crocodile followed, shepherded by their three faithful teachers.

And where did they go first? To church of course, where they were received by the Rev White with Mrs White, an able musician, at the organ. A short service of praise and thanksgiving followed. Then the round started, this time accompanied by the parson who stayed with them all day. How they loved him and his gentle humour.

Wherever the garland stopped the children sang. The people admired the garland and greeted the children with their teachers. Maybe a quiet word as to how our Willie or Rosie "was doin'".

At the Hall, which was usually visited in the morning, the children were regaled with milk and buns – three cheers given for the gracious donors. In the afternoon similarly, tea was given either at Sedgebrook by the late Miss Markham or at Moulton Grange at the other end of the village by the late Mrs Manfield. The infants did not go to the outposts, but with the "big room" children went the parson and he helped count the contributions in the May Ladies' dorothy bags – always so generous.

Then as a sequel came the May treat, usually held either on the rectory lawn or in the event of wet, in the coach house there. Piles of bread and butter (no thought of margarine in those days) were cut by willing helpers. Pounds of cake duly apportioned, and gallons of tea consumed. Later games and competitions were held in the rectory field. Sweets were scrambled for, the children madly hanging on to the coat tails of the rector who was so obviously enjoying himself. About 6.30 pm the games ended. The last "Ring-a-Roses" was played and the final handkerchief dropped. The moment of reckoning came. The money left over from providing for the treat was meticulously shared according to the age of the children. Never was there a murmour of discontent, and so ended with cheers for the hard-working willing helping band.

The big occasion of the year most people will remember was May Day, not only for the maypole dancing but for the procession of the garlands culminating in the crowning of the May Queen, as shown here at Sywell in the 1950s.

Another May Day! What a pity to see this traditional simple, happy family day fall into disuse and decay.'

BOWER ON STOCKS HILL

'May Day was a very special occasion in Moulton. The dances were practised for weeks before and on 1st May the Queen's throne and bower was set up on Stocks Hill and the schoolchildren walked there in procession for the crowning ceremony. Afterwards they went around the village centre, pausing to dance in various places. The girls all looked so neat and dainty in their white frocks, the boys as far as possible in white shirts and plimsolls. It must have been a great struggle for the mothers during the depression years to send the children out properly clad, but they nearly all managed to do so. In "Boss Eynon's" day the parents were probably as much afraid of the headmaster as were the children under his care!'

OUR LOVELY DAY

'Each year as May 1st draws near, my thoughts return to those early days spent at Whittlebury village school. May Day was an extra special holiday. The previous evening excitement mounted as I, a member of a small group of scholars, happily visited villagers' homes to beg a few flowers for our May garland. Oh! the pretty cottage gardens and the aroma of primroses, hyacinths, bluebells etc pervaded the air. What joy. Later we adjourned to our Parish Rooms where we decorated our large hoop and pole.

May Day was seldom sufficiently warm to wear summer dresses but were our shivers due to breezes or excitement? The boys were fortunate, they wore best suits. Our May Queen, after her crowning ceremony, led the procession through the village, calling at each house to sing the fine old May Day folk songs. The monetary gifts were given to a charity for children. Our lovely day culminated in a feast of buns, cakes and lemonade provided by our parents.'

WHAT RICHES

'I was born in Long Buckby in 1925. One of the most outstanding features of the year was the build up to May Day. We made our May garlands on the last day of April, and proudly took them round to neighbours and friends to have a look at the lovely arrangements we had made in either a hoop or basket, or even a doll's pram. All of them were dressed up with spring flowers and ribbons, and some of Mum's net curtains. For the pleasure of looking at the garlands we were usually given a penny or twopence, or even a sixpenny piece if we were lucky – oh! what riches.'

MAY DAY SONGS

'May Day was always a splendid affair at Duddington in the 1920s. and held on 1st May no matter what the weather. I remember some very chilly ones! We girls wore white dresses and had garlands of spring flowers on our heads. I especially remember a lovely wreath of crab apple blossom my mother made for me one May Day. Many of the songs we sang were composed by Miss Abbott, the headmistress of the village school. I can still sing them to this day. The day began with the crowning of the May Queen in the school playground, followed by the songs and dancing around the maypole. Four boys carried a flower-filled garland around the playground, setting it down at intervals for the admiration of the parents and villagers who had come to watch the fun. The garland song went –

'We've a beautiful garland, a garland of flowers,
A garland sweet scented and gay,
Of flowers we've gathered from nature's own bowers,
To welcome the coming of May.'

After the playground ceremony we toured the village singing May songs and collecting. After lunch, we walked to Tixover Grange, then along the Ketton line to the village of Tixover, again singing our songs. A tea was waiting for us on our return, set out on a long table in the school room. I cannot remember feeling tired, but we must have walked a few miles on those May Days of my childhood.'

'At Benefield the garland was carried, two by two, around the village. Train bearers wore crowns of buttercups and daisies and they sang the May Day songs. One of these went as follows –

'The first of May is garland day
So please remember the garland
We don't come here but once a year
So please remember the garland.'

The collection was counted and shared out between the children by Grannie Pyewell. The May Queen and King were crowned and there were games and races, and Charlie and John Leighton played fiddles for the dancing.'

FROM QUEEN TO QUEEN

'A Queen and consort for Grafton Underwood was chosen by the children in school. The garland and crown was made by the mothers. The garland consisted of two hoops fitted together to form a sphere. Flowers were tied to it to completely cover it, and two of the oldest lads carried it by means of a broom handle pushed through the sphere. On May Day morning the children walked to Boughton House, about a mile away, and sang May songs to whoever was in residence. One one occasion, Queen Mary was there so she had the pleasure of meeting the village Queen. A collecting box was taken with the children. In the afternoon the procession went round the vilage singing and afterwards finished the day off with a tea party in the village hall or the school, where the money collected was divided up between the children, the Queen and King having the largest share.'

THE BBC COW

'In the 1920s May Day was celebrated in a big way in Yarwell and Nassington. One year in Nassington a four-wheeled flat cart was borrowed, its usual function being to carry hundredweight sacks of coal. The local wheelwright put a frame of wood on, this was decorated and the May Queen rode round the village on it. In the early days at Yarwell, there was just a May Queen and Maids of Honour, but later, with a different teacher, there was also a May King with Soldiers and once, when the proceedings were televised by the BBC, a cow was included!'

CROWN O' PEARLS

'The Crown Imperial Lily featured prominently in the May garlands. Its name, passed on by word of mouth, became "Crown o' Pearls", as one old gentlemen from Everdon called it.'

OLD MAY DAY

'May Day at Greens Norton was always held on Old May Day, 12th May. This dated from 1752, when Parliament introduced the Gregorian Calendar and England "lost" 11 days – but not at Greens Norton. The May Queen was crowned on May morning and then there was a procession through the village, stopping at any house where anyone was ill or invalid. One year someone provided a white horse for the Queen to ride and on another occasion Miss Vinning, the rector's sister, lent her little cart, drawn by two white ponies.'

I'VE BROUGHT YOU A BUNCH OF MAY

'May Day was to the children of Great Houghton a delight to look forward to. The previous evening, mums and friends and older children met at the old school in the Cracknuts to make preparations. There were two hoops, a long pole, plenty of may blossom from the hedgerows and spring flowers from the cottage gardens with which a beautiful garland was made. On the big day we all started off early with the boys carrying the garland and we sang this little song at every door –

"I've brought you here a branch of May,
And at your door it stands
It is but a sprout, but it's well budded out,
By the grace of our Lord's hands."

In the afternoon we would walk to the Britannia Inn, passing the railway level crossing, where the gates were operated by hand and where we would sing at the crossing keeper's cottage. We then carried on to the tannery to sing at the owner's big house – at that time Mr and Mrs Parker Grey. On our return to the village we had a big tea party. A few years later we were taught maypole and country dancing and a May Queen was picked from both Little Houghton and Great Houghton. The crowning of the Queen at Great Houghton was first and later again at Little Houghton, followed by singing and dancing. In the evening we did two more performances so that our Dads could come along after work to see it all.'

AN UNUSUAL MAY DAY

'We started at Stanion school in 1922, when Mrs Kathleen Thompson was the infants teacher. We looked forward to May Day, always held on 1st May, or the Monday following if the 1st was a Saturday or Sunday.

All the girls wore their best dresses, often white, starched and frilly. "My mother," said Connie, "had a crimping iron, rather like old fashioned curling tongs, with a wavy bed and straight prong. You pressed the frill between them".

Boys wore shirts with rounded collars, short trousers, and a sort of knitted tie with horizontal stripes.

In the late 1920s there was an unusual May Day; it began as always, with a church service taken by the vicar, the Rev Percy Lidster, who was fond of children and always rejoined us at teatime. The night before our parents had made garlands with garden flowers and bluebells and primroses we had picked in the woods. We climbed a stile at the top of Little Lane, crossed two fields, and there were the woods.

After church, and the register, we picked up our own garlands and went all round the village in a procession; some very young children would have their mothers with them. If someone in the village was ill, the whole procession stopped outside the house and sang May Day songs – *Early One Morning*, or *The Cuckoo is a Pretty Bird*.

Six or seven older pupils collected money in a cocoa tin with a slit in the top. Later on this was shared equally between the children, and spent at Leadbetter's, at the bottom of Little Lane, or Wally Land's shop in Chapel Yard.

After walking round Stanion, the older pupils and all the Little Oakley children visited Little Oakley; by about 12.30 pm we were home for lunch.

This particular year – was it 1927 or 1928? – Miss Fairy, the head

239

teacher, had trained the older children in country dancing, and we were in the team that went to Delapre Abbey; our team won a certificate.

There were only a few places available on the bus for parents, so Miss Fairy arranged a display on the cricket field behind Home Farm, where Grange Road is now.

Miss Fairy's high chair, from the big school room, was carried through the stock yard and draped in red for the crowning of the May Queen. And this was different too, that year, we had a May King, as far as we remember, for the first time. And the May King, Bob Headland, crowned the May Queen, Sylvia Greenwood, and led her into the dancing.

All the girls were in white, with black plimsolls; the boys in white shirts and grey trousers. We danced the Gallopede and Gathering Peascods. It was quite intricate.

Then it was back to the schoolroom where mothers had prepared the sandwiches, the cakes, and *Jellies*. Jellies were very important. After tea the money collected was distributed; all in coppers, the share-out organised by mothers. "I think the most I ever got was four shillings – a fortune!" says Sylvia.

By six o'clock the mothers had cleared up – no kitchen in the school, bring your own plate and spoon – and collected their children.

"We were pretty tired and grubby," and Connie and Sylvia smile now with the pleasure of a May Day a long time ago.'

THE MERRY COMRADES

'May Day was celebrated in Cold Ashby for about 40 years, money being raised for the Merry Comrades. This was an organisation run by the *Mercury and Herald* newspaper to pay for extras for people in hospital in Northamptonshire. The King and Queen of the May would be chosen and taken to be crowned in the playing field or in later years the grounds of the Hall. The girls would be dressed in white frocks with garlands of flowers. Before the crowning they would go off to pick bluebells to give to the old folk and to use to decorate the maypole area.'

FEAST DAY

The other great day in the village calendar was the Feast Day, when church and chapel services were held, processions wended their way through town and village, and the fair arrived, to the great glee of the children.

THEY CAME FROM MILES AROUND

'At Harvest Festival time, Michaelmas (29th September), came Creaton Feast. The fair would arrive and park on the grass verge opposite The Bricklayers until the stroke of noon, Sunday, and then they would go on to the green and set up the swings etc, opening on Monday and Tuesday and leaving Creaton on Wednesday. Later on they came on Saturday and stayed until Tuesday. Finally they moved off the green to a field. But Creaton Feast during the 1920s and 1930s was something people came to from miles around, the music being heard at Spratton and elsewhere.'

ESCORTING THE FAIR IN

'The Greens Norton Feast was held every year on the Monday between 6th and 14th September. Towcester Band played on the green on the Sunday evening (the only remaining celebration of the Feast today), and on the Monday afternoon, Billings Fair would be open on the village green. Often the children of the village would go out to meet the fair on the old turnpike (now the A5 Watling Street) and escort it back to Greens Norton. Almost every house would have visitors for the Feast and those who had left home would do their best to return for that one day.'

FAYREFIELD

'On Denford Feast Day in June we used to go to chapel and it was so full that we had to have chairs up the side. The children sang special hymns and we all had new dresses. Thrapston Band used to come and start playing about seven o'clock outside the pubs or sometimes in the vicarage garden. The pavements outside the pubs used to be full of people who had come to listen to the band. The fair was set up opposite the village hall in what was called the Fayrefield, the huge steam engines having quite a job to turn into the field. Later on, in the late 1920s and early 1930s, the fair was held by the ford.'

IT'S COME!

'All Saints Day, the first Sunday in November, was Harpole Feast Sunday. We usually had relatives from Kislingbury to tea, but the highlight of the Feast was the arrival of the George Billings Fair in the village. It arrived on the Thursday morning and we used to rush across the jetty at dinnertime from the school to see if it had come. Great excitement and shouts of "It's come!". Back to school after dinner, then down to Park Lane to see if they had got "it" up at teatime. Friday night, the big night, "it's going around". That was the wooden horses. Side shows went all the way down Park Lane to the White Swan; Feast Rock and a go on the "White Mice". On "Free Ride Night" or "Hospital Night", George Billing used to shout "Free ride" and we all scrambled on the wooden horses. On Thursday afternoon Mr Marston, the baker from Kislingbury, used to scramble pennies. I wasn't very big so I didn't manage to get many pennies, the big boys got them all.'

THE EVENT OF THE YEAR

'The Feast at Long Buckby was regarded as the event of the year, only equalled perhaps by Christmas in the excitement it generated. Traditionally, the Feast was held in August, running from Saturday to Saturday, with Feast Sunday being that Sunday which followed 21st August. Three families – the Billings, Thurstons and Abbots – were particularly associated with the large fair which came to the village during the week of the Feast.

At some point in the previous week, great excitement would mount among village youngsters on holiday from school. The fair vehicles, at first horse-drawn then later, motorised, usually approached the village from the Daventry Road. Where this road crosses the brook at Surney, the vehicles would stop to take in water. At this point, children would join the procession, even helping to push the heavier vehicles up Rockhill (for this they received one free ride on the fair).

The fair was set up on the village square, completely covering it and even extending into the surrounding streets. Power for the roundabouts and other stalls was supplied by gleaming steam-engines and music was supplied by a large fairground organ. There were many sideshows, swingboats, cakewalk, skittles, hoop-la, roll-a-penny etc, as well as refreshment stalls selling candy, brandy

242

snaps and pease pudding. The fair was thronged by dense crowds throughout the week, not only locals but also people brought in by special buses from neighbouring places such as Daventry, East Haddon and Ravensthorpe.

In many ways, however, Feast Sunday was the high point of Feast Week. This was the day when natives of Long Buckby who had moved away came back to the village to see friends and relatives. Such meetings were often marked by eating Feast Pudding – a kind of Christmas pudding which was baked and eaten cold. On Sunday, the fair, for obvious reasons, did not "go round". Instead, the two village bands gave concerts on the square, one before the church services and one after. Large crowds attended both evening concerts.

There was, however, much more to Feast Week than this. During the week, there would be a large Flower Show and a Bird Show, which attracted a large number of entrants. Children from the school would give displays of maypole dancing.

The Feast would end at midnight on the second Saturday when the fairground organ always played "Christians Awake, Salute the Happy Morn".

I first knew the Feast in 1940 when it was already diminished by the war. Dodgems replaced steamhorses gradually and although there was a post-war revival, more modern attractions have seen the gradual decline of the Feast.

There was still a band concert by the late 1950s but the final blow was the alteration in the August Bank Holiday date. The fair now arrives in October, is a very small fair and all that is left of Buckby Feast is a happy memory.'

CROW FEAST

'The big event in Wootton was the celebration of St George's Day, or Crow Feast as it was known locally. The actual day that this Feast was celebrated provides interesting evidence of the independence of the people of Wootton in resisting the introduction of the Gregorian Calendar. In 1752, to correct an error of eleven days in the calendar, Parliament changed 3rd September to 14th September, but Wootton refused to lose eleven days and so celebrated their Feast on the Sunday following 4th May instead of 23rd April, which was now St George's Day. This continued until at least the 1930s, as did the strange custom of hanging a dead crow outside licensed premises for the weekend of the Feast. No one now knows why this was done, but it seems probable that it had something to do with warding off evil.'

COLLECTING FOR THE HOSPITAL

'Moulton Feast was held early in November. The fair came and was set up in Bluebell Field. What joy it was to go on Saturday night with one's father – thrilling rides on the roundabout and cakewalk, being treated to goes on the hoop-la, coconut shy, swingboats etc, and sticky toffees liberally sprinkled with dust. Just to be out late in the dark was exciting. Next day we stood to watch the big procession through the village to the church, led by the Moulton Brass Band, with the Oddfellows huge banner and all the uniformed organisations taking part. A collection was made for the hospital, still largely maintained by voluntary contributions until the coming of the NHS.'

THE CLUB FEAST

'The Club Feast was held at Easton on the last Sunday in September. There was a joint procession of the friendly rivals, the Oddfellows (who met at the Exeter Arms) and the Forresters (who met at the Blue Bell), to church, and then they returned to a splendid feast laid out in the clubrooms of the public houses.'

MORE VILLAGE DAYS

◄⑤►

When holidays away from home were few and far between, special days in the year were eagerly looked forward to as a break from the monotony of everyday life. Though May Day and the Feast Day were the high spots in the year, there were other celebrations to be anticipated, from Plough Monday through to Christmas.

PLOUGH MONDAY

'Plough Monday is the first Monday in January after Twelfth Night, and my mother would remark that we would have the "plough boys" calling tonight. On this day, those farm labourers responsible for ploughing the fields would ring our front door bell and be invited into our home at Duddington and given a half crown or so by my father. Mr Harry Dolby was one I remember and after a glass of my mother's home-made wine, many a tale was told that evening!'

244

'On Plough Monday at Grafton Underwood the boys put dirt on their faces and went round the village knocking on doors and saying "Could you please spare a penny for the poor plough boy?'

'In the 1920s the life of Clipston village was mainly based on agriculture, with the blacksmith, the saddler and the wheelwright providing their essential services to the community. Plough Monday was celebrated each year and I recall peeping from behind my mother's skirts as she answered a knock on the door from a group of boys with blackened faces, who asked if she could "spare a penny for the poor old plough boys".'

PANCAKE DAY

'On Pancake Day at Middleton Cheney they used to ring the bells from 11.30 am to noon so that the mothers would know to start cooking the pancakes. We didn't have much but we liked to keep the old traditions. A book of local customs says that the bells were originally rung to call the faithful to be shriven (an old term for confession).'

MOTHERING SUNDAY

'The girls at Grafton Underwood always tried to get a few violets for their mothers on Mothering Sunday, but it was not always possible, dependent on the weather.'

EMPIRE DAY

'At Sywell on Empire Day (24th May) we were assembled in the school yard, the Union Jack was hoisted and we then marched round the yard, saluting the flag as we passed beneath it. Our excitement grew as the day approached, not so much as to what we were about to do, but more because of what also took place. There was a family living in the village at that time who were of Communistic leanings and their children were forbidden to take part in this ritual, although of course none of us had any idea what it was all about. There was usually a bit of an affray between the parents and the teacher (I can't remember which side won) and it provided extra excitement to our day.

I can only remember one verse of the ditty we sang as we marched round the flagpole –

Today we bring our flags to school
And proudly march along,
For this you know is Empire Day
So join in choir and song.'

'Lois Weedon and Weston children all had to file past the flagpole
and salute the Union Jack on Empire Day. We would also have a
school play, all the costumes provided by the school.'

'When the Union Jack was raised at Woodford, the children would
gather round and sing patriotic songs. For the finale they all faced
the flag and saluted and sang a song that ended "We salute thee and
we pray, God will bless our land today".'

TEA DRINKING

'Tea Drinking brings back many memories for me. This was held in
June – church one week, chapel the next. Collection point was Broad
Green, Wellingborough. From there we marched round the town,
then everyone branched off to their own place of worship. We sat
down to tea, which was bread and butter, jelly and cakes, followed
by games.
    We also had "Penny Bank Tea" which was for children who
saved their pennies at the Co-op Bank. This also started from
Broad Green. Besides walkers there were floats advertising Co-op
wares. We walked to a field in London Road near the Dog and Duck
pub. Tea was a bag containing white and brown bread and butter, a
piece of plain cake, a piece of fruit cake, an orange, apple and a bar
of chocolate. For this party we had to take our own cup and saucer
– I don't think many arrived home intact.
    These were always hot days so our new white socks managed to
get splashes of melted tar on them – not very popular when mother
saw them! Sadly these events were not revived after the Second
World War.'

'Every year in July a Tea Drinking was held at Irthlingborough and
every Church school child was given a cup and saucer tied in a
handkerchief at home and they all marched through the streets of
the town. There were more breakages on the parade than whole
cups and saucers ever arrived at Dr Robb's lawn. (Dr Robb lived
half way up Station Road and his garden was often referred to as
"Dr Robb's lawn" and parties and gatherings were held there.) At
the Tea Drinking, there would be a speaker and there would also be

246

races and games for the children, as well as the tea party. Everyone dressed up in their best clothes for this event.'

FAIRS, FETES AND CARNIVALS

'The annual Woodford garden fete was held in the grounds of one of the farm houses, where there was a mixture of stalls and competitions, but the highlight of the evening was the dance that was held on the tennis courts, which had been decked with fairy lights. Band Sunday was another eventful day, when all organisations met on the village green for a band concert, all the proceeds going to charity.

The event of the year was the carnival. It started with a pre-carnival dance, to choose several girls who would be the Queen and her attendants. The crowning ceremony took place later in the rectory gardens and the villagers turned up in droves to watch, as until this moment no one knew which of the girls would be crowned Queen. When the crowning ceremony was over, preparations were made for the carnival parade. Carnival bands came from miles around to join in the fun and there were numerous floats from different parts of the county. A lot of jazz bands also took part. The parade took a long time to get through the village, but they slowly made their way up to the recreation field where there were stalls set up for hoop-la, roll-a-penny etc. At the end of the day plans were laid for the following year.'

'The house known as The Firs stands on the edge of Stanion village, still shaded by huge chestnut trees, an impressive stone building. In the early decades of the century it was surrounded by fields and orchards, the extensive grounds and paddock an ideal venue for garden fetes, a very popular way of raising money for good causes and eagerly reported with all the details by the local papers.

The fetes were popular not only with the inhabitants of Stanion; a considerable number of people travelled from the surrounding area, and according to reports, the events could be not only well-attended, but quite grand.

Even in war time, in 1917, a fete in aid of the Red Cross Fund seems to have been largely unaffected by any food shortages; perhaps not so surprising in a country area probably self-sufficient in fruit, vegetables, cheese, eggs and the ingredients for cakes – all there for sale in abundance. These sales, together with the bran-tub, skittles, the name of the doll and the time the watch would stop were the money raisers, these and the collection taken while the procession paraded through the village, led by a band "of the ragtime sort, in grotesque garb, which, with their remarkable music created immense merriment" as the newspaper put it. The serious brass bandsmen were away on sterner duties.

And what a procession! Of course, in 1917, "there were the decorated cycles and cyclists depicting the Allies", the wounded soldier (children, first prize), the Anzac and the Belgian. There were several Japanese ladies, an early Victorian lady, a cowboy (Miss Maud Swingler) and the "Stanion Witch", black cloaked, peak hatted, carrying a model of the Dun Cow's rib. There was Hubert Swingler as the Pied Piper and George Swingler as a Red Indian; Miss Constance Hector as a Japanese lady, the second daughter of Mr and Mrs Thomas Hector who lived at The Firs, won a special prize and had her picture in the paper.

Under the trees in the garden the catering committee served teas, in the paddock the children raced and chased for prizes, and the energetic adults tugged away at either end of a rope; even the ladies liked the tug-of-war, and the single girls (or as the *Evening Telegraph* has it "those who wore not wedding rings") proved stronger than their married sisters.

It wasn't over yet. After the auction of left-over fruit, after the speeches of thanks, "the pleasure-seekers wended their way to the schoolroom for a whist drive". Indefatigable, weren't they?

Everyone liked garden fetes at The Firs; possibly it was an annual occasion. Mrs Thomas Hector died in 1917, not long after the Red Cross Fete; the following year her youngest daughter, Florence, married Herbert Tansley, and together they hosted more "successful fetes" on "glorious summer days" in the "charming and picturesque" grounds of their home through the early 1920s, in aid of the Church Restoration Fund.

Sometimes the merry-makers were treated to a rather lengthy disquisition on the history of Stanion church (September 1922), but the grounds were illuminated in the evening.

Victorian ladies still carry off the fancy dress prize (1923), and hitherto unreported competitions surface: "Slashing the Ham – all you slice you have". In the old photograph it looks dangerous – the competitor is blindfolded and seems to be armed with a sword, slashing at a ham hung on a rope well above his head, while barely a yard away a spectator grins.

Four year old Bobby Headland and Sylvia Greenwood start to make their appearance, this year, as Darby and Joan. They were to repeat their success in various guises for many years.

In 1924 Dr Clapperton of Corby judged the baby show; all afternoon and evening St Barnabas' Glee Party from Leicester entertained on the steps of the house, and Mrs Bandy judged

248

the waltzing competition. Sylvia Greenwood and Bobby Headland won a special prize as Tiny Bride and Bridegroom. The ham-slashing competition was in the charge of Mr Keeble. I am still puzzling over the second prize winner in the Ladies' Section of the parade: "Mrs H S (Sutton's Long Pea Pod)" – how did she manage to walk?'

HARVEST FESTIVAL

'The Harvest Festival service was an important event in the church calendar at Little Addington, and followed the gathering of the harvest in the surrounding fields. This was the climax of the year's work and horse and binder were used; all available manpower, including the children, was used to complete the harvest. Only in later years was the Harvest Supper included in the celebrations.'

'When we had our Harvest Festival at Everdon, we didn't sell the produce. It was all taken to Northampton General Hospital by the village carrier in his horse and cart.'

A lesser known annual event was the Nutting Outing at Great Houghton when the men went off to gather walnuts in a waggon loaded with beer.

249

'Harvest had particular meaning for the farming community at Hargrave, signifying survival and a measure of prosperity – even if during the hymn "All is safely gathered in", a voice might murmur "Except the draggings" '

NUTTING

'Nutting was an annual event at Great Houghton. It is recalled that at one time there was a two-horse waggon loaded with beer, and a two-horse waggon carrying the men. They'd be gone all day nutting in the woods. At Houghton Feast in October one could stand almost ankle deep in walnut shells in the taproom at the Old Cherry Tree inn.'

REMEMBRANCE DAY

'Remembrance Day was always a big day in Deanshanger, with parades through the village. What I remember most was that everyone observed the two minutes silence, work stopped and wherever they were, people stood still at 11 am.'

CHRISTMAS

'At Christmastime at Easton on the Hill there would be a lot of whist drives, known locally as the "Fur and Feather". People would attend hoping to win their Christmas dinner. The Collyweston Silver Band used to serenade the village on Christmas Eve. The hospitality meted out to them was lavish, resulting in headaches the next morning.'

'At Christmas at Everdon there was some carol singing, but it wasn't organised like nowadays. Men would go round carol singing when they came out of the pub to get more money for a drink or two.'

'For a number of weeks before Christmas, during Advent, the bellringers at Middleton Cheney would go to the church every Monday morning at five o'clock in the morning and ring the bells until six, then going to work. My father told us that Father Christmas lived up with the bells and it never occurred to us to question this, we just accepted it. We used to write proper letters to Father Christmas and give them to Dad to take to the church. We'd hang up our stockings by the fireplace, not in the bedroom – we daren't have him in the bedroom! I remember one particular Christmas morning, my Dad was up early getting ready to go to work to tend his horses and he heard me and my sister talking.

"Be quiet," he said, "he's coming!" We hid under the bedclothes and Dad must have got a stick and rattled it up the chimney so we'd think Father Christmas was on his way down. "He's gone," Dad called, "he's gone over the fields to Purston!" We'd look in our stockings and there'd be an apple, an orange and a few sweets and always a doll. My sister always had the same as me. If we were very lucky there would be a new school bag or satchel.

My father used to go and muffle the bells ready to ring the old year out at the end of December; he had to climb up the belltower to do this. Then the bellringers rang a muffled peal. Come midnight, he'd go up the belltower again, take off those muffles and they'd ring the new year in.'

Index